America's Road to Fascism: From the Progressives to the Era of Hope and Change.

By Peter Suciu and John Kullman

PSB Publishing
Melbourne, Australia
New York, USA

Copyright © Peter Suciu and John Kullman 2010.

The moral right of the authors has been asserted.

All rights reserved.

No part of this publication may be reproduced, stored in a retrieval system, or transmitted, in any form or by any means, without the prior permission in writing of the authors, nor be otherwise circulated in any form of binding or cover other than that in which it is published and without similar condition including this condition being imposed on the subsequent purchaser.

ISBN 978-0-9806567-1-8

Copy by Peter Suciu and John Kullman.
Design, layout by Stuart Bates.

Cover design by Chris Armold.

Printed and bound in the U.S.A

Table of Contents

Preface	iv
The Myth of Fascism	1
The History of American Fascism Part I	12
The History of American Fascism Part II	33
The Rise to Power of President Barack Obama	46
The Rule of the Land Under President Obama and the Comparison to Fascism	61
Forced Fitness and Health Under Fascism	76
Eco-Fascism and the Green Takeover	91
Small Matters, Big Steps: The Fascist Way	101
The Business of Fascism	114
Fascism at the Community Level	123
The Enemy Within	132
The External Enemy	151
Islamic Fascism	161
The Road Ahead	177
About the Authors	192
Notes	193
Bibliography	216
Index	229

Preface
The Long and Winding Road

There is an irony in the "popularity" of President Barack Obama. Supporters like to point out that he won an overwhelming majority, and that he is among the most respected presidents in recent history. How can it be then that demonstrators began protesting against the POTUS soon after he took office?

Could it be that he isn't as popular as his supporters make out, and that perhaps this "support" throughout America and the world is really just a smokescreen? Of course those demonstrators, often called "tea baggers" or far worse, are dismissed as being racists, angry that a "black man" is in the White House.

Ironic say the critics of the tea baggers is that Mr. Obama has been compared to Adolf Hitler by these demonstrators, because according to his supporters the POTUS is a man of peace (he won the Nobel Peace Prize) and is a man who wants to reshape America.

No, we say the irony is that the demonstrators are more on the mark than it appears. While it would be easy to criticize any politician and label him or her to be like "Hitler" if you don't agree with their policies, in the case of our 44th President of the United States, it is the policies that speak loudest. Mr. Obama, his supporters and those in government who follow him are taking America down a road to fascism.

Hitler and his ilk didn't seize power. They were duly elected and slowly dismantled the fledging German democracy into a totalitarian state with a charismatic supreme leader ruling, not by fear but by a cult of personality. The Nazis in Germany controlled all aspects of life in Germany, but it wasn't taken by force, the people of Germany happily gave it away to their Führer or "leader."

So today we stand at a crossroads. One road leads back to the freedoms our founders knew were important for a great nation to grow. The other leads to a fascist dictatorship that strips individual freedom in return for government-subsidized cradle to grave care. Patriots, the Republic is in danger! Rally to Old Glory with the authors and persuade relatives, friends and neighbors that the road back to freedom is the only choice worth making.

Peter Suciu & John Kullman

January 2010

Chapter One
The Myth of Fascism

One of the greatest myths and misunderstandings about Fascism and National Socialism as practiced in countries such as Italy and Germany respectively is that these are extreme right ideologies. This is a curious belief given that the Nazis, as in National Socialists, even state their clear intention towards socialism right in the name! How can any ideology that is based on the pretext of socialism be a right-wing concept?

The answer is that it cannot, but for decades this is how it has been seen, and thus it has made it hard to label the true Fascists and national socialists as such. In the United States, it is a historic mistruth to label the policies of the right as being "fascistic." Those opposed to conservative initiatives usually use the term as a way to impugn the character of conservatives. This is a very Fascist thing to do. Truth gives way to political expediency.

Communists were among the first to attempt to define fascism. Even before Mussolini consolidated power, the followers of Marx created convoluted phrases that labeled fascism. During the reign of Stalin a formula was hit upon that became communist orthodoxy for fifty years. "Fascism is the open, terroristic dictatorship of the most reactionary, most chauvinist and most imperialist elements of finance capital."[1] While this may be adequate for those nostalgic towards the Stalinist period, it is an inadequate definition. Ancient history can give us clues to a political movement that started in the 20th Century.

First we need to understand the meaning of the word, and ironically it dates back to an era of republicanism in ancient Rome. The term "fascismo" comes from the Italian word "fascio," which is based itself on the Latin word "fasces." The meaning was "bundle" or group, which makes sense for a political party, which is typically a group. However, American scholar Gilbert Allardyce argued that "fascism is not a generic concept," and that the word 'fascismo' has no meaning outside of Italy," despite the fact that clearly in the

1930s Oswald Mosley, founder of the British Union of Fascists, thought it did![2]

The fasces of Rome during the Roman Republic were bundles of wooden rods that were tied together, with an axe head at either the side or top. This was a symbol of authority for civic magistrates, and in time was carried by military leaders as a sign of strength. A single rod is easily broken but a bundle is not. The Roman Legions throughout the Republican era, as well as in the early Empire, carried it much the way a flag might be carried today. For centuries the fasces was a symbol of power. This icon was adopted by the Italian Fascists following the First World War, and in a strange twist of fate, has been used by the United States of America practically since its founding.

It is a symbol that is surprisingly spread throughout the corridors of power in the United States, and yet one that hardly gets a second glance. The American mercury dime, which was in widespread circulation from 1916 until 1945, bore the fasces, while more ominously there are two fasces on the walls to either side of the flag of the United States in the House of Representatives. This is meant to represent the power of the House and of the people, but in the future could represent the total control over its people by the government.

On the back of the dollar, an American eagle clutches a bundle of arrows in one claw and a bundle of olive branches in the other. This symbolizes strength of the republic during times of peace and war. Interestingly, the eagle was an icon used by the Romans.

Forebodingly, there are also fasces above the door leading to an exterior walkway in the Oval Office. This example does however lack the axe. In ancient times the axes were removed before the bundle could be carried into Rome. This symbolized the rights of citizens over absolute power by its rulers.

Unlike the swastika, which was adopted by the Nazis (but also used throughout the world for centuries for commercial purposes as well as by dozens of cultures [3]), the fasces had no mystical ties. Instead, the founders of the United States of America adopted it because it represented the classical age of the Roman Republic.

In this regard, it fit with the Greco-Roman architecture, but it is worth wondering whether these founding fathers ever considered that the classical city states of Greece were constantly warring with one another, or the fact that Rome's republic died at the hands of ambitious men who eventually established rule by one man?

Regardless of what the founding fathers considered or did not, they could not have looked into the future to see that a 20th Century leader would use the same symbolism and memory of Rome to claim power, and lead his nation to near destruction. This of course was Benito Mussolini, dictator of Italy from 1922 to 1945, who founded the National Fascist Party, or in Italian "Partito Nazionale Fascista."[4]

As with the Nazis in Germany, whom we will get to shortly, the Italian fascists have constantly been referred to as an extreme right wing party, but again this is not a fair or accurate assessment. Part of Mussolini's prime mantra from his founding of the National Fascist Party would be that the party would form an economic policy that was a "third way" between traditional capitalism and socialism. "Presented as a 'Third Way' between the anarchy of the liberal market economy and the strictures of the Bolshevist planned one." [5]

Given the global economic crisis of the past year, this "third way" type of policy is one brought up time and time again by the left wing in the United States as a way of "correcting the wrongs" of capitalism, but without a full-fledged redistribution of wealth along Marxist lines.

During the presidential campaign of 2008, critics of Barack Obama routinely compared the man to a Marxist, communists or the less threatening socialist. But as we will soon see, his "third way" types of policies are indicative of Mussolini, and as we will further explore, some policies and approach aren't that far off from the Nazis as well as many other Fascists throughout the 20th century.

This is because again, the modus operandi of the Fascists and Nazis is really based on left wing concepts as much as right wing ones. While a number of historians have erroneously viewed fascism as a right wing ideology, and in the post-World War II world it was seen as a radical right wing movement, the fact is that fascism at its core is opposed to many right wing values. These include free trade, free speech, individual liberty, small government, freedom of religion and market-driven capitalism. Some historians have noted that fascism is actually an ideology that is opposed to established movements, whether on the left, the right or the center. It is like a hurried diner at a salad bar who puts mismatched foods on his plate. Putting Catalina dressing on mashed potatoes is not a problem. Ideological purity gives way to a rush for political power despite a lack of cohesive taste for the movement.

While it is safe to say that fascism typically rejects the classless society advocated by Marxists, it also objects to unregulated capitalism; including free trade, open stock markets and private ownership that may conflict with the needs of the state.[6] Some historians and economists have noted that fascism is actually an anti-Marxist form of socialism, especially as it favors class collaboration and supports the concept of nationalism - the latter being something that Marxists could never support. A diehard Marxist leader wouldn't get on a plane and fly half way around the world to try and win support for the Olympics to be hosted in his country, even his hometown. But a tried and true Fascist might do so.

Fascist leaders such as Mussolini further described fascism as an economic system of corporatism that was both state capitalism and state socialism. It was referred to as the corporate state. Yet this was not entirely a new thought by these leaders. The concept of state capitalism vs. state socialism is actually one that has been debated since the 19th century by economic thinkers like Wilhelm Liebknecht. In 1896 he stated that in Germany, "State Socialism is really State capitalism."[7]

Considering the volatile economic and social state of the 2nd Reich in the late 19th Century, it is not hard to see that this was a pre-Fascist portent of things to come. But it would take the Kaiser's downfall, a crushing defeat in the First World War, a world depression and the failure of the Weimar Republic to seed the soil for a Nazi takeover in Germany.

It was Mussolini who pronounced that fascism's path "would lead inexorably into state capitalism, which is nothing more nor less than state socialism turned on its head."[8] Mussolini also theorized that capitalism would go through three stages. In the final stage the extremes and decadence of capitalism would be replaced by state socialism. Given the recent global economic crisis, company bailouts and news stories about Wall Street fat cats feasting off capitalism's failure, Mussolini's theory is foreboding. "[A] capitalist enterprise, when difficulties arise, throws itself like a dead weight into the state's arms. It is then that state intervention begins and becomes more necessary. It is then that those who once ignored the state now seek it out anxiously."[9]

Mussolini's brand of fascism allowed private enterprise to control production, but it was supervised by the state. Corporatism was used to preserve private enterprise and private property rights. But the state had the power to intervene whenever the needs of the nation called for trampling over an individual's rights. Given the sub-prime mortgage failure, bailouts of banks and government ownership of the auto industry, this type of "private enterprise failure" and state intervention sounds familiar.

So is it safe to just label fascism as state socialism? Not entirely. As we've seen, fascism under Mussolini was really seen as a "third way." Traditionally fascism is hostile to Marxism, but it is also hostile to liberalism (could this even explain why many hardcore liberals are somewhat disappointed by the policies and performance of President Obama) and more importantly conservatism. Yet, the interesting part of fascism is that while hostile to these ideologies, it also manages to borrow heavily from all these.

Fascism rejects the Marxist principles of class struggle and proletarian internationalism, which are viewed as threats to societal unity and nationalism. Fascism rejects the status quo as a failure and desires to bring change. The past is romanticized as a utopian time. Mussolini invoked the glory of the Roman Empire, while Hitler called for a return to blood and soil. It is only natural that icons of the past were high jacked for state propaganda.

President Obama has stated that one of his goals is to return America to greatness. He had been compared by his supporters to Presidents Lincoln, Kennedy, Roosevelt and Reagan, after only being in office for a few months. How is this different from Mussolini's evocation of the glorious Roman past? But that's something we'll explore in detail later.

When the status quo is deemed to be broken fascism presents itself as an answer to the crisis. Fascism's allure is its promise of national rebirth and an end to societal chaos through government action. Fascists capitalize on the public's clamor for something new but are short on concrete policy changes. Instead they rely on emotionalism and icons of the glorious past.

During the 2008 election, Obama's campaign slogan was "hope" and "change." The candidate was short on what the public was to expect when the change came, only that it would be different and therefore better. The message was clear: America is failing but citizens can put their hope in one man to make life better.

In the case of Italy and Germany, the Fascists and Nazis came to power following the First World War capitalizing on the perceived failure of democratic liberalism. Today, American fascism is being brought on by the so-called failures of capitalism and conservatism. In this book, when we speak of American conservatism think 18th Century liberalism embraced by the founders. The cornerstones of American conservatism are individual liberty, small government, free trade and individual responsibility. This is different from European conservatism and shares elements with European liberalism.

National upheaval is an important element leading to a strong fascist movement. Germany, France and Portugal were disillusioned with liberalism during the world depression of the 1930s. High unemployment, hyperinflation and a loss of national pride grew Fascist movements that promised to heal the national psyche. This same formula affected the United Stated as well.

Because fascism is a national movement, it doesn't look the same in every country. A glaring example is how Italian Fascists treated Jews differently from German fascists. The Nazis were murderously anti-Semitic, while Mussolini had Jews in high positions in his party until late into WWII. American fascism has been stereotyped along European lines but this is erroneous. Fascists come in many shapes and sizes - not just large bald Italian men - and as we can see from the past, there are many blends to fascism.

Some historians have noted that fascism typically rejects standard religious teachings, but this is not entirely true. The Iron Guard of Romania was almost founded on a religious belief as much as a political one.[10] The Iron Guard, which was briefly in power in Romania from September of 1940 through January of 1941, was founded by Corneliu Zelea Codreanu in 1927 as the "Legion of the Archangel Michel" or Legiunea Archanghelu Mihail. His group utilized elements and beliefs of Orthodox Christianity into the group's political doctrine. As with the Nazis, this also ventured deep into ultra-nationalism and violent anti-Semitism. The Guard's failure was mostly based on the fact that it was "congenitally vicious, incompetent and anarchic."[11] So when the Germans had to choose whom to back, they ended up supporting Romanian dictator Ion Antonescu over the Iron Guard's Horia Sima and his 300 leading supporters, with the latter being "held in Germany as a potential alternative government to Antonescu should his adherence to the Axis falter."[12] It will be interesting to see if such "alternative" power structures are formed in Iraq and Afghanistan if current or future governments go against American interests.

One of the paradoxes of fascism is that while it is a national movement it has international appeal and is with us still. For example the Peronism or Justicialism of Argentina, created by former President Juan Perón, is still active today! Derived from the Spanish words for "social justice," this party is focused on a strong centralized government with authoritarian leanings, wants freedom from foreign influences and combines nationalism with social democracy. Moreover, Perón called for a "third way" approach to economics that was to be neither capitalist nor socialist. He instead called for ways to merge the two together to create a corporatist system.[13]

Argentina's neighbor Brazil also had its own homegrown version of fascism known as the Brazilian Integralism under Plinio Salgado. As with the Romanians, it too incorporated religion. Catholicism was mixed with the traditional Fascist ingredients of anti-capitalism and anti-socialism to serve up corporatism. Like other Fascists he adopted the usual symbolism, but publicly rejected racist ideologies. "Salgado successfully merged indigenous Brazilian historical imagery (including the Tupi Indian culture) with the more overtly fascist aspects of his program, such as dictatorship, nationalism, protectionism, corporatism, anti-Semitism, goose steps, a proposed Secretariat for Moral and Physical Education, green shirts and black armbands with the Greek letter *sigma* (the symbol of integralism), to form an authentically homegrown overtly fascist movement."[14] As with many Fascist groups, Salgado's support came from the lower middle class, as opposed to the working class that typically supports Marxist elements.

Salgado followed a path that is common with fascism. He used his widespread support to legitimately come to power, only to become so ambitious that he threatened Brazilian President Getulio Vargas, who had essentially established his own full dictatorial powers.[15] In this case, Salgado was a failed Fascist leader, as he never achieved leadership of his nation. Instead he was sent to exile in Portugal for a while, ironically at a time when the Estado Novo were in power.

Founded by António de Oliveira Salazar, the Estado Novo came to power after the failed Portuguese First Republic (1910-1926). Salazar's Portugal borrowed heavily from Mussolini's Italy, and while this is another example where religion was maintained - again Catholicism in this case - the authoritarian regime tried to control the economic powers to maintain control over the people. Salazar also predated Mussolini in founding his movement. The Academic Centre for Christian Democracy (CADC) was founded in 1901, but "revived in 1912 after a long period of inactivity by right-wing Catholic intellectuals, including the two men who were destined to be the twin pillars of Church and state in dictatorial Portugal: António de Oliveira Salazar and Manuel Gonçalves Cerejeira."[16] Ironically Salazar's Portugal was probably far more brutal to its people, and used its secret police as a means of repression far more than other Fascist states. During the Spanish Civil War the Portuguese secretly (and not so secretly) supported the Nationalists under Franco, but did lend some support to the Allies during World War II - in part because Salazar never trusted Hitler's Nazi Germany.

This brings us to the Nazis. First, it must be stressed that many historians and political scientists argue that Nazism, or National

Socialism, is not truly a valid form of fascism. The Nazi's extreme racial policies and emphasis on racial purity ran contrary to many Fascist ideologies, but it is hard to ignore that both reject liberalism, Marxism and democracy while championing national rebirth.

More importantly, the Nazi's economic policies were, at least in the beginning, much in line with those of Fascist Italy. In May of 1933 the Nazis even formed the National Socialist Institute for Corporatism, with the understanding that corporatism was a policy that was a key part of National Socialism. Hitler believed that National Socialism and National Socialist corporative ideas would be the way to end what the leader called "ruinous class warfare."[17]

It could be argued that much of this talk in Germany was really about propaganda, and true corporatism was not instituted. But given the fact that Germany's industry and various merchant based industries had been powerful long before there was a unified Germany; it is not hard to understand why the Nazis did not fully embrace corporatism.

Yet, the Nazis did use the power of German industry to rebuild the nation following the devastation of the First World War and the harsh sanctions of the Versailles Treaty. While much of the world, including Europe, went through an economic depression throughout the 1930s, Germany's brand of fascism used public works and rearmament as a way to pull itself out of the depression. And when war did come in 1939, Germany was essentially on a peacetime economy until 1942, when Albert Speer took over the job of running the economy and advocated total war.

Another facet of the Nazis that is necessary to look at is the concept of "property rights," which the Nazis saw as conditional upon the mode of use; in other words, property needed to be used to further Greater Germany's and more importantly the party's goals. If it was not being used to "better" the nation's needs, it could be nationalized. Here is some of the duality of saying one thing and doing another, a situation that rings true all too much with fascism. The Nazis stressed the notion that private property should be protected, and owners compensated, unless of course it interfered with the big picture and the direction of the nation - which was stated as being good for the many. Individual rights were trampled by the state because of the perceived needs of the group. This is the antithesis of what American conservatives believe.

Under the Nazis private property remains private in name, but not in substance. Various firms were taken over and run by the Nazis - often with the argument that the state could do it better. Quickly the economy of Nazi Germany was taken over, and was essentially state directed. Today some firms that worked with the Nazis - such as Hugo Boss, Bayer, Opel, Volkswagen and Krupp, downplay their role.[18] In fairness, it could be argued that in this instance they really had no other choice! This is a topic we'll address later and in greater detail.

The other facet of Nazism that is generally misunderstood is where its support came from - because there is now a strong belief that it was actually supported as much by the lower classes, as it was the middle class (the typical largest supporters of traditional fascism).

Neil Gregor discusses this support in his book *Nazism*: "If Nazism's mass support was rooted in its promises of a Germany free from the discontents of capitalism, rationalization and the eclipse of traditional values, its historical function was to exorcize the traditional patterns of culture which conflicted with modern modes of production."[19] Gregor maintains that the people further affirmed this shift in the 1920s.

Here is where we need to take another look at who was supporting the Nazis. Michael Burleigh, in his book *The Third Reich: A New History*, describes that the "electoral profile of the National Socialist Party has been described as an integrative people's party with an accentuated middle class, or, less pretentiously, as having a profile of a man with a pot belly."[20]

It is worth noting that the concept of "working man" vs. "middle class" is also one that likely rings true today to the average American. When the Nazis rose to power in the late 1920s and early 1930s, "millions of prudent people had been ruined by the hyperinflation".[21] In other words, people that once felt safe and secure were suddenly without their savings, and facing economic uncertainty. During the 1920s Germany saw a massive period of what today would be considered "layoffs," but in fact were just flat out dismissals. In other words, the Nazis drew from those who looked towards a change, but we'll get to the coming of power of the Nazis in the 1930s and President's Obama's election later on.

For now, it is safe to say that the followers of fascism throughout history, even the Nazis, were not extreme conservative fanatics in the American sense. They were instead every day people, mostly from the lower middle class and those aspiring to reach beyond the class they were born into, who were looking for "hope" and "change." And this was the promise offered by these various charismatic leaders, time and time again. *Hope, Change and a better way of life* through a system that was neither capitalistic - which according to the Fascists had failed - nor socialistic, which was feared by those who weren't *have-nots* but certainly didn't feel they were the *upper class*. As we explore the topic, this "third way" may be the direction America is headed towards at an ever-alarming speed.

Chapter Two
The History of American Fascism Part I

Today the extreme "right wing" movement in this country that includes the Ku Klux Klan, white supremacists and other "neo-Nazi" organizations is typically lumped under the banner of fascism. Yet, as with fascism nothing in this movement is inherently right wing - ultra or otherwise. Consider that among these groups the doctrines and dogmas are typically against core "right wing" values, including free trade, capitalism and fiscal conservatism.

A tried and true "skin head" would not fit in with those at a Republican Party mixer at a country club any more than he would blend in at a hip hop show in Harlem. We have been told by the press and others that these movements are right wing but this is not true. The root word for conservative is to conserve or to keep from change. Conservatives believe that the founders were correct in setting up a nation based on the ideals of 18th Century liberalism. While it is true that women and slaves didn't enjoy this liberating force at the start, over time the country evolved to include them.

Fascists don't like the status quo and demand change. In the case of white supremacists, they are angry over the nation's power sharing with non-whites and Jews, and fear contamination of the race. True conservatives don't care about the color of one's skin but the content of one's character.

Unfortunately in the United States the concept of fascism is one that is often misunderstood, misreported and just wrong. Authors such as Chris Hedges, with his book *American Fascist: The Christian Right and the War on America*, try to argue that the right wing is somehow a Fascist movement, but Hedges cites points that are libelously incorrect. "The movement has sanctified a ruthless unfettered capitalism."[1] As we have seen, unfettered capitalism is hardly what Fascist leaders such as Mussolini, or Nazis such as Hitler, approved of. In fact, this notion of unfettered capitalism is exactly why Fascists call for their "Third Way," one that we have touched upon and will explore in greater detail.

The History of American Fascism Part I

Fascism is not new to America. In his 1935 published semi-satirical political novel *It Can't Happen Here* author Sinclair Lewis warned of the possibility of a Fascist being elected to the highest position in government. "Lewis outlined the new structure of state and local government in *It Can't Happen Here*. In so doing he gave expression to some of the fondest dreams of American political scientists and public administration experts."[2] In the novel President Berzelius "Buzz" Windrip is elected on a populist platform, where he promises to restore the United States to prosperity and greatness. He also makes the pledge to give each citizen five thousand dollars a year - sort of sounds like recent tax rebate checks- but of course once elected he changes the Constitution, dismantles democracy and takes total control of the United States. As the book's title says, it can't happen here!

Consider for a moment the many things that seem like they couldn't happen here; including slavery, a civil war, women treated as property, domestic terrorism and race riots. Sadly all of those things are part of the history and tapestry that is the United States of America. So, could "it" happen here? Well, the fact is that while it hasn't happened like it did in early 20th century Europe, it has happened.

When the first Hollywood blockbuster was released in 1915, it was met with some controversy but hardly to the level it would if released today. This is of course D. W. Griffith's *The Birth of a Nation*, a film about the rise of the Ku Klux Klan, and the highest grossing silent film of all time. The irony is that Griffith wasn't a racist or supporter of the Southern cause following the American Civil War, which the film depicts.[3]

The film was so controversial at the time that it sparked riots and murders in a number of American cities. The NAACP protested the film and launched an educational attack pointing out the various historic inaccuracies and racist point of view of the movie (of course protests continued to the current time: "a planned showing at Brown University in 1989 was called off after local protests."[4]). The mood of the country at the time can best be summed up by a quote attributed to President Wilson after a White House screening: "[I]t is like writing history with lightning. And my only regret is that it is all so terribly true". [5]

We've grown as a people, and controversial films are just that, controversial. Still, the fact that a film could ever be made - by a racist director or not - about the origin of the Ku Klux Klan serves as a reminder of the deep roots of racial hatred in the United States, one that many groups still embrace.

While racists groups have fascist leanings and trappings, the current American trend towards fascism is from another direction entirely. It comes from the left; which embraces the nanny-state, political correctness and redistribution of wealth, where the rights of the individual are sacrificed for the good of society. If the nation is to move forward, the individual must sacrifice for the good of all.

The earliest example of American-style fascism goes back to the days of reconstruction and includes the seemingly benign adoption of the Pledge of Alliance. Author R.G. Price, in his Web article on the "Rise of American Fascism", notes that American society is reflected by the evolution of the pledge.[6]

The Pledge of Allegiance was written by Francis Bellamy in 1892 for a national Columbus Day celebration (the 400th anniversary of Columbus' "discovery of the New World"), and was subsequently published in *The Youth's Companion* magazine. For the record, the current version of the Pledge of Allegiance reads:

> "I pledge allegiance to the flag of the United States of America, and to the Republic for which it stands, one Nation under God, indivisible, with liberty and justice for all."[7]

Today the pledge is known throughout the United States by school children. It is also used to open Congressional sessions, recited at local governments meetings and gatherings of the Boy Scouts of America. It is akin to a second national anthem, and while the text - which has been revised four times - doesn't swear allegiance to an individual, who is to say that it couldn't be revised yet again? Consider that there is a highly unofficial (at least at this point) American flag that replaces the 50 stars with an image of Barack Obama.[8]

The History of American Fascism Part I

The chilling *I Pledge Video* by Demi Moore and Ashton Kutcher, which has been widely circulated online since the late summer of 2009, is an example of how a pledge can be corrupted by a Fascist movement. The popular celebrities surround themselves with other artists who all pledge to do something that is perceived by them to be helpful. For example, not using plastic bags and not flushing the toilet after urinating, may seem as a positive step and give the viewer a benign way of "doing something," but there are those that are a bit more extreme. At the end, Moore pledges, "to be a servant to our president."[9]

This is a stark contrast to what conservatives believe. The president is supposed to be a servant of the people for the people, not an autocrat who demands service from the citizenry. The whole point of the American Revolution was to break free from absolutist rule so individuals would be able to exercise their freedom. Under Fascist rule, the individual is subservient to the group and its Great Leader. Service to, and sacrifice for the Great Leader is expected from all for the good of the nation.

It is true that oaths of allegiance are required for newly naturalized American citizens, and this is considered the "Oath of Citizenship," and more importantly this isn't just an American tradition and/or requirement. Additionally, many nations require oaths when joining the armed forces or assuming public office. President Obama did himself take such an oath when he became POTUS. But this concept of oaths of allegiance, which does go back to medieval times, was something embraced by those with more sinister notions.

How would this be different from the oaths offered to individuals? For example, the oath for Dutch Members of Parliament says:

> "I swear (affirm) allegiance to the King, to the Statute for the Kingdom of the Netherlands, and to the Constitution."[10]

Is it thus not hard to believe that the Pledge of Allegiance in the United States - again, one that has been rewritten four times - couldn't be further changed to swear allegiance to an individual. President Obama is so popular, why not swear a Pledge of Allegiance to him, or at least the office that he holds. Given that there is a division in this country already, it might not seem so strange. What better way

America's Road to Fascism

to bring all American's together than by a simple act of fidelity. If it is good enough for our celebrities it must be good for everyone. But of course the road where it leads is a frightening one.

In Hitler's Nazi Germany, there was an "oath of allegiance" that was sworn not only by German Wehrmacht (armed forces) officers and soldiers,[11] but also by civil servants. This lasted throughout the Third Reich's reign of terror from 1933 to 1945. Unlike our military's oath to uphold the constitution, the German oath was one made to the Hitler persona, not the national constitution. The oath that was used by the military read as follows:

> "I swear by God this sacred oath that I shall render unconditional obedience to Adolf Hitler, the leader of the German state and people, supreme commander of the armed forces, and that I shall at all times be ready, as a brave soldier, to give my life for this oath." [12]

The oath that was used by civil officials:

> "I swear: I will be faithful and obedient to Adolf Hitler, leader of the German state and people, to observe the law, and to conscientiously fulfill my official duties, so help me God."[13]

Neither of these oaths seems particularly dangerous; accept in hindsight when we know of the terrible crimes committed by Hitler. But in a nation such as Germany's it resulted in a terrible situation, where good men found themselves bound by honor to Hitler! How many officers and soldiers were just "following orders" because of this oath and their sense of honor? In fact, it has been argued ever since the end of the war that the reason that the soldiers did not and could not act against him was out of this sense of loyalty. To do so would require them to break their very sense of military and civil service honor.

In America we have never had a loyalty oath to a president but there have been loyalty oaths. After the Civil War, Southerners were required to swear an oath to "faithfully support, protect and defend the Constitution of the United States, and the union of the States thereunder"[14] as a condition for a Presidential pardon. During the Great Depression, 100,000 school children marched to Boston Common and swore a loyalty oath administered by the mayor, "I promise as a good American citizen to do my part for the NRA (National Recovery Administration). I will buy only where the Blue Eagle flies."[15] Similar oaths were administered during WWII and the early years of the Cold War. In the 1960s and 1970s the Supreme Court wrestled with the constitutionality of such oaths.[16] The last case was heard in 1972, and found constitutional a requirement that State of Massachusetts employees swear to uphold and defend the Constitution and to "oppose the overthrow of the [government] by force, violence, or by any illegal or unconstitutional method."[17]

The emotional outbursts of enthusiasm that the Obama presidency creates isn't any different than the throngs of cheering crowds that met Hitler at his pre- and post- chancellorship rallies. Both men had a message of hope and change for a better future and a plan to change the political status quo that was perceived to be broken. A simple loyalty oath to serve the Great Leader isn't much to ask when utopia is so close.

This sense of hope actually fosters itself at dark times. The United States, while being the land of the free and home of the brave, has needed to heal at times. The Pledge of Allegiance was introduced at such a time, when the wounds of the American Civil War had still not fully healed. As the 20th Century dawned, western nations were full of hope. Economies were booming, science and technology were making life easier and the rich were getting richer along with the poor. Major war was something most believed couldn't happen on a civilized continent like Europe. It was a time when anything was possible.

The painful truth is that the war did happen, and the cream of an entire male European generation was killed and broken by the trench warfare of WWI. The physical and psychological destruction of this so-called "Great War" killed the hope and ambition that opened the century. In Russia a revolution toppled the centuries old monarchy, and resulted in a civil war far worse and bloody than any the world had seen. The Bolshevik Revolution and the ensuing Russian Civil War was a wake up call to those opposed to far left wing Marxism.

This course of events brought on the Nazi movement in Germany and the Fascists in Italy. In the United States it resulted in the first "Red Scare," as many European socialists and communists fled the old world for the new. The national fear that swept through the United States saw potential communists in every left-leaning organization. This included the labor unions, which had been gaining in strength and power in the decades leading up to the First World War.

There were fears that a Bolshevik Revolution would spread to the United States. According to Karl Marx, communism would first take root in highly developed industrial countries, which the United States led at the time. This would destroy American life by ending free enterprise, expropriating private property, dismantling religious freedom and discarding the traditional family structure. This fear was started by strikes in the United States throughout 1916 and 1917, brought on by the Industrial Workers of the World (IWW).[18]

In 1919 authorities in the United States discovered that 36 bombs were to be mailed to highly visible businessmen and prominent American politicians, including the likes of John D. Rockefeller and Supreme Court Justice Oliver Wendell Holmes.[19] Later that same year eight bombs in eight cities exploded at the same hour! "Most of the bombs erupted in cities with powerful Italian anarchist movements: Boston, New York, Patterson."[20] And in September of 1920, decades before the 1993 World Trade Center bombing or the tragedy of September 11, 2001, lower Manhattan was rocked by an explosion perpetrated by anarchists that killed 38 people and injured 400 others. At the time it was the deadliest terrorist attack on U.S. soil.

A worldwide left-wing revolution was supposed to begin on May 1, 1920 (May Day or International Worker's Day) but never happened. Instead the Communist Party of the United States lost many members and the roaring 20s washed away these fears, at least until the Great Depression arrived. The first Red Scare resulted in new laws that were meant to protect Americanism from the red menace. This included the passage of laws that limited free speech and targeted certain ideologies for investigation and prosecution.

The 1920s also saw a period that has been classified by some as an era of lawlessness, which saw a rise in organized crime. Movies and TV shows dramatize and even romanticize the "gangsters," and while entertainment might evoke images of Tommy Gun wielding bank robberies and shootouts, the truth is far less colorful. To combat the lawlessness of this era, Washington greatly increased the powers of the Federal Bureau of Investigation (FBI). As with many cases where power is given, it is usually not taken back when the crisis is over.

The 1920s also saw a polarization in American society. This was a fast paced decade of stock speculation, gin and jazz: fortunes were made - only to be lost in October of 1929 with the stock market crash. It was also an era when racism and what have been labeled "right wing" organizations gained a new foothold. By the First World War, the Ku Klux Klan's power had waned but it reached its peak of power in the 1920s. Figures suggest that the organization had nearly 4.5 million members by 1924. The Klan was a national movement that reached far beyond the rural south where it was born. At the time it wasn't anti-government but a movement that tried to take the reins of political power. There was membership in states such as Ohio, California and Oregon. The Klan's stronghold was in Indiana, where Klan member Edward Jackson was elected governor in 1924.[21]

The KKK's rise to power in the 1920s is similar to fascist movements in Europe at the same time. On August 8, 1925, between 30,000 and 35,000 Klan members marched on Washington, D.C.,[22] reminiscent of Mussolini's march on Rome. This shows that large sections of the American population are willing to embrace anti-democratic political movements when conditions are right.

It is easy to point to the white-sheeted men marching on Washington in the 1920s and suggest that this was part of American fascism but the violence that the KKK advocated didn't sit well with most Americans. A more insidious form of fascism, if you will velvet fascism, has deep roots in the political movements of America. You know this as progressive politics.

The progressives can be traced back to the early 1800s, before the American Civil War. Abolition, better treatment of the mentally ill and prison reform were signature causes that progressives championed. Some attempted to start communal communities where non-violent anarchists could withdraw from the rest of the nation and experiment with utopia.

These early causes were targeted at state and local laws; and exercised the 10th Amendment to the Constitution. After the Civil War, progressives aimed at changing the American landscape on a national level. The country went through the industrial revolution at this time, and millions moved from the farm to the city. Millions more emigrated from the old world looking for a better life.

Muckraking journalists backed the progressives by telling stories of poverty, child labor, evil robber barons and unclean food production. National laws like the *Interstate Commerce Act* and the *Sherman Antitrust Act* federally regulated business for the first time. The hand of big government was just starting to reach from its Washington crib.

The progressives jettisoned religious institutions as a means for change and instead looked to government intervention. They were convinced that the government must play an active role in establishing economic fairness and the solving of social problems. Black citizens and those living on reservations weren't included in such protections.

The racial bias of progressives isn't surprising considering that prominent progressives supported eugenics as a way to initiate national regeneration. The powers of government were used to sterilize tens of thousands of women in the United States between 1907 and 1940. Most were poor uneducated minorities or mentally ill white women. When the Nazis started their eugenics program they looked to American methods and law as a starting point.

The progressives scored a major victory in 1901 when President William McKinley was assassinated and Theodore Roosevelt became the youngest president at age 42, after "a quarter-century of change had swept the field of its attachment to purely literary narrative and Romantic expression."[23] Having made a name for himself in the Spanish-American War, Teddy Roosevelt was a rising star of sorts, and those who worried about his progressive leanings placed him in a position where he could do little harm, namely in the office of the Vice President. But when McKinley was assassinated in September 1901, Roosevelt rose higher than anyone had expected.

He was known for trust busting and increased federal regulation of business. He attempted to move the Republican Party into the progressive camp with his Square Deal, where he emphasized that his domestic policies would give the average citizen a fair shake. In Roosevelt's words:

> "I stand for the square deal. But when I say that I am for the square deal, I mean not merely that I stand for fair play under the present rules of the game, but that I stand for having those rules changed so as to work for a more substantial equality of opportunity and of reward for equally good service."[24]

He was also an early environmentalist and set aside large stretches of land for national parks. Like Obama, Roosevelt won the Nobel Peace Prize. Unlike Obama, Roosevelt actually negotiated a peace, that between Russia and Japan during their war over Manchuria in 1905.

Roosevelt served out the rest of McKinley's term and ran for re-election, then helped his successor William Howard Taft to the White House. However, as Roosevelt became angered by the direction the far more conservative, and suddenly independent, Taft took the nation, Roosevelt tried to regain power.

Thus, the second progressive president was elected in 1912 when Roosevelt's Bull Moose Party split the Republican vote, with Democrat Woodrow Wilson winning the election. During his first term, Wilson increased the powers of the federal government by passing the *Federal Reserve Act* (1913), *Federal Trade Commission Act* (1914), *Clayton Antitrust Act* (1914) and the *Federal Farm Loan Act* (1916).[25] He also passed the first American progressive tax. You know this as the income tax.[26]

Wilson was narrowly reelected under the banner, "he kept us out of the war." A year later he changed his mind and dragged the country into the horrors of the First World War. In his declaration of war speech, on April 2, 1917, Wilson feared that if the Central Powers, which included Kaiser Wilhelm II's Germany, won then western civilization could be destroyed. He promised this would be the "war to end all wars." This idealistic view is typical of progressives but isn't based in reality. In fact, the defeated Germany eventually followed World War I veteran Adolf Hitler down the path to World War II.

Despite Wilson's promise, and that fact that Germany clearly expected America to enter the war as that nation began a policy of unrestricted submarine warfare against all ships sailing to Great Britain (including those carrying neutral passengers), there remained a large peace movement at the time that opposed U.S. entry into WWI. To suppress these movements Wilson passed the *Espionage Act* of 1917 and the *Sedition Act* of 1918. The U.S. Post Office refused to carry any written material that was seen as critical of the war effort. Around sixty periodicals lost their second-class mailing rights. "The Sedition Act, passed in May 1918, permitted the jailing of citizens who uttered anything, 'disloyal, profane, scurrilous, or abusive' about the government of the armed forces."[27]

The Committee on Public Information, the nation's first propaganda office was set up. Known as the Creel Commission, the United States was flooded with pro-war anti-German messages. The Commission also conducted a range of censorship measures.

A quasi-private organization, the American Protective League assisted federal agents in rooting out unpatriotic citizens. At its height, the League had 250,000 members in 600 cities. The group was backed by the Wilson administration and issued Government badges. Members conducted warrant-less searches and interrogations with Wilson's blessings. Anyone considered pro-German, a slacker or critical of the government was investigated. Even refusing to buy Liberty Bonds could lead to an unfriendly knock on the door.

A lesser-known but more insidious group, the Anti Yellow Dog League was made up of schoolboys over the age of 10, "and claimed thousands of branches throughout the country."[28] They set out to find disloyal people in their communities, perhaps even a parent.

Flash forward 20 years and it is easy to compare both American Leagues to the brown-shirted SA and Hitler Youth of Nazi Germany.

Wilson also created intrigue where there was none, and created fear where there needed not be. "Because there had been no direct attack on the United States, and no direct threat to America's national security, the Wilson administration needed to create an 'outraged public' in order to arouse Americans to enlist, contribute money, and make the many other sacrifices war demands. This was the first and perhaps the great challenge to the administration. Not surprisingly, this led to one of the most fiercely repressive periods in American history."[29]

Towards the end of the war Wilson issued his Fourteen Points, which were to create a lasting peace. He helped negotiate an armistice with Germany and went to Paris in 1919 to shape the Treaty of Versailles. Like Obama, Wilson also won the Nobel Peace Prize. Unlike Obama, Wilson was instrumental in forming a worldwide organization to promote peace, the League of Nations. The hope and goal of this group was to ensure that the world would never face a war like the Great War. But of course the League's power was far from lasting. The Great War gave way to the Roaring '20s, and put the progressive movement on the sidelines for a while. But it wouldn't be the last time that a progressive headed to the White House.

The third progressive president was Herbert Hoover, who of course is seldom seen this way due to his handling of the Great Depression. However, as we shall see, many of his policies did not differ all that much from his successor.

It would be apt to say that Hoover was between a rock and a hard place when the Wall Street crash came, and it should have been a place he knew well. Hoover was actually a mining engineer and tried to translate this to governmental problems. He championed government intervention into the private sector as economic modernization.

As with Teddy Roosevelt, Hoover also found himself in the center of war at the turn of the century. In Hoover's case, he was a "25-year old American mining engineer who, along with his wife, had taken refuge in Tientsin" in China during the Boxer Rebellion in 1901.[30] This could explain how throughout his life Hoover was usually seen to be quite calm under pressure.

Hoover was elected president never having held an elective office before, although he had held the cabinet position of United States Secretary of Commerce under Presidents Warren Harding and Calvin Coolidge. In that capacity, he had promoted government intervention to modernize the economy under scientific economic models. "Hoover never forgot that his main responsibility as commerce secretary was to serve American business, though always with an eye on how to improve it. With his encouragement, the Bureau of the Census in July 1921 launched *Survey of Current Business*, an invaluable monthly periodical."[31]

He believed in the Efficiency Movement, an idea held that government and the private sector was naturally inefficient and wasteful. The movement further stressed that only experts could identify these shortcomings and create solutions to solve them. "That nation, so it was argued, needed cooperative programs that would help to reduce industrial costs, allocate resources to their most productive uses, and iron out harmful fluctuations in employment, output, and demand. And government, so the argument continued, could and should play a limited role in launching and nourishing such programs."[32] These experts can be seen as forerunners to the "czars" that infest modern presidencies.

As a progressive, Hoover treated the presidency as a way to improve the living conditions of all Americans by federal regulations and a call for volunteerism. He attacked laissez-faire thinking and advocated direct government action. Eighty years later Americans would hear a similar message from candidate Obama.

In November of 1928, President-Elect Hoover went on a seven-week goodwill tour of several Latin American countries, a move that seems to be similar to Obama's multiple international goodwill tours. During it Hoover outlined his economic and trade policies that he wanted to see implemented throughout the Western Hemisphere.[33] While not as geographically ambitious as Obama's whirlwind tours of the world to date, transportation and international realities were different than today. And unlike Obama, there is no evidence that Hoover apologized or bowed to the foreign leaders he met during his travels. However, "in Nicaragua, Hoover told the leaders of two hostile factions that he planned to end Uncle Sam's military presence in their country. Holding true to that pledge, he refused to send forces into the interior - even when incursions by the anti-American rebel August Sandino, whom Hoover thought 'a bandit beyond the pale,' took American lives. On January 2, 1933, the last detachment of marines pulled out of Nicaragua."[34] The same year Hoover would leave the White House.

Hoover failed to win reelection in 1932 mainly because of the Great Depression, which hit America in October of 1929. He attempted to battle the economic downturn by raising tariffs, taxes and increasing government spending. His opponent, Franklin D. Roosevelt attacked these measures, and Hoover was accused of spending and taxing too much, as well as placing millions on the government dole. Roosevelt attacked Hoover's attempt to increase the powers of the Federal Government and blasted him for outspending any administration during peacetime in the history of the United States. Roosevelt's running mate John Garner even accused Hoover of "leading the country down the path of socialism."[35]

This may seem ironic, when you consider the New Deal that followed, but clearly the fourth progressive president, Roosevelt, didn't mind running to the right of his opponent. The truth is policy didn't play a large part in the 1932 election. Hoover was so unpopular that the cartoon character Betty Boop could have beaten him.

Not exactly liberal, but certainly not conservative, the progressives had policies that embraced the "third way" and falls under the roof of fascism. The irony here is that many American businessmen believed that Roosevelt was openly hostile to them, but some liberal-minded critics believed he was far too friendly.

FDR's attempts to get America "moving again" and out of the Great Depression included tactics that could - at least in hindsight today - be viewed as Fascist. One of the most glaring is the *National Industrial Recovery Act* (NIRA). In his memoirs, former President Herbert Hoover stated that the NIRA was reminiscent of Mussolini's corporate state, and "in 1935 former President Herbert Hoover was using phrases like 'Fascist regimentation' in discussing the New Deal."[36]

The comparisons go deeper. FDR was a master politician, one who knew how to manipulate the media - to the point that he used (or as Michael S. Sweeney contends misused) the Office of Censorship during World War II. He hid his affair with Lucy Page Mercer Rutherfurd and concealed his deteriorating health from the public.[37]

FDR was a relentless campaigner, both before and after getting elected. He used rallies, parades and the new media of radio to promote his agenda, notably his economic policies. Today it is credibly argued that many of the policies and practices of the New Deal that went into effect between 1933 and 1935 may have actually had the opposite effect of those intended. Government interference in the economy extended the length and severity of the economic downturn.

While most European countries recovered from the worldwide depression after two or three years, the U.S. economy saw little or negative growth throughout the decade. It was believed by some that Great Britain would outstrip the U.S. in industrial output. It took America's entry into the Second World War in December of 1941 to finally snap the country out of the Great Depression.

During the 1930s there were many critics of the New Deal. To the classical liberals (think modern conservatives) the New Deal was a sign of big business controlled by bureaucrats with the usual bureaucratic waste. One result of the New Deal that is still with us is the expanded role of the Federal Government. Does this sound familiar to the situation facing us today? On the other end the far left saw the New Deal as business as usual for large corporations, with the government picking up the check while the rich got richer. One notable supporter of the New Deal was Italy's Mussolini, but this isn't a surprise, since it was just a brand of American fascism at its very best.

Progressive regulation of business creates a paradox. While the politicians give lip service to the importance of small businesses and entrepreneurs, big business profits the most from regulation. Large corporations are better able to absorb the extra costs of government interference. The small business owner can't, and has to close shop. The large corporation is then able to take over that market share and become even larger.

One of the core pieces of the New Deal was the National Recovery Administration, which was created as part of the *National Industrial Recovery Act of 1933* (NIRA). The intention was to create "codes of fair competition," and to reduce "destructive competition," a common theme repeated time and time again as being good for business; regardless if it means holding back a successful company just to help a less successful one. Supporters of the New Deal claimed this was just leveling the playing field.[38]

One problem the Great Depression created was falling prices and wages. This is known as deflation. We are used to inflation, where the purchasing power of the dollar shrinks over time. In the 1930s, the dollar increased in purchasing power. To combat this, the New Deal created the first minimum wage law and price controls. One side effect of this hurt black laborers. Business owners weren't willing to pay blacks the minimum wage when there were so many whites unemployed.

The links between fascism and the New Deal, or at least the NRA (never to be confused with the National Rifle Association), are even closer when we examine Hugh Samuel Johnson, the first NRA director. Like today's czars, Johnson was appointed by FDR to administer the National Recovery Administration. Johnson believed that the NRA was akin to its farming counterpart in the Agricultural Adjustment Administration. "As bold as the NRA was in conception, it was more audacious in action."[39]

Johnson was a retired brigadier army general and a successful businessman. He also helped organize the Democratic Party in 1932. These traits; businessman, general and organizer came together in a unique way. Johnson developed a solid interest - and possibly admiration - for Mussolini and the Fascists. He suggested that FDR take on Mussolini-like policies when it came to the economy. Critics of Johnson have noted that he embraced Fascist corporatism, and even suggested to Labor Secretary Francis Perkins that copies of *The Corporate State*, a suitably Fascist look at economics, be given to the Labor cabinet.[40]

As director of the NRA, Johnson helped draw up codes for trade associations and industries. He believed the organization was crucial to restoring jobs and to fixing the economy. For his efforts *Time Magazine* named him as Man of the Year for 1933.

One of his initiatives to boost support for the NRA was the "Blue Eagle," which was part of a PR campaign meant to be used by business and labor. The concept was that all companies that accepted FDR's Re-employment Agreement or the Code of Fair Competition would be permitted to display a poster showing the Blue Eagle. The icon proclaimed that the business was an "NRA Member," and that "We Do Our Part." Of course consumers were encouraged to buy products or obtain services from companies that displayed the banner. Author Jonah Goldberg sums up the symbol quite well. "The Blue Eagle was the patriotic symbol of compliance that all companies were expected to hang from their doors."[41]

Consider that at the same time in Nazi Germany, a similar campaign was being waged *against* Jewish owned businesses. The SA hung posters pointing out Jewish owned businesses that the public was supposed to boycott. The Blue Eagle may thus seem sinister in hindsight, but anyone venturing into some large American cities a year after Election Day will find campaign posters of Barack Obama still proudly displayed.

Fortunately the Blue Eagle fell from the sky soon after the campaign was launched. Johnson faced his own downfall, much of which was blamed on heavy drinking. But he had major disagreements with NRA policies and his reported drinking may have been a cover story. "By the middle of 1934, Johnson's increasing incapacity began to rouse concern at the White House."[42] He was even labeled as having Fascist leanings by Perkins, and was subsequently reassigned to the Works Progress Administration. While he supported FDR in the 1936 elections, Johnson failed to agree with some of the President's policies. He eventually supported Republican challenger Wendell Willkie in 1940.

As for the Blue Eagle, it lasted until September of 1935 when the compulsory code system was invalidated, and the emblem was prohibited. The U.S. Supreme Court unanimously (how often does that happen) declared in *Schechter Poultry Corp. v. United States* that the NIRA was unconstitutional.[43] The high court ruled that the NIRA violated the separation of powers as an impermissible delegation of legislative power to the executive branch. The Court also held that the NIRA provisions were in excess of congressional power under the Commerce Clause of the Constitution.

It is interesting to note that the owners of Schechter Poultry were the Schechter brothers, who sold kosher chickens. The government originally charged the brothers with sixty violations of the NIRA and conspiracy. At a time while the Nazi's were boycotting Jewish businesses, our government was using unconstitutional powers to prosecute them.

It is also worth noting when former National Football League commissioner DeBenneville "Bert" Bell formed the Philadelphia Eagles - which replaced the defunct Frankford Yellow Jackets - he named his team the Eagles in recognition of the NRA.[44] However, he went with green and white colors instead of blue, but the team retains this name to this day.

The death of Franklin Roosevelt in 1945 resulted in the end of what could be considered the final progressive president and possibly first American Fascist leader. To ensure that no other president could attempt to gain the same power the U.S. ratified the 22nd Amendment in 1951. The Amendment makes a person ineligible to be elected for a third term, or to be elected for a second time after having served more than two years of a previous president's term. While Harry S. Truman, who became president following the death of FDR, was exempt due to a grandfather clause in the amendment; it was a moot point. Truman did not run for reelection after his second term.

The wording of the 22nd Amendment on these points:

Section 1. No person shall be elected to the office of the President more than twice, and no person who has held the office of President, or acted as President, for more than two years of a term to which some other person was elected

President shall be elected to the office of the President more than once. But this article shall not apply to any person holding the office of President when this article was proposed by the Congress, and shall not prevent any person who may be holding the office of President, or acting as President, during the term within which this article becomes operative from holding the office of President or acting as President during the remainder of such term.

Section 2. This article shall be inoperative unless it shall have been ratified as an amendment to the Constitution by the legislatures of three-fourths of the several States within seven years from the date of its submission to the States by the Congress.[45]

It is still debatable as to what were the intentions of the founders as pertaining to the length that the POTUS should serve in office. George Washington started the trend of running for two terms, and choose not to seek a third term. Thomas Jefferson, James Madison and James Monroe all followed the two-term principle.

It is worth noting that Jefferson wrote about this very point in 1807. "If some termination to the services of the chief magistrate be not fixed by the Constitution or supplied in practice, his office, nominally for years, will in fact become for life; and history shows how easily that degenerates into an inheritance. Believing that a representative government, responsible at short periods of election, is that which produces the greatest sum of happiness to mankind, I feel it a duty to do no act which shall essentially impair that principle; and I should unwillingly be the person who, disregarding the sound precedent set by an illustrious predecessor, should furnish the first example of prolongation beyond the second term of office."[46]

What Jefferson didn't know at the time was that progressives would come along later and disagree with his limited government concept. The good of the collective takes precedence over the liberty of the individual. Only a strong leader with no term limit can reform the country along these lines as quickly as possible.

In fairness, FDR was not the first president to run for reelection a second time, he was just the first to succeed. Republican Ulysses S. Grant first sought a third term in 1880, but was unable to win his party's nomination. Theodore Roosevelt had succeeded to the office after the assassination of William McKinley, and subsequently was elected to a full term. He stepped down from office, but unhappy with his successor, William Howard Taft, ran for office as a third-party candidate. Roosevelt's split with the Republicans allowed Woodrow Wilson to win with less than fifty percent of the popular vote.

The Constitution also forbids a former two-term president, such as Bill Clinton or George W. Bush, from serving as vice president. This is based on the 22nd Amendment combined with the 12th Amendment, which was ratified in 1804. The 12th Amendment states, "no person constitutionally ineligible to the office of president shall be eligible to that of vice president of the United States."[47]

There have been arguments made that term limiting the POTUS essentially limit's the power and influence of the president. Dwight D. Eisenhower, to whom the amendment first applied, was the first to express concern that it eroded the power of the office. And in recent years, there have been movements by several congressmen to repeal the 22nd Amendment, including House Democrats Rep. José Serrano of New York, Rep. Barney Frank of Massachusetts, Rep. Howard Berman of California and Senator Harry Reid of Nevada. Below is an example of such a bill introduced by Rep. Serrano in January of 2009:

> H.J.Res.5 - Proposing an amendment to the Constitution of the United States to repeal the twenty-second article of amendment, thereby removing the limitation on the number of terms an individual may serve as President.[48]

This is only the newest proposal to repeal the presidential term-limit. Various members of Congress and the Senate have offered similar proposals for repealing the 22nd Amendment. To date 21 attempts have been made over the last 20 years. Serrano's is just the most recent. For the Constitution to be amended, two thirds of both federal houses have to agree. Alternatively, two thirds of the states must vote to call for a Constitutional Convention. Once this hurdle is overcome, three fourths of the states must ratify the Amendment.

It is unlikely that the 22nd Amendment will be overturned anytime soon. A super-majority has to be reached just to bring a change to the Constitution to a vote by the states. For now none of these proposals have even reached a point where a vote was brought before Congress. Some have been referred to committee but went nowhere. But it does beg the question as why anyone - on either side of the aisle - would even seek to introduce such legislation?

One answer could be that this deflects calls for congressional and senatorial term limits. Currently, while the president may only serve up to 10 years in total - considering that he or she could finish out up to two years of a predecessor's term, plus be reelected twice more - there are no term limits in the House or Senate. These professional politicians often stay in office for decades, and only death keeps them from winning reelection. Even death isn't always an obstacle. There is at least one example of a dead senator beating his live opponent.

Supreme Court justices too are appointed for life, but at least they aren't allowed to hear cases after they die. All of this is part of the checks and balances created by the founders to ensure that the nation continued down the road of a democratic republic.

Chapter Three
The History of American Fascism Part II

While the media today regularly reports about "extremist" groups, and over the past 20 years it has been commonplace to find white supremacists, Neo-Nazis and other "hate" groups on talk shows, the truth is that the original American Fascists date back to before the Second World War. Many of these groups actually had ties to the German NSDAP, and as such were more of an imported brand of fascism, rather than a truly homegrown version.

To understand this, we must understand that the United States is really as much a nation of Germans as it is a nation of Englishmen. While it is easy to see our historical ties to England, the fact is that the Germans have deep roots here as well, going back to the colonial days. "In 1608, the first German settlers arrived at Jamestown, Virginia, thus marking the beginning date in German-American history, and in 1683 group immigration began with the arrival of the first group of German immigrants, who established the first permanent German settlement in America at Germantown, Pennsylvania. The stage was thereby set for the beginnings of the German immigration on a massive scale, and this occurred in the early 1700s with the immigration from southwest Germany, especially from the Palatinate."[1]

There was continued immigration from Germany. "The United States was well advertised by the second quarter of the nineteenth century in Europe as the 'common man's utopia.' Shippers and American consuls circulated guidebooks on the young country, and letters from relatives and friends in America fed an 'immigration fever.'"[2] In the late 19th and early 20th Centuries, German speakers made up the largest contingent of U.S. immigrants.

"From 1816 to 1914, about five and a half million Germans came to the United States."[3] German language periodicals and later radio stations could be found in larger cities. Some feared this migration, especially during the First World War. At one point Hitler commented that U.S. culture would eventually become German because of this immigration. However, he later changed his opinion based on Nazi racial-mixing theory, in which so-called lower races would pollute German stock. There was real fear in the United States at the time that these new arrivals would gain political power and change the character of the country.

The earliest group, at least to adopt what would be correctly labeled as Nazism, was the Free Society of Teutonia (FTS), a German-American organization that was founded in 1924 by German immigrants in Chicago. "The threat of Nazism had hardly permeated the American consciousness. But in the heartland of America, a shadow was being cast that would be felt for years to come. America had witnessed its first sign of native fascism when four German immigrants founded the Free Society of Teutonia in Detroit."[4] FTS included actual Nazi Party members Fritz and Peter Gissibl, who began the group as a club. Of course the concept of a "club" being disguised for other methods has a long and dubious history in the United States, with everything from Latino gangs that are called "clubs" by members in Los Angeles to Italian social clubs being a front for organized crime. Regardless of whether this was really a club, or the foundation of a political movement; it soon followed the patterns of the Nazis in Germany. "During the next two years, the Society attracted hundreds of new members, most of them German immigrants, many of them formerly active in Hitler's circle. By 1932, the Teutonians had established branches in five American cities."[5]

The FTS's membership include a weapon wielding force that mirrored the SA (the Sturmabteilung or brown shirts in Hitler's party), and this group was used as muscle as the organization became critics of Communists in the United States, the Treaty of Versailles as it related to the "Fatherland" and of course Jews. The FTS never grew in size and it was eventually absorbed into a larger pro-Nazi German-American movement.

At the same time that Hitler gained power in Germany, a new organization was founded. This was the Friends of New Germany. It was actually authorized by Nazi Deputy Führer Rudolf Hess in May of 1933; only three months after Hitler became Chancellor of Germany. Working with Hess and the German consul, Heinz

Spanknobel, a German citizen living in New York City, formed this Nazi American group. Spanknobel had been a longtime member of the Teutonia Society.[6] It was based in the New York City area, but eventually partnered with the FTS, which maintained its own strong presence in Chicago. "Spanknobel called himself Führer and instructed his followers to do the same. The Newark branch of the Friends became one of the largest in the country,"[7] and was the site of a major rally and subsequent raid by the police. Despite this minor setback the Friends were doing well, at least for a while. The Friends of New Germany eventually absorbed the FTS, as well as the Gau-USA, another German-American based Nazi organization. By the middle of the 1930s it was the largest Nazi group in the United States.

And while the Nazis in Germany had their own power struggles, so too did the groups in the United States. Spanknobel was ousted from power, but this was not the only setback the group faced. As the organization followed the German model, the Friends of New Germany worked to gain a foothold with German immigrants, and even called on a Jewish boycott in the heavily German populated neighborhood of Yorkville in Manhattan's Upper East Side.[8]

Instead of bringing on widespread support, this was a public relations disaster for the group. The boycott led to an investigation as well, brought by Samuel Dickstein, who was a Democratic Congressman from New York. He would go on to help establish the committee that eventually transformed into the House Committee on Un-American Activities. While this committee would later be remembered for its Red Scare tactics in the post-war years, in the mid-1930s it looked at not only suspected communists, but Nazi sympathizers and fascists as well.

Dickstein's investigation of the Friends of New Germany didn't sit well with the true Nazis in old Germany, and soon Berlin pulled the plug. "Nervous that the Nazis' activities were attracting too much negative attention, Hess issued a new directive in December 1935 that effectively disbanded FONG."[9]

By 1936, the Friends of New Germany was without friends, and the group ceased to be - at least in name. Instead, Hitler appointed

Fritz Julius Kuhn as the head of the American Nazi Party, and the group was reborn as the German American Bund. "As Kuhn conceived it, the Bund would build within the United States a solid core of support for Nazi Germany (a mission Hitler cared about) and would instill in German-Americans a respect for their cultural heritage."[10]

The Bund eventually established training camps outside New York, in nearby Sussex County, New Jersey and on Long Island in Suffolk County. New recruits could be schooled in techniques for spreading fascism to America.[11] There was little, if any, paramilitary training at these camps. They were more like retreats, where members would be schooled in the group's ideology. This shouldn't be confused with Middle Eastern terror cell training camps that have been repeatedly shown on cable news.

Hitler wanted the group to take a low key. He didn't want the American Nazi's interfering with his diplomatic moves and eventual conquest of Europe. Kuhn had other plans. The group grew in size, and reached its peek with the President's Day, February 19, 1939 rally at Madison Square Garden in New York City. This rally is so well known it served as the basis of an early episode of TV's *Seinfeld*, where the characters accidentally end up traveling to a similar meeting at the current MSG. The Madison Square Garden event is included in the propaganda film *Why We Fight*, which was shown to American soldiers going off to fight WWII. In fact, the 1939 rally drew some 20,000 people, close to the number of Klansmen who marched on Washington fifteen years earlier.

It was marked by Kuhn appearing on stage with large Nazi flags and oversized posters of first American President George Washington. During his speech, Kuhn criticized the New Deal, reportedly calling it the "Jew Deal" and referred to FDR as "Franklin D. Rosenfeld." While the group never seemed stronger, this would also be the turning point, as protestors and Bund storm troopers clashed, resulting in harsh criticism and outrage throughout the country.

It was not hard for the group to be labeled as "anti-American" and while it staggered on with the outbreak of World War II, by

The History of American Fascism Part II

the time of the bombing of Pearl Harbor on December 7, 1941, the opinion of all things Germany changed. But Kuhn and the Bund had their own troubles well before Germany became an enemy of the United States.

Kuhn was investigated for embezzling money from the Bund. On May 26, 1939 he was arrested in New York and charged with forgery and grand larceny. The indictment alleged that he had stolen Bund funds.[12] But the Bund operated on the concept that the leader's powers were absolute, so it did not want to prosecute (a fact that might seem ironic today given the way that banks operated after Barack Obama's bail out). While the group didn't seek to bring down Kuhn, the New York City district attorney's office did. Kuhn suffered a downfall, and while other leaders replaced him, it was the House Committee on Un-American Activities that basically made it impossible for the group to have any significant influence during World War II. "During the barely remembered 'Brown scare' of the 1940s, everyone from real Nazi supporters - the German-American Bund, for example - to misguided isolationists was targeted and harassed."[13]

By the end of the war the German American Bund was as much history as the actual Nazis. Unfortunately, this would not be the last time that the ideology of Nazism would appear in the United States of America.

Not all of the original Fascists and proto-Fascists were imported. While many of the groups were made up of imports, there were homegrown versions that lasted briefly as well. Among the most notable was the Silver Legion of America, also known as the Silver Shirts. Founded just days after Hitler came to power in January of 1933 by William Dudley Pelley,[14] the group sought to draw on membership from the lower classes - and in this way mirrored the direction that the New Party, and later the British Union of Fascists took under Oswald Mosley. As with Mosley, the Silver Shirts looked to Mussolini and Hitler for cues on ideology and symbolism. The group was eventually linked to a host of other anti-Semitic groups.[15]

The Silver Legion, Pelley's avid followers, used a scarlet "L" as its symbol. This icon evoked the concept of "Loyalty to the

American Republic," "Liberation from Materialism" and "Loyalty to the Silver Legion". The group had its own version of storm troopers, who wore a uniform based on their German idols. The uniform was made up of blue trousers, leggings, silver shirt and tie with the scarlet "L" over the heart.[16]

The group was clearly based on the black shirts of Fascist Italy. The black shirts were a reflection of the "redshirts" worn by Italian nationalists during Giuseppe Garibaldi's Mille expedition. The redshirts were volunteers to the unification cause,[17] and Mussolini adopted the term "black shirts" for his own movement. Other fascistic movements adopted their own shirts, notably Mosley's black shirts (no originality there) and Hitler's brown shirts. The moral is watch out for any movement that features single colored shirts!

Pelley, who has been called the "Star-Spangled Fascist," not only adopted a movement that was similar to Mussolini's, but he also came from the same type of background. He was a journalist - whilst Mussolini was a newspaper editor - and Pelley was widely respected for his articles and writing style. He gained notoriety as a foreign correspondent, and traveled widely throughout Europe and Asia following the First World War. This included travels to Japan and on to Russia during the Russian Civil War, where he no doubt witnessed first hand many atrocities committed by both sides. However, he developed a hatred for communism, which he feared would dominate the globe and lead to the destruction of civilization.[18]

As with many proto-Fascists of the era, he too saw the Jews as somehow behind this vast conspiracy - likely because there were Jews in notable positions within Communist groups. Interestingly, Pelley did not immediately opt to start a political movement, but instead went to Hollywood where he became a screenwriter and novelist. He wrote two films that starred silent actor Lon Chaney, including *The Light in the Dark* and *The Shock*.[19]

However, Pelley never fully "went Hollywood," and in 1929 left the movie business. He moved to North Carolina, where he had what he described as an out-of-body experience. This surreal turn of events led him to gain an interest in both Christianity and metaphysics. While this may seem like mutually exclusive concepts today, these were instrumental in the path that Pelley took next. He soon founded the Silver Legion and the Christian Party.

Pelley soon was attracting membership to his new movement from the lower classes, and by 1934 had some 15,000 members. Pelley's tactics included "railing against the takeover of the United States by these 'alien locusts in human form.'"[20] But this peak did not last long, and within four years the membership had fallen by a third. Despite this fact, Pelley ran for president in 1936, although he was only able to get on the ballot in the state of Washington, and reportedly had less than 1,500 votes.

While he didn't gain much in the way of votes, his campaign did attract interest from FDR and his supporters. Pelley continued to oppose both the President and the government, labeling Roosevelt as a warmonger, and like others - notably Charles Lindbergh (it is believed that the two never met) - called for a policy of isolationism. This led to charges being drawn up against the Silver Legion following the outbreak of World War II in Europe.

Unlike Pelley, who may have believed he had power, FDR actually had power, and called upon J. Edgar Hoover and the FBI to investigate the Silver Legion. In 1940, Pelley's Asheville, North Carolina headquarters were raided by U.S. Federal Marshals, and many of his followers arrested. He was even called to testify before the House Committee on Un-American Activities. The Japanese attack on Pearl Harbor sealed the fate of the Silver Shirts. With the declaration of war on the United States by Nazi Germany and the Kingdom of Italy under Mussolini, almost all support for the Silver Legion was gone.

Just before American's entry into the war Pelley started two magazines. For the metaphysical followers he published *Revelation*, but it ceased publication in the fall of 1941. Pelly's *Roll Call*, advertised as the "voice of the loyal opposition," attacked the government's policies. Notably, it took on issues that were being censored at the time. "Pelley devoted his weekly's pages to defending Hitler and to detailing American foreign policy and Roosevelt's role in drawing the United States into the European war."[21] This being a time of war, the First Amendment didn't protect Pelley. He was arrested and charged with high treason and sedition in April of 1942. "The Silver Shirt chief was one of twenty-eight people indicted in Washington, D.C., in July 1942."[22]

During the subsequent trial the most damning charges against Pelley were dropped, but for the minor charges he was still sentenced to 15 years in prison. Due to his financial situation - the original trial had cost Pelley almost all of his money - he was unable to launch an appeal. He remained in prison until 1950, when relatives and his few remaining supporters were able to raise enough money for an appeal.[23]

Pelley was paroled that same year, on the condition that he would never engage in political activity. He instead returned to Nobelesville, North Carolina and founded Soulcraft Press, where he published books and magazines on the metaphysical as well as those of a political nature. These included writings that criticized FDR's policies and lasting legacy, as well as tomes that were anti-United Nations, pro-segregation, and anti-communist. During his final years, he fought off charges of securities fraud that had been brought against him. Pelley died on June 30, 1965, just in time for a new wave of American Nazis to take root.

Many of the post-World War II Neo-Nazi movements in the United States cannot entirely be labeled as "true" Fascists, but these groups did use the symbolism and in many cases the rhetoric of the earlier movements. Thus for the sake of clarity, these groups are included here (albeit briefly and in passing).

The first true Neo-Nazi group in the United States was George Lincoln Rockwell's World Union of Free Enterprise National Socialists (WUFENS), which was founded in 1959, with its headquarters in Arlington, Virginia. As the name suggests it even had the pretext of "socialism" as the original Nazis saw it. Rockwell, always one to crave the media spotlight, renamed the group in 1960 to the American Nazi Party (ANP).

He based his group's policies on those of Adolf Hitler and of the Third Reich, yet at the same time attempted to maintain allegiance to the American Constitutional principles and to the nation's founding fathers. Rockwell was also a hardened Holocaust denier.[24]

The History of American Fascism Part II

It is possible that Rockwell saw parallels between himself and Hitler. Rockwell was a former soldier, who became a commercial artist. While studying at Pratt Institute in New York City, he encountered modern art, which he saw as being both the work of Jews and supported by Jews and Communists. Hitler believed modern art was subversive and decadent. Rockwell preached that Jews controlled the U.S. media, government, banking and commerce. His interest in art drifted toward politics, and he was highly motivated by Senator Joseph McCarthy's crusade against communism. "He believed that those he considered the twentieth century's most enlightened race leaders - Henry Ford, Charles A. Lindbergh, Charles E. Coughlin, Joseph McCarthy - were subverted by the Jews, whom he repeatedly characterized as sneaks and liars."[25]

Rockwell also supported Douglas MacArthur for president, but felt he didn't go far enough with his politics. "He (Rockwell) believed that right-wing leaders - including Hart, Hargis, McIntire, and Carto on the fringe and William F. Buckley Jr., Douglas MacArthur, and the die-hard segregationist bloc in Congress closer to the political mainstream - secretly shared his conspiratorial and anti-Semitic views."[26]

A supporter sent Rockwell a Swastika flag, which he soon adopted.[27] In part he knew the Swastika would upset any Jewish protesters he encountered. The topic of race and ethnic purity was one that he would base his entire political movement on. In this way it actually runs counter to the traditions of fascism. There is no third way concerning economics, an important aspect of fascism. But it is important to briefly discuss Rockwell - as well as those who came later - to understand how fascism has been labeled an extreme right-wing movement.

Upon founding the World Union, Rockwell takes a path that is actually quite different from that of traditional fascism, notably an opposition to state ownership of property. As we have seen, for true Fascists, such as Mussolini, the concept of state and corporate was one that was intertwined, but not with Rockwell's ideology.

Throughout the 1960s, during the era of the Civil Rights Movement, was when Rockwell was part of the not exactly loyal opposition. He regularly protested the White House, but at the same time supported the war in Vietnam. In fact Rockwell could be considered quite an enigma, part counter-revolutionary and part extreme reactionary. "He made contact with the Nation of Islam leader Elijah Muhammad and exploited their common desire for racial segregation,"[28] and reportedly admired Malcolm X. But by 1967, Rockwell changed the American Nazi Party's name to the National Socialist White People's Party (NSWPP), replacing the traditional Nazi "Sieg Heil" with the equally inflammatory "white power" slogan. This move was not embraced by all of his followers, and on August 25, 1967 the man who has been labeled as an "American Fuehrer" was shot dead by John Patler (née Yanacki Christos Patsalos), a former supporter of Rockwell's who had been expelled after developing Marxist leanings.

While Neo-Nazis would make news again, and as mentioned become staples on daytime talk shows, the truth was that with Rockwell dead the organization that he founded floundered and died. The mantel of hate was picked up by various followers of Rockwell, notably Matt Koehl and William Luther Pierce - the latter being the author (under the pseudonym Andrew MacDonald) of the infamous book *The Turner Diaries*, which was believed to have been a key motivation to Oklahoma City bomber Timothy McVeigh.

Koehl succeeded Rockwell as "Commander" of the NSWPP, which he renamed the "New Order," and serves today as de facto leader of the World Union of National Socialists, a loose group of international Neo-Group organizations. Despite this fact, Koehl is far more low key than Rockwell and today is an old man who rarely grants interviews. "If gold watches were awarded to Nazis for longevity of service, Matt Koehl would be among the first of the generation that came into the movement under George Lincoln Rockwell to receive such a golden handshake."[29]

"After Rockwell was assassinated in 1967, Pierce became a leader in the Nazi Party and then, in 1974, went on to establish the (National) Alliance."[30] In addition to founding the white separatist organization the National Alliance, Pierce also founded a religion he called Cosmotheism, which preaches white racism combined

The History of American Fascism Part II

with pantheism and eugenics; teaching that the white race should be separated from the other races. He is noteworthy also for taking a different approach from Rockwell on the issue of the holocaust. "Pierce loathed Holocaust denial," and "claimed to have talked with Nazi veterans who had assured him that they had shot Jews."[31]

While Koehl and Pierce are no doubt "Neo-Nazis," their cut is not true to fascism. They have been included here to understand what fascism is by discussing what it is not. Today, because of the likes of Koehl and Pierce, as well as groups such as the Aryan Nations, The Order and Brüder Schweign (Silent Brotherhood), a white nationalist revolutionary group that existed in the mid-1980s, we have a misunderstanding of what fascism is. As we have seen, the tactics of these groups and individuals are quite different. Even if the symbolism is the same, their messages and goals are vastly disimilar.

In the case of the latter two groups, very little can be considered truly fascistic about them. While those groups that preceded them were no doubt of great inspiration, these organizations hardly seek the type of state socialism and the third way politics that is a core tenet of the Fascist doctrine. Nor was another insidious group that made a return following the Second World War. This would be the Ku Klux Klan, which we looked at in the previous chapter, and will now examine in a bit more detail.

Following its peak in the 1920s, Klan membership declined during the 1930s and 1940s, to the point that the group might have eventually faded away completely. But the Civil Rights Movement of the 1950s spawned a number of hate groups that claimed the mantel of the KKK. These groups were loosely organized and there wasn't a national head. Instead, individual cells operated locally. In some areas of the country the Klan operated with impunity.[32]

In Birmingham, Alabama, during the Bull Conner era, there were so many bombings of homes by the Klan that the city's nickname was "Bombingham," and "Blacks were now bitterly calling their section of town 'Dynamite Hill.'"[33] In states such as Alabama and Mississippi the KKK formed political alliances with governors. At the local level, all white police and juries were unwilling to investigate and prosecute Klan members. Bombings and assassinations targeted social activists and those who refused to follow the racist convention, but often-innocent bystanders and victims of random violence were murdered.

Eisenhower was the first president since Reconstruction to seriously tackle segregation. In 1952 the Eisenhower administration declared racial discrimination a national security issue, and therefore in the domain of the federal government. When Arkansas Governor Faubus refused to desegregate the Little Rock Central High School in 1957, Eisenhower took control of the Arkansas National Guard and sent paratroopers to escort nine black students to school.[34]

President Johnson made even more progress with the *Civil Rights Act of 1964* and the *Voting Rights Act*. According to legend, Johnson put down his pen after signing the *Civil Rights Act* and said to an aid, "We have lost the South for a generation."[35] The Klan feared black voters and saw the quick erosion of segregation. After the murder of civil rights worker Viola Liuzzo, Johnson went on television to announce the arrest of four Klansmen. This was the first federal prosecution of a Klan member since Ulysses S. Grant's presidency.

Johnson also unleashed J Edgar Hoover's FBI on Klan groups. The FBI groomed informants, stole membership information, conducted psychological warfare and investigated Klan crimes. Much of this activity was unconstitutional and amoral, but it broke the Klan in the late 1960s.

With civil and voting rights protected by federal law, Klansmen turned to issues like forced busing to desegregate schools, affirmative action and immigration as rallying points for a rebirth of the movement. For example, in 1971 the KKK bombed ten school buses in Pontiac, Michigan.[36]

During the 1980s and 1990s, the Klan became a staple for daytime talk shows. KKK members spouting their hate and babies dressed in Klan garb made for high ratings, at least for a while. This exposure made the Klan seem more prominent than it was. So much so that one of the authors of this book even had a High School History teacher claim the KKK was the best-funded terrorist group in the world. Maybe this was true, but a more important fact is that the Klan may be more in the public eye, but their influence is actually fairly insignificant than in past decades. While there were some vicious murders and acts of violence in these decades, Klan membership never came close to the millions who took up the cause in the 1920s.[37]

Today, there are roughly 5000-8000 Klansmen distributed across 179 loosely organized chapters. In the 21st Century the KKK has seized upon illegal immigration, urban crime and same-sex marriage as rally points. But there is no centralized authority: no great leader to bring the chapters together to create a viable political movement. Despite this fact, the road to fascism in America still has a solid foundation, one that supports a far more mainstream movement.

Chapter Four
The Rise to Power of President Barack Obama

November 4, 2008 was a night that too many Americans saw as a new beginning. Millions of people took to the streets to cheer as Barack Obama was elected 44th President of the United States. It was proof that democracy in the American fashion continued to work.

Certainly this should have silenced anyone who believed that the events of September 11, 2001 were an "inside job" that former President George W. Bush and Vice President Dick Cheney instigated in an attempt to create a dictatorship. The people spoke and the nation elected the first African-American (albeit half African-American) to the highest office in the land.

To many this wasn't just a new beginning, but an era of "hope," "change" and a new direction; with the audacity to do so. But as we have stressed already, others with similar dubious tactics have used the same message. Ominously, the crowds that gathered in New York's Times Square and in other urban areas throughout the country were reminiscent of the crowds that gathered for other charismatic leaders, notably Italy's Mussolini and Germany's Hitler.

Even the acceptance speeches had a similar tone. In 1933 Adolf Hitler described the situation in Germany as "having seen the unity of the nation vanishing away, dissolving in a confusion of political and personal opinions, economic interests, and ideological differences." Contrast this to Obama's statements that promised unity and peace.[1]

Hitler spoke of how "the misery of our people is horrible to behold," while Obama stated that "we know the challenges that tomorrow will bring are the greatest of our lifetime."[2] The words are startling in their similarity and in their delivery. Thus should there be any surprise when detractors of Obama compare him to Hitler? And the similarities do not end there.

While Hitler was a soldier, and this point is addressed time and time again, the two men had upbringings and careers that were not all that dissimilar. They were both outsiders of sorts, and were both driven by relentless ambition and both could be considered radicals that were appealing to the mainstream.

From their births, there are fundamental similarities. Neither Adolf Hitler nor Barack Obama were close to their fathers. Hitler's father Alois was an Austrian civil servant who wanted young Adolf to work for the government. Adolf wanted to become an artist. Alois often had harsh words directed at young Adolf because of these artistic dreams and would occasionally beat him.[3] Obama's father worked for the Kenyan government's bureaucracy after returning from the United States.[4] The one time Barack Senior visited his son in Hawaii, the two argued over Barack Junior's laziness when it came to doing homework.[5]

Hitler was close to his mother, notably so after his father died when Adolf Hitler was just shy of his 14th birthday. Barack Obama only really knew his mother and seldom saw his father, who died when he was just 17 years old. Both men endured the loss of the mothers that they were close to as well. Hitler's mother was just 47 years old when she died of breast cancer in 1907, while Obama's mother was 52 years old when she died of uterine cancer in 1995.

These similarities can of course be written off as coincidences, but it is hard not to imagine how these events shaped the lives of these two men. Likewise, while it may seem like just another coincidence, it is worth noting that neither man was truly an everyman of his respective nation. Barack Obama was born in Honolulu, Hawaii, and although there is still a "debate" raging whether he was in fact born in Kenya, the fact is that it really doesn't matter in the end. What is more important to consider is that Obama actually lived in Indonesia, and later returned to Honolulu to live with his maternal grandparents. Thus it could be argued that he never really had an American childhood, and his experiences in his youth shaped his vision of what his "adopted" country should be, or become.

For example, American elementary school children were reciting the Pledge of Allegiance, while in school in Indonesia Obama was reciting the Arabic call to prayer.

The opening lines of the Adhan, the Muslim call to prayer, translates as follows:

> *Allah is supreme! Allah is supreme!*
> *Allah is supreme! Allah is supreme!*
> *I witness that there is no God but Allah.*
> *I witness that there is no God but Allah.*
> *I witness that Muhammad is his prophet ...*[6]

Contrast this to Adolf Hitler, who was born and raised in Austria, and as a young adult lived a life that could be best described as "bohemian." He reportedly loathed Austria, so much so that he moved to Munich to live in a real German city. When World War I broke out he petitioned to serve in the Bavarian Army, which was part of the Imperial German Armed Forces.

There are notable differences between the two men that are impossible to ignore. From youth, and his return to Hawaii, Barack Obama lived a life of privilege. Not only did he spend his teenage years growing up on an island paradise, but he went to private schools and took an editorial journey that eventually included Occidental College, Columbia University and Harvard Law School. Hitler of course was famously rejected not once but twice from the Academy of Fine Arts Vienna, and it was suggested to the aspiring "artist" that he should consider a career in architecture. Yet one fact that is typically overstated is that Hitler was a failure as an artist. This isn't quite the whole picture. "He (Hitler) sat the two tough three-hour examinations in which the candidates had to produce drawings on specified themes. Only twenty-eight candidates succeeded."[7]

Thus in the issue of education, Obama and Hitler are very different men. Despite Obama's success in school, and as a university professor, where for 12 years he taught constitutional law at the University of Chicago Law School, nor Hitler's early failures, there is however another fact that cannot be ignored. Simply, neither man ever really seemed destined to lead their nations into "new directions." Politics drew both men to the cause; they did not head to it.

There are many books that chart the move towards politics of both men, and for this reason it is not worth repeating in detail. The purpose of this book is not to retell the careers of either man, but to examine the political nature of the men instead.

What is fundamental to understand is that Hitler, Obama, and Mussolini have differences because of the eras and countries they came from. But at the same time there are important similarities that can't be ignored. History may not repeat itself but we've seen similar movies in the past.

President Obama's entry to the political world and rapid rise would seem something like a work of fiction. The man was only elected to the Illinois Senate in 1996, representing the state's 13th District. He bravely took on controversial issues by voting "present" 129 times, or about 3% of the time.[8] The road to the White House began in 2002, when Obama hired political media consultant David Axelrod to help in the 2004 race for the United States Senate.

Obama was victorious in the March 2004 primary election, capturing 53 percent of the vote, which was notable given that there were seven candidates in total. This, along with the keynote speech at the 2004 Democratic National Convention in Boston, Massachusetts put Obama on the national stage. Interestingly, the major commercial broadcast networks did not televise the speech; the coverage from PBS and the cable news networks was enough that more than nine million people saw it.

The presidential election of 2008 is now remembered as practically a slam-dunk for Mr. Obama, but in fact was a highly contested race even before the general election. Just slightly over six months prior to taking office, Barack Obama wasn't even the presumptive nominee for the Democratic Party. This shows just how divided the Democrats had been throughout the primary season, and just months earlier the Democrat's candidate could have been Hillary Rodham Clinton.

So too in pre-Fascist Italy, pre-Nazi Germany, no one could have guessed that six months before Mussolini or Hitler took office respectively that these would be the nation's leaders. Here too there are differences, Mussolini had his so-called March on Rome, where the National Fascist Party came to power in Italy, ousting Prime Minister Luigi Facta. This "march" wasn't so much a rebellion, as it was a quasi-bloodless coup d'état. King Victor Emmanuel III refused to support Facta, and essentially handed over power to Mussolini, a man who had practically no political leadership qualities, but yet was strong with vision and more importantly strong with words.

Mussolini has been called a man who was somehow simultaneously a revolutionary and a traditionalist, and who based his politics on what he called "The Third Way." With his newly founded National Fascist Party, Mussolini was elected to the Chamber of Deputies in 1921, just a year before his march on Rome.

Hitler too was essentially a political outsider, notably so after his failed "Beer Hall Putsch" as he rebuilt his political party. He had originally entered the German Workers' Party after attending many meetings as a Verbindungsmann (police spy). But instead of merely watching and reporting back, he joined Anton Drexler's small political party, and soon was speaking at meetings. While not the founder of the Nazis, he was one of the earliest members, and used his power to follow Mussolini's lead and seize power.

This coup was not bloodless, and instead of ending up as a new leader, Hitler ended up in prison, where he began work on his book *Mein Kampf*. After serving just over a year in prison, Hitler was pardoned and began to rebuild his political organization.

While the Nazi Party had achieved mixed results in actual elections, Hitler used his power and influence to finally persuade the German President Paul von Hindenburg to obtain the office of Chancellor. On a chilly evening, people took to the streets to cheer that hope and change were coming to Germany, which had suffered through economic downturns and bank failures. In less than a year, Hindenburg was dead, and Hitler essentially became a dictator in Germany.

The rise to power is thus very different, and Hitler and Mussolini are easier to compare in this regard than either man is to Obama. Yet, the similarities in the campaign styles of both Hitler and Obama are also worth comparing. Each man was a master of manipulating the media, and in the case of both Hitler and Obama, books played a very important part on their grabbing of power.

Even the titles offer an ominous similarity with a promise of a better tomorrow: *Mein Kampf,* or *My Struggle,* and *The Audacity of Hope.* Both books are known, but in each case, far fewer have ever actually bothered to read the books. Yet, in both cases, many followers of each man will certainly tell you what the book meant, again without ever actually opening the covers.

For Hitler his writing was a way of rebuilding his political career following his imprisonment. The result was a two-volume book that was as much about his personal motivations as those that his adopted nation faced. Much of the emphasis is on what Hitler saw as the great twin evils, communism and of course Judaism. Despite its now notorious reputation, the book was actually quite popular when it was written, and was soon translated into several languages. So popular was it in fact that Hitler became a millionaire, despite the fact that the book was given free to every newlywed couple, as well as soldiers serving during the Second World War. Some 10 million copies had been sold or otherwise distributed throughout Germany by the end of World War II.

The power of this book also cannot be dismissed either, as it was written in an era before the Internet or even television, and certainly before an era where politicians are under a constant microscope as they are today. Yet, despite this fact, *Mein Kampf* doesn't try to hide Hitler's goals or ambitions, and looking back it is difficult to understand why all the signs and portents leading up to World War II were essentially ignored until it was far too late.

Of course, there are those on the right who would, and in fact, do say the same thing about Obama's *The Audacity of Hope: Thoughts on Reclaiming the American Dream,* which essentially built upon the man's keynote address from the 2004 Democratic Convention. The actual title was "borrowed" from a sermon delivered by Obama's former pastor, Jeremiah Wright, while the book seems to be long passages of speeches.

But rather than ignore Mr. Obama's book, some have begun to question whether he even wrote it. It was not Barack Obama's first book, and he had previously published *Dreams From My Father: A Story of Race and Inheritance,* which was essentially a memoir of his life so far. Published in 1995, after Obama was elected the first African-American president of the Harvard Law Review, and well before he was on a political path, the book covers his early life and struggle to fit in. It was republished in 2004 after his speech at the 2004 DNC.

Some critics have noted that the passages of the two books are extremely similar, so much so that some have questioned how much of *The Audacity of Hope* is repurposed writing from his earlier book, while others have questioned how a new Senator with small children found the time to write the 216-page book in a short amount of time. For *American Thinker,* writer Jack Cashill even questions whether the book was made up of speeches written by Obama speechwriter Jon Favreau.[9]

Whether Obama wrote the book, or whether Favreau "helped out" isn't the point at the end of the day. The book, helped by an endorsement from TV's Oprah Winfrey, propelled then Senator Obama onto the national stage, even more so than his keynote speech.

Much has been made of the fact that Senator Obama began his bid for the White House almost three years before the election of 2008. However, as we have already touched upon, Mr. Obama wasn't even the Democrat front runner at the beginning of 2008, and most political pundits were predicting that then New York Senator Hillary Clinton would likely face off against former New York City Mayor Rudy Giuliani, with the latter burning out in the primaries rather quickly.

By contrast Obama and Clinton faced a major showdown, but even here these two senators were not the only candidates in a hotly contested field. John Edwards, the former senator and 2004 vice presidential candidate, as well as New Mexico Governor Bill Richardson and Indiana Senator Evan Bayh, all threw their respective hats into the arena.

It is also necessary to stress that Edwards was actually the first to formally announce his candidacy, which he did on December 28, 2006, followed by Clinton on January 20, 2007 and finally Obama on February 10 of that year made it official. Throughout much of

2007, Clinton led the in the polls, followed by Obama, and she was the frontrunner through January of 2008.

It is not necessary to recap the play by play of the elections, but there were some interesting facts in the election of 2008. This was the first time in 56 years that neither the incumbent president nor a vice president ran for election, and it was first time that two sitting senators ran against each other.

American democracy also played a major role in this election, and 2008 saw the highest voter turnout in more than 40 years. However, while the media - and numerous authors - have attempted to play this as a solid, unquestionable victory for Obama and the Democrats, and more so have suggested that this was the death of the Republican Party, this is far from the case.

Yes, the Democrats took control of the White House, and strengthened their hold on the House of Representatives and the Senate. But both houses of the legislative branch were already controlled by the Democrats prior to the 2008 elections, so the media's hype - or even at times cheering - the GOP downfall is certainly exaggerated. Here is where the biased liberal media plays a major role in America's road towards liberal fascism, something we will continue to touch upon later.

For now it is worth revisiting the campaign, just to clarify points that have been either forgotten or washed over by the media. The most notable is that it wasn't so much Obama's popularity that resulted in his victory, as much as concerns over the economy.

We must go back and look at the election results over the past several decades. The notion of "change" is not entirely a new one, except that again the media seems to believe, and worse reports, that the ideals of "hope" and "change" are concepts exclusively attributed to Obama.

It is also fair the say that outgoing Republican President George W. Bush was not a popular president. While he had won re-election in 2004, his popularity had been on a downward spiral since even before the midterm elections in 2006, when the Democrats captured the House of Representatives and the Senate, effectively making President Bush a lame duck.

Both Senator John McCain, who had previously run for president in 2000, and Senator Obama campaigned on a platform of change and reform in Washington. However, it is not hard to see that Senator McCain was at a disadvantage for his guilt by association - not only for being of the same political party as Bush, but also for having previously endorsed President Bush in 2004. And while Bush did endorse McCain in March of 2008, the sitting President made no appearances with the GOP candidate.

The issues of the campaign also centered on the war in Iraq, but more importantly focused on the economic crisis, which began in full just as the race for the White House heated up following the two national political conventions.

More importantly, what has not been fully reported on by the media is that it isn't so much that President Obama ran a good campaign, as that Senator McCain ran a very bad campaign. The Senator from Arizona was uncertain of how many houses he and his wife Cindy McCain actually owned - not the sort of thing that probably was sitting well with voters as the housing bubble burst and many were on the verge of foreclosure. Worse for McCain he chose to say, "the fundamentals of our economy are strong," on just the same day as Lehman Brothers filed for bankruptcy.

Thus it was a black September for McCain, who saw his poll numbers sink sharply. What had been a clear path to the White House for the man with far more experience, especially in the key area of foreign policy, became an uphill battle against a less experienced legislator, who told the Americans what they wanted to hear.

But as with many other Fascists and proto-Fascists, there were promises made with the vaguest of notions, and with little actual specific details on how this change would come about. Was it too much to hope for to know what exactly did Mr. Obama mean during the campaign? But of course, this is a classic tactic with Fascists. The vaguer the promise, the easier it is to keep the promise. This is where skullduggery and propaganda came into play, far more than in many previous elections. While 2008 may not have had the accusations and counter-accusations (ala "Swift Boats"), the Obama campaign called in on imagery to make a make a powerful statement.

The concepts of "hope" and "change" were hard to miss during the campaign season, but again what does it actually mean? It doesn't mean anything in hindsight, but that's not the point, OR is it? Some could question what did the swastika actually mean as well. Today, the symbol is notorious with the Nazi party, but for centuries it had been a simple symbol used around the world, from Buddhists in Central Asia to Native Americans, and even to Jews in Ancient Israel. More recently, at the beginning of the 20th century the symbol was used in advertising and consumer products. Steven Heller, a senior art director at *The New York Times*, and author of more than 70 books on graphic design as well as *The Swastika: Symbol Beyond Redemption?* described the swastika as being "one of the most visually powerful symbols every devised." [10]

Hitler and the Nazis therefore didn't create the symbol, which was already in use by German Free Corps (Freikorps) paramilitary troops at the end of the First World War. Flash-forward to the current day, and it is hard to think of the Nazis without thinking of the swastika.

Less sinister of course is the Fasces symbol, which as we previously discussed is already used in the corridors of power within the United States. But here is where we must examine how the Fascists often adopt and take past symbols, and notably colors, and twist them to make something new while evoking the national tradition. Mussolini's use of the Fasces symbol was to connect to the glory of the Roman Republic and later the Roman Empire. Hitler opted to retain the red/white/black colors of imperial Germany, but downplayed the traditional "Prussian" eagle in favor of the swastika. Knowing that he couldn't completely remove the eagle, it was retained, but today the Nazi eagle is remembered in passing, as the bird that holds the laurels with the swastika.

Obama too played a similar game when crafting his signature campaign logo. Sometimes known as the "hope and change" symbol, or the "Obama O," it was created by "a team of Chicago graphic designers," including "Sol Sender of Sender LLC and five others in his firm." [11]

While Sender, as quoted in *Crane's Chicago Business* said he was "unsure if the logo would remain intact if Mr. Obama (won) the Democratic nomination," [12] the symbol actually had some serious staying power. It even replaced the American flag on Obama's campaign plane - a move notable as key Nazis, such as Hitler typically flew around in aircraft decked out in swastikas.

Few in the mainstream media even picked up on that fact that the painted American flag was removed from the tail of the then candidate's plane, and replaced with the trademark "O." Notably the p757 was shown to the media just prior to Obama's trip to Amman, Jordan, which was part of a campaign trip to the Middle East and Europe. [13] And as with the Nazi's swastika flags, the "O" symbol retained the national colors. Likewise, long after taking power it remains still a symbol that can be found on t-shirts, flags and posters. It is a powerful symbol that has been examined online and throughout the blogosphere, with notable comments about the "meaning" being made, including this one:

- "The O represents Obama and he can use the logo without his name next to it. He's claiming the O as George W. Bush claimed the W

- The blue O and the red stripes represent the flag

- The red stripes represent the plains, the American farmland

- The O's whitespace represents the sun, shining over the plains. Because it's white, it evokes sunrise, not sunset." [14]

Whether this opinion is even correct is of course debatable, just as what the swastika meant to the Nazis, but it is notable that few presidential hopefuls completely disregarded our nation's flag in favor of their own symbol, no matter how powerful it seemed, or even how insightful.

Yet, this wasn't the only memorable symbol from the Obama campaign. As with past proto-Fascists, Obama went all out to send a visual message. Thanks to the buttons, posters and websites, the images were everything. One in particular showed the pensive Obama looking upward, suggesting he was looking to a brighter

The Rise to Power of President Barack Obama

future - ala the 1950s everyman who was ready to take on the world. Contrast this with a red, white and blue background that evoked such artists as Andy Warhol, and this was clearly meant for those who believed the hype.

The concept was designed by Shepard Fairey, a Los Angeles-based street artist, who apparently hoped it would make him popular. The long repeated story is that Fairey found an image online, downloaded it without bothering to determine the original source and created the image. As it was similar to the Warhol style, it became popular and soon was everywhere. But it seems that neither Fairey, nor the Obama campaign, ever actually paid the Associated Press, nor the original photographer, for use of the image. This must be what the campaign had in mind when the question of wealth redistribution came up!

This image has those subtle traces that are just very much a part of fascism, and it is questionable whether this is a coincidence. It features the would-be ruler's face, and the oh-so-patriotic colors to make the viewer/voter see that this man is truly one of the people. More than a year after the election, this image, along with many other examples still proudly hang in shop windows throughout New York City - evoking that same sort of Blue Eagle symbol that we've previously touched upon.

Also, while Obama's campaign may not have spent much money to actually buy the rights to the photograph that served as the basis for the Fairey image, the campaign did spend a pretty penny to get to the White House. During the 2008 presidential race, Barack Obama raised nearly $530 million and spent a record $513 million - or roughly $7.39 per voter. Contrast that to the $5.78 per voter that McCain spent and you begin to wonder whether it was really an issue that McCain owned more houses than Obama (Source: Federal Election Commission).

This is an especially interesting issue to discuss, because Obama had no shortage of wealthy supporters, including those in the ranks of Hollywood. Why exactly would these "fat cats" support the candidate that promised to raise the taxes for the wealthiest Americans? This is an ongoing debate, and of course part of the answer is that the Hollywood elite may play powerful thinkers in the movies and on TV, the truth is that they aren't exactly the cream of the crop when it comes to being at the intellectual forefront in our country. These people begin to think that their devotion to niche causes somehow makes their actions more enlightened than those of the so-called "special interest." But truth be told, what could be more "special interest" than supporting efforts to reduce the carbon footprint, while jet setting around the world, and buying massively oversized houses?

Yet, this is another example of how the extended media, or the celebrity, often goes hand in hand with the rise to power of dictators and corrupt rulers. Consider actor Sean Penn, who denounces our own government, while praising a proto-Fascist such as Venezuela's Hugo Rafael Chávez Frías. Of course, as we have seen how many celebrities already took part in their so-called "pledge" to be better and to support the president - by which of course they mean President Obama. These same celebrities could only say bad things about President Bush, and often times America in recent years.

Much of this is because of the cult of personality with the media. Many in Hollywood believe themselves to be the intellectual superiors they play, and jump onto their causes. Thus it is easy for them to listen wholeheartedly to the promises of hope, change, a better tomorrow, a world without wars, a world without poverty, etc. But just because these celebrities have played the downdraught, doesn't mean they actually relate in real life.

Thus they are easily drawn to these fast-talking do-gooders. The danger here is that it is very easy in our culture of personality for the average citizen to further get sucked in. Why question what the leaders are saying if the guy who played Milk thinks Obama is all right? More worrisome is the fact that these same celebrities would like to silence the loyal opposition, a point we shall also get to shortly.

For as worrisome as the celebrity bandwagon can be, more disturbing is the direction that the media has taken. A Pew Research Center found that 70 percent of registered voters actually believed that the mainstream media wanted Barack Obama to win the election, while only nine percent felt that the media showed favoritism towards John McCain.

It is hard not to see this media bias. From election night, when Obama took the stage for his acceptance speech it was clear that this was a very different sort of candidate. The imagery, again back to imagery, was not hard to miss. Rows of American flags - meant to look patriotic, meant to remind you that this man, who was born in Hawaii, raised by a Muslim in Indonesia was a true American - had a sinister look that could be compared to Hitler or Mussolini. But the media only ignored it.

The cheering in the streets on election night, which we have compared to the cheering when Hitler took power, was instead compared to New Year's Eve. The media highlighted the vast turnout and over-the-top parades for Obama's inauguration on January 20, 2009. But they failed to suggest that it at all appeared to have the organization and look of the massive Nazi rallies in Nuremberg from the 1930s.

Maybe here we're looking for something that isn't there; maybe we're seeing ghosts where there is nothing. But we did see something else. In 2001, when George W. Bush headed down Pennsylvania Avenue the mainstream media in the United States showed the protestors, who argued that Mr. Bush wasn't really the duly elected president, but had essentially pulled off a coup d'état. No such protesters were shown on TV in 2009. Was it because they weren't there, or did the media just not want to cover it?

When President Bill Clinton left office in 2001, the media duly covered his farewell speeches - all of them - but when President Bush left office in 2009, the media practically cut him off before he boarded *Marine One*, the presidential helicopter.

In 2001, there were also editorials in various papers that called for the inauguration to be canceled, as the country was in the grip of mild recession. So imagine one's surprise when the same media highlighted (endlessly it seemed) about how Washington was going to have the biggest party ever for President Obama. The arguments of spending too much were thrown out the window. Likewise, when President Bush was set for his second inauguration, there were calls

America's Road to Fascism

that due to the wars in Iraq and Afghanistan that the inauguration should be somber and downplayed. No such calls were made in 2009.

Moreover, the media treated Obama with kid gloves when he took office. The rules it seemed change. There had been statements by comedians - who never let up on Clinton or Bush or for that matter any president in recent history - that Obama was going to be different. Was it really because he was "too smart" as some said, or simply because he was too black? But even making that statement would come under the microscope in this new Obamanation.

The same celebrity protestors, such as Janeane Garofalo, who made statements that it was patriotic to question the nation's leader and government, did an about face and said that it was suddenly unpatriotic to question Obama. Filmmaker Woody Allen apparently wasn't joking, and we weren't laughing, when he said, "it would be good... if he could be a dictator for a few years because he could do a lot of good things quickly." Continued charges of racism were leveled at anyone who dared raise questions, but this is a point that we'll also cover in more detail.

For now we'll say that the rules changed in how Obama and the office of the President were covered. And when the rules change, you know you're solidly on the road to somewhere different. The question we must continue to ask is where is the country headed?

Chapter Five
The Rule of the Land Under President Obama and the Comparison to Fascism

Within months of the inauguration of Barack Hussein Obama II, the 44th President of the United States, there was a significant crack in his once unbreakable foundation. The cheers on election night that suggested he brought the nation together were being drowned out by cries from those opposed to those not wanting this change. There was distain with the president and it seemed that to many this was completely unexpected. But is this really a surprise? While Obama had won the election by some 10,000,000 votes, more than 60,000,000 had voted for someone else. To many liberals, as well as the White House, it was shocking that there was such early opposition to this photogenic and charismatic president.

Since the election, political pundits, liberal thinkers and of course the left-leaning media praised the new direction for the country. Among those cheering the aftermath of the election was liberal moviemaker Michael Moore, who wrote on his website:

> In a nation that was founded on genocide and then built on the backs of slaves, it was an unexpected moment, shocking in its simplicity: Barack Obama, a good man, a black man, said he would bring change to Washington, and the majority of the country liked that idea. The racists were present throughout the campaign and in the voting booth. But they are no longer the majority, and we will see their flame of hate fizzle out in our lifetime.[1]

But has the so-called "hate" really fizzled out? We will explore who the likes of Michael Moore and his liberal ilk believe are the real villains, the enemy within, and who is doing the real hating. But for now it is worth noting that because of this change there was a new sheriff in town, and the rule of law would change, and that the hard line approach of President George W. Bush and Vice President Dick Cheney would be a thing of the past. Reaching across the aisle, listening to the ideas of the Republicans and hammering out change with bi-partisan tools were promised by the Obama campaign. The nation would heal under his rule.

Questions were immediately raised, such as whether Gitmo, or more accurately the Guantanamo Bay Naval Base prison would be closed, and how suspected terrorists would be interrogated. Many Bush detractors claimed that his policies allowed suspects to be tortured. This in itself has led to a massive misunderstanding, one that the mainstream media has failed to correct, time and time again.

The media has failed in its job. Little has been reported that before the dark days of September 11, 2001 that the United States has essentially been at war. This is a war unlike any other, because the enemy is for all intents and purposes an army without a nation. This is a war that started during the administration of President Bill Clinton, and in truth began on February 26, 1993 with the first bombing of the World Trade Center.

This attack was planned by a group that included conspirators, at least a half a dozen individuals, who received their funding from Khaled Shaikh Mohammed, who himself was a member of Osama bin Laden's al-Qaeda terrorist network. A car bomb was detonated below the North Tower of the World Trade Center that failed to bring down the towers but did kill six people, while another 1,042 people were injured in the attack.

While this event should have been a wake up call for the United States, the nation under Clinton essentially hit the snooze button instead. And did so again in August of 1998 when American embassies in Kenya and Tanzania were bombed, and yet again when the *U.S.S. Cole* was attacked in the port of Aden in Yemen. "Seventeen U.S. sailors were killed aboard the USS Cole on Oct. 12, 2000, when two al-Qaeda terrorists set off explosives as they pulled their fishing boat up to the destroyer."[2] All of these events occurred under the watch of Clinton, and other than a few missile launches to Afghanistan and Sudan, the United States response was nonexistent.

During the Bush era, it is true that the United States became involved with two wars on the ground. The first was in Afghanistan to root out bin Laden and al-Qaeda, and the latter was to remove Iraqi warlord and Dictator Saddam Hussein from power, for allegedly stockpiling weapons of mass destruction. In the latter case, while no major weapons were found, the amount of small arms recovered - as well as those that have continued to fall into the hands of insurgents - suggests that Hussein was certainly stockpiling a great deal of weapons, and in violation of UN sanctions. This followed Hussein's policy of using chemical weapons, which he had done in the Iran-Iraq War (1980-1988), and also against member of his own Kurdish population - which he considered to be rebels and insurgents.[3]

The wars were not popular. Wars in the modern era have not been popular, but in this age of instant news with 24-hour cable news channels, embedded journalists and of course the Internet, these were not far off conflicts, these were practically prime time entertainment. But yet while many people continue to be outraged by the state of how these wars were, and still are, being conducted, more viewers know more about who were the last five winners of American Idol, than can place either of the aforementioned nations on a map.

The more important facet to consider is that Fascists use these wars as a way of getting power. Mussolini rose to power after Italy, being on the winning side at the end of First World War, failed to be - at least what it considered - duly rewarded. Germany, by contrast, was ripe for the Nazis after signing an armistice, which brought down Kaiser Wilhelm II, the nation's monarch, who fled to the Netherlands. The nation had lost the war, but it didn't expect the harsh treatment it received, which put the blame for the war squarely on Germany.

Yet because German forces were still deep in French territory, and more importantly had soundly defeated the Russians, in the process seizing the Ukraine and other eastern territories, there were those in power who felt that politicians had stabbed the army in the back. The situation wasn't exactly the same in the United States, but the wars resulted in a change of attitudes in the United States.

Just as the Vietnam War had become a cross to bear for President Lyndon Johnson in 1968, so too had the wars in Afghanistan and Iraq been crosses to bear for any Republican that supported them.

Following the banking crisis of 2008, the election went to those who promised a new direction.

Those who claimed Bush had orchestrated the wars to seize dictatorial power were proved wrong, but with Bush out of office, many liberals claimed the nation would be peaceful and ready to work with the rest of the world again. Here again, is where those who didn't like Bush liked to point out his "Nazi-like" ways.

And this is where one of the most common misconceptions of the Nazis must be addressed. The movies and TV programs - again something far too many Americans use as their basis for history - often show the black trench coat wearing Gestapo agent asking, "papers please," and suggesting, "we have ways of making you talk." Yet, this is far from accurate.

While there is absolutely no doubt that for most Germans the Nazi regime was the darkest time in their nation's history, the truth is that the Nazis didn't actually rule through fear and intimidation. The Gestapo was the creation of the Nazis, and its name is actual a contraction of Geheime Staatspolizei or "Secret State Police." In fact the story is that "an obscure post office employee who had been asked to furnish a franking stamp for the new bureau suggested that it be called the Geheime Staatspolizei, simply the 'Secret State Police' - GESTAPO for short - and thus unwittingly created a name the very mention of which was to inspire terror first within Germany and then without."[4] As with the Czar of Russia's Okhranka, or Department for Defense of Public Security and Order, also known as Secret Police, which were created in 1880, much of the truth is shrouded in the fact that it is almost a contradiction to have a secret police that isn't so secret, but this has essentially added to its mystique. Furthermore, works of fiction, such as George Orwell's *Nineteen Eighty-Four* and its use of the Thought Police, further confuse the issue, and make it harder to determine the truth. This is a case where fiction needs to be separated from the facts.

In the case of the Gestapo, it was created in 1934 and was under the administration of the Schutzstaffel, or SS, under Heinrich Himmler. He was charged with leading this private army for the German Nazi Party, and as serving as the Chief of the German

Police. By the outbreak of the Second World War, administration of the Gestapo was given to the Reich Main Security Office, or the Reichssicherheisthauptant (RSHA), and in practice was a subordinate branch of the Sicherheistpolizei (SIPO) or the Security Police.[5]

While certainly no one would want a knock on the door from the Gestapo in the middle of the night, consider that today would anyone want a knock on the door from the FBI or Department of Homeland Security? The difference is that the Gestapo was given in 1936 the ultimate authority to investigate crimes not only against the state, but also those against the Nazi Party. Essentially the Gestapo was exempted from any authority of administrative courts.

Here is where many have tried to counter that Bush and Cheney used "Gestapo" tactics, but it is worth noting that the Gestapo's authority was not limited to foreign nationals or terrorists. Anyone could be arrested under the Gestapo's authority, while Americans under President Bush maintained their constitutional rights.

What must also be remembered is that then candidate Obama had said in a speech during the campaign that he called for a civilian force to free up some of burden of national security from the military. This issue has been mostly dismissed by the mainstream media, but was brought to the forefront following Obama's election by Rep. Paul Broun (R-Georgia). "Broun cited a speech Obama gave in Colorado during the campaign last July (2008) calling for 'a civilian national security force that's just as powerful, just as strong, just as well-funded' as the military."[6] While others have fired back that Obama didn't intend that this would be a private military, but a civilian reserve corps meant to help with post-war reconstruction in Iraq, this is still a point that needs to be watched with cautious eyes.

What is an even more interesting comparison is how Hitler essentially became a power broker, and gave out semi-official positions to his cronies, much the way Obama has done since taking office. In the case of Hitler, when he was "appointed" Reich Chancellor - again he was never actually elected to that position we must remember - he was part of a coalition government with President Paul von Hindenburg. However, that didn't stop the Nazis from essentially creating new positions, ones with virtually no government oversight and those that were also for all intents and purposes outside of the German constitution at the time.

Among the first to be "rewarded" for his loyalty was a man who would go on to be lapdog for Hitler to the final days. This of course was Joseph Goebbels, who had served as the propaganda head for the Nazis, and who after Hitler had taken power, believed himself to suddenly have an official office within the government. This included taking charge of the state radio for a live broadcast when Hitler assumed the office of Chancellor.

Within months a previously nonexistent cabinet position was created, that of Reich Minister of Public Enlightenment and Propaganda or Volksaufklärung und Propaganda, or simply known as the Ministry of Propaganda - a now ominously sounding title. "As a former journalist, Goebbels took a keen interest in print journalism too. Germany's press culture was rich and varied, with nearly three and a half thousand newspapers and ten thousand periodicals in 1933. However, global statistics concealed an industry in trouble, while the circulation of many parish-pump papers was derisory."[7]

The parallel here to the state of the American media is disturbing to say the least, especially given that we are losing many voices, who offer opinion about our government. Who watches the watchers if the media is gone? And while there is, as we have touched upon, a clear and present media bias, the fact is that fewer papers and magazines makes this that much more a danger, as there are now fewer voices. To date Obama has not appointed anyone to look into this matter, but that seems to be about the only entirely made-up position that the POTUS hasn't created! A fact we will cover in a moment.

For now consider how the media covered the leaders. While the Nazis took this a step further, with Goebbels believing the role of the press "was that the people should 'think uniformly, react uniformly,'"[8] it does evoke the White House's stance that FoxNews was not a legitimate news organization. It was after all, Anita Dunn, White House Director of Communications, who said in an interview in October of 2009 with *The New York Times*, "we're going to treat them the way we would treat an opponent. As they are undertaking a war against Barack Obama and the White House, we don't need to pretend that this is the way that legitimate news organizations behave."[9]

Goebbels took matters further, offering instructions on the size of headlines, and going so far as to order what photos may accompany an article. But there was also a lighter side to the media's coverage of the Nazis as well. "By contrast, illustrated or women's magazines extended coverage of film stars to a laughing Führer on the telephone or admiring the exhibits at the Automobile Show, and to the wives and children of other Nazi leaders."[10] So we ask, how many times have Barack Obama and his immediate family appeared on the cover of numerous magazines since the election? There may not be a directive from the White House communications office for such coverage, but again it is hard not to see the eerie similarities.

More importantly, unlike many of the cabinet positions, the White House Director of Communications is part of the senior staff to the President and in that way becomes a face to the world, yet only reports to the POTUS. This should not be especially disturbing in itself yet; as seen by the poor choice of words spoken by Ms. Dunn, can have ramifications that go far beyond a mere staffer. Additionally, President Obama has looked to expand the role of the Office of Communications, noting the role that the Internet played in his campaign, and has noted that he would like to see greater interaction through social media such as Facebook and Twitter.

Apparently, expanding the role of certain offices and creating new positions in the government is somehow Obama's way of reducing "big government." But how is creating so many "Czars" really making government smaller? In fairness, President Obama did not start the practice of appointing Czars, he had merely taken advantage of the practice beyond any previous president.

The term Czar of course is derived from Caesar, and goes back to the founding of the Roman Empire, when all Emperors were called Caesar in honor of Julius Caesar and his nephew and first Roman Emperor Octavian Caesar or Augustus. During medieval times the term Czar meant Emperor, or one who had the rank of a Roman

Emperor or other supreme ruler. In Germany the title became Kaiser, and in Russia it was Czar, both of which had their "Imperial" dynasties fall by the end of World War I. But the term was later applied to those in various appointed positions in government by the media. Yet it must be stressed that this use of the informal title for high-level officials in the United Kingdom and in the United States, has never been official. No office doors say "Czar" on them in the halls of Washington, D.C.

More importantly, the individual may have an official title such as representative advisor, director or administrator, but are generally just known as Czars, as in "Auto Czar," who is Ed Montgomery, who actually holds the official title of Director of Recovery for Auto Communities and Workers. More importantly, the issue here is that this powerful sounding position is part of the executive branch, and was appointed by the president without Senate approval, thus making them answerable only to the POTUS.

To understand this notion of czars, we must go back to the founding of America. Today, the cabinet, which was established in Article II, Section 2, of the Constitution, is there to advise the POTUS on any subject he may require relating to the duties of each member's respective office. With the exception of Vice President, the Senate has to approve of all cabinet appointments with a majority vote. Today the cabinet includes the Vice President and the heads of 15 executive departments, including the secretaries of Agriculture, Commerce, Defense, Education, Energy, Health and Human Services, Homeland Security, Housing and Urban Development, Interior, Labor, State, Transportation, Treasury, and Veterans Affairs, as well as the Attorney General.[11]

Many of these positions were created over time, and originally George Washington had a cabinet that consisted of only the Attorney General, along with the Secretaries of State, War and Treasury. Various presidents turned to their own trusted advisors, including those who often did not hold official positions. These included Andrew Jackson's "Kitchen Cabinet," Grover Cleveland's "Fishing Cabinet," Teddy Roosevelt's "Tennis Cabinet," Warren G. Harding's dubious "Poker Cabinet," and Herbert Hoover's strangely named "Medicine-Ball Cabinet."[12] But these terms were not always even used by the respective president. For example, the "Kitchen Cabinet," was a term used by those political opponents of President Jackson, to describe his unofficial advisors, while the official cabinet then became known as the "parlor cabinet." This however began a trend where presidents would turn to these unofficial advisors, and it was not always a group opposed to the official cabinet. It was just an extension of the official advisors, and one that has become increasingly more common.

The Great Depression can further be seen as a time when a president felt the need to increase the number of offices to handle the issues pressing the nation. Thus President Franklin Roosevelt was the first president to appoint individuals to the position we today call czar. In his 12 years in office he appointed 19 individuals to 12 positions. Roosevelt used this "cadre of advisers to oversee the New Deal."[13]

His successor, Harry Truman had a total of six appointments to six positions, and this number remained low until President Bill Clinton appointed 10 individuals during his eight years to a total of seven positions.

There is also a case of liberal bias in this matter as well. It has been reported that former President George W. Bush had 47 czars, but many of these were just labeled as such by the media, and these positions had previously existed, only to be renamed as "czars" during the Bush years. In fact, while Bush did appoint individuals to 31 "czar" posts, he did so over eight years. In less than six months in office, President Obama had created 32 czars, with only seven previously existing.

According to a report from TV commentator Glenn Beck's website, there are 32 positions, ranging from Afghanistan Czar (or Special Representative for Afghanistan and Pakistan) to Climate Czar (or Special Envoy for Climate Change) to Green Jobs Czar (or Special Adviser for Green Jobs, Enterprise and Innovation at the White House) to Information Czar (Federal Chief Information Officer) to Technology Czar (Chief Technology Officer), the latter not to be confused with the Science Czar (or Assistant to the President for Science and Technology, Director of the White House Office of Science and Technology Policy, and Co-Chair of the President's Council of Advisers on Science and Technology).[14]

While each administration since FDR has used czars differently, it must be stressed that these are still just political appointees. These individuals should not make decisions, nor determine policy. And while many of them report to department heads, or a specific secretary in the cabinet, by law they aren't required to. Their power comes directly from the president not a cabinet member. This is a convenient way of dispensing Executive power to friends of the president without a vetting by the Senate.

The founders wouldn't approve of the term Czar, even though it is unofficial. They were revolutionaries and Article I section 9 of the Constitution prohibits the granting of any title of nobility by the government. Napoleon started his career as an anti-noble but in the end couldn't resist crowning himself the French Czar. Why the press and others think Czar is appropriate is difficult to understand. Friend of the President would be a more appropriate title.

One Friend of the President who had an early downfall was Anthony "Van" Jones, who held the position of Special Advisor for Green Jobs - or Green Jobs Czar - for membership in a socialist group, and for supporting Mumia Abu-Jamal, a death row prisoner. If the Senate had the power to examine Jones as a Czar he probably would have been rejected.

Whether other presidents - Bush included - utilized czars is not the point. Throughout the campaign then Senator Obama promised to reduce the size of government, but within just a few months on the job he had instead followed the same pattern of his predecessors and actually increased the role of these semi-official individuals. Even some Democrats have taken issue with so many Czars. "Sen. Robert Byrd, (D-W.Va.), the 91-year-old dean of senators known for carrying around a pocket-sized copy of the Constitution, warned Obama in a letter that the czars 'threaten the Constitutional system of checks and balances.'"[15]

Here too is where past leaders such as Hitler can once again be compared to Obama. Despite the fact that his title essentially became

"The Leader," Hitler never really led - at least until the outbreak of the Second World War. While he was always a big picture guy, he allowed many others to do the actual governing, instead focusing on other projects, many of which seem to be completely outside the role of the leader. These included taking the time to consider the designs for a future Berlin - a city to be rebuilt as "Germania," a vision that many architects and city planners think was solidly over ambitious,[16] but in fairness this came from a man who thought he could defeat the combined forces of Great Britain, the Soviet Union and the United States during the war.

In his pre-war roles, Hitler traveled the country; constantly reaffirming his message to the masses, oftentimes traveling either by his private train or by air. In fact, Hitler is generally regarded to be the first world leader to fly by plane while in office, although Britain's Winston Churchill had also had a keen interest in flying as early as 1912.[17]

But even before American candidates used airplanes as a means to campaign, it was a tactic pioneered by the Nazis. During his campaign for a position in government, Hitler took to the skies and flew from city to city, "holding twenty major speeches in different venues before huge audiences, totaling close to a million persons."[18] This was a practice that Hitler continued even after being appointed Chancellor, although by the outbreak of the war, flying became too dangerous and the Nazi leader instead was left to rely on the Führer's Special Train, or *Führersonderzug*, which was named "Amerika" in 1940. Through 1941 it was even used as the Führer Headquarters.

Consider how much American presidents travel. In the case of President Obama this method of campaigning has continued even after he had taken office. In the spring of 2009, as the economy was downright bad, and millions of Americans were losing their jobs, the President took flight time and time again, flying to so-called "town hall meetings" to tell the people what he'd do, instead of actually doing anything. This is reminiscent of FDR's fireside chats with a modern twist. The public is bombarded with TV news sound bites meant to make American's feel hopeful but can't possibly explain Obama's policies.

By the fall of 2009, this had even become a joke, with the weekly comedy sketch TV show *Saturday Night Live* making fun of the president's efforts, where comedian Will Armisen offered his take, playing the embattled president, saying basically, "look at what I've accomplished... nothing."[19] The irony is that CNN had to then "fact-check the skit" for errors![20]

However, we could recap what the POTUS has done, and it actually looks far worse than nothing. One promise made by President Obama was that unemployment would not go above eight percent. But by the fall of 2009 the number had reached 10 percent, a number not seen since 1983. And this doesn't factor in those whose unemployment benefits may have lapsed but were still unemployed, or those who saw their freelance work fall off, or those who simply were under-employed - in other words those who were working for less money and doing more.

Additionally, during the campaign and after the election Obama said he would not hire lobbyists. According to *USA Today*, Obama promised to "Prohibit lobbyists from working in the administration on issues related to their prior employers for two years." But the result: "Obama signed an executive order on his first full day in office that restricted former lobbyists from performing such administration work for at least two years. Since then, the White House has granted several waivers allowing ex-lobbyists to work in the administration. Among them: William Lynn, a former Raytheon lobbyist who became deputy secretary of Defense."[21]

There were also talks of a middle class tax cut, even as a health care bill was being written that would almost certainly necessitate a raise in taxes somewhere. In this case, it is also worth stressing that part of the health care bill would require everyone to get medical insurance or face a fine, which could be read by some as a tax on those in the middle class who have no health insurance and opted for whatever reason to go without!

And while one promise made about health care is that there would be no rationing, that no one would be left untreated, as of the fall of 2009, there had been massive rationing of the H1N1 flu vaccine.[22] This of course can be blamed on any number of factors, including the amount of time it takes to prepare a vaccine, but it is still somewhat ironic that a health care bill was being debated as many elderly people had to wait for hours, only to be told that flu shots were not available.

There was also supposed to be greater transparency and openness, changes Obama made when he came into office. Among the first promises the new President Obama made, via a blog post from Macon Phillips, the Director of New Media for the White House, was that the public would have the ability to review and comment on legislation:

> One significant addition to WhiteHouse.gov reflects a campaign promise from the President: we will publish all non-emergency legislation to the website for five days, and allow the public to review and comment before the President signs it.[23]

It sounded like a good promise, but by April of 2009, Jim Harper of the Cato Institute noted that Obama had signed 11 bills into law, and only one bill spent the five days online. This was the DTV Delay Act, a bill we will discuss in an upcoming chapter, and it was cleared by presentment by Congress on February 4, with the President signing the bill into law on February 11. However, while Harper noted that this may satisfy the five-day promise through presentment, which is a constitutional step in the legislative process, Congress did not actually present it until February 9, thus the time when the five-day clock should have begun.[24]

Harper further added that several times the White House had posted a bill while it remained in Congress as an attempt to satisfy the five-day rule, and that several versions of bills were linked to from Whitehouse.gov, but not posted in final form. Additionally, the POTUS has signed most bills within a day or two of their presentment from Congress, and as of April of 2009, had signed two bills after the five-day period, but ironically these were not posted on Whitehosue.gov either![25] Clearly here was an example of just one campaign promise not kept, and now virtually ignored by everyone including the mainstream media.

America's Road to Fascism

This is not to say that even his supporters welcomed all of Obama's campaign promises with open arms. Among one of the most controversial was the promise to "close Gitmo," or at least to close the prisoner detention at Guantanamo Bay Naval Base. And we do need to be clear that by closing Gitmo, it was intended that this only referred to the detention center. To even consider closing the whole facility would be nonsense! Still, there are probably many Americans who have no idea what Gitmo even is, or know anything about its history. For that reason, we need to offer a quick recap.

There is much more than just prisoners at Gitmo, which was also the backdrop location of the Tom Cruise and Jack Nicholson film *A Few Good Men*. This is the oldest overseas U.S. Navy Base in the world, and it is located on 45 square miles of land and water in - as the name suggests - Guantanamo Bay in Cuba, where U.S. Marines landed during the Spanish-American War in 1898. It has been leased as a fueling station since the Cuban-American Treaty of 1903, which followed the 1901 Platt Amendment that was passed by the U.S. Congress and included a provision where Cuba would have to provide long-term leases on naval bases.[26] Since 2002 Guantanamo Bay has been used as a military prison for enemy combatants captured in Afghanistan and Iraq who are considered to be unlawful combatants, and who are more importantly not protected under the Geneva Conventions.

It is also important to note that as the United States does not have diplomatic relations with Cuba, and has not since Fidel Castro took power in 1961. For this reason, it is the only base of its type that exists in such a political void. In fact, while the United States continues to maintain that the lease is valid, and continues to pay the rent for the land directly to the Cubans, the government there opposes the presence of the base, and claims the lease is invalid! One story even suggests that Castro had keep every check, except one, in his desk and un-cashed! The base was of major strategic importance to the United States military during the Cold War, and remains important today.

Thus even the idea of closing the detention center is a rather questionable one, given that the base has a unique status in the world, and that it is essentially away from any American civilian population center. It would seem to be the perfect place to house dangerous suspected terrorist, but as questions of torture have been raised - an issue that falls outside the scope of this book - there are those who see this as a good public relations move, without considering the ramifications of moving these prisoners to American soil.

However, it is a campaign promise that has not been resolved, and shows no sign of being resolved. It is also ominous to consider that the United States government would seek to create such a detention facility within the continental United States, unless it expects to capture even more enemy combatants, or perhaps believes there will be domestic terrorists that will need detaining. That is a topic we'll be exploring shortly, but the failure to meet campaign promises shows that Obama the community organizer was better at organizing a plan than following through with one. And as we have seen from other Fascist leaders this is a common problem. There is a vision, and a sense to do the impossible, but in a world of possibilities even these leaders promising hope and change, find that it is hard to follow through.

Chapter Six
Forced Fitness and Health Under Fascism

In October of 2009 many comedians took to the airwaves, and pranksters on the Internet declared that Obama couldn't become Hitler, because the former failed to get the Olympics. So while Obama lobbied for his adopted hometown of Chicago, going so far as to fly to the International Olympic Committee session and XIII Olympic Congress, which was being held in Copenhagen Congress Center in Denmark, in the end the 2016 Summer Games will head to Rio in Brazil. But the truth is that Hitler never actually brought the Olympics to Germany.

While 1936 marked the only year that both the winter and summer games were held in the same country - something that cannot happen again, as the winter Olympics have been since moved to fall two years apart from the summer games - both Garmisch-Partenkirchen in Bavaria, and Berlin were chosen prior to the ascent of power by the Nazis. Despite this the Nazis took every opportunity to show the world the progress the nation had made since coming to power in January of 1933.

The twin villages of Garmisch and Partenkirchen played host to the games, which were the most popular winter Olympics to that point. There were 755 competitors from 28 countries and over half a million spectators who watched the 17 "official" and two demonstration events.[1] The 1936 Summer Olympics, also officially known as the Games of the XI Olympiad, was a far more controversial event, even before the Nazis had gotten involved. The IOC chose Berlin over Barcelona, which ironically was the location where the group had gathered in April of 1931 for actual voting to determine the host city. This was only the second time such an event had occurred, previously being held in Paris, which determined that the 1896 Olympics would be in Greece, with the 1900 Olympics to be held in Paris.

Hitler has often been credited with "bringing the Olympics" to Germany, and of course we see that this is now certainly not the case. Thus any claims that Obama failed where Hitler succeeded is of course off base. Hitler did not succeed in bringing the games to Garmisch-Partenkirchen or Berlin, because he had nothing to do with it in 1931. But in 2009, President Obama did take the time to travel to Copenhagen to lobby support for Chicago, and most certainly failed!

What is also clear is that while Hitler didn't bring the Olympics to Germany, he did use it as a propaganda tool, putting the best Nazi face forward, and it paid off. "The Reich invested one hundred million reichsmarks in the Games and took in a half billion. Once it was realized what was to be gained from the Olympics, everything possible was done to guarantee its smooth course. During this time, foreign policy provocations and negative headlines were intentionally avoided, and the Reich saw to it that the Berlin Olympics, even after they ended, would remain a positive memory in the minds of all those who participated."[2]

However, the Berlin Olympics were probably one of the most political ever, and "throughout Berlin there were thousands of swastikas and martial music was played everywhere. The streets around the stadium were cleaned up and decorated with flags and garlands of flowers."[3] Likewise the Olympic village was larger and grander than past locations, and the arrangements for the events themselves superb, with the track and field events being held in the stadium intended for the 1916 games, but subsequently enlarged and improved.[4] And while there had been calls for advocating the removal of the games from Berlin, or for the boycotting of it, notably by the United States and Great Britain, in the end the games went on, with it being a major success for the host country, which won a total of 89 medals.

Much too has been made of the fact that Jesse Owens stole some of the thunder away from the Nazis, but this is really a post-World War II revision, not actual history. The Jesse Owens controversy actually began in the United States, a nation that was still very much segregated in the 1930s, and he likely encountered more freedom in Berlin than he might have in many southern states back home. While he would have had to ride in the back of a bus, and would have been kept from "whites only" establishments, Nazi Germany had none of these restrictions. While this isn't an endorsement of Nazi Germany, it is just a fact, and one that didn't change in the United States even after Hitler and his ilk were defeated.

Nor is there much truth in the story that Hitler had "snubbed" Owens. Hitler may not have personally congratulated Owens for his Olympic victories, but the German leader did not congratulate any athletes during the games, including Germans ones after the first day. This was part of the IOC guidelines requesting that the host country maintain Olympic and diplomatic neutrality throughout the games. To clarify the position the Chancellery in Berlin even released a statement the following day:

> "As the Fuehrer and the Chancellor of the Reich could not be present at all the final competitions and was therefore unable to receive the winners of the different nations, receptions of the winners after the individual finals in the Fuehrer's box will no longer take place; only German winners will be introduced to the Fuehrer in the case of his being present at the victory of a German in the final."[5]

The bigger snub for Owens, who had won the gold medal for the 100-meter dash, 200-meter dash, 400-meter relay and long jump, came when he returned to the United States. Despite his accomplishments, which at the time included winning more medals by a single individual in any Olympic games to that point, he was never invited to the White House by President Franklin D. Roosevelt. Owens offered his own take on this, "Hitler didn't snub me - it was FDR who snubbed me. The president didn't even send me a telegram."[6]

The point is that the Nazis went all out with the Olympics to win favor with the world, which to a large extent they actually did. Thus there is no doubt why Obama took the time to campaign for Chicago.

And in fairness, President Obama was not the only national leader to travel to Copenhagen, as Japanese Prime Minister Yukio Hatoyama and Brazil's President Luiz Inácio Lula da Silva, the latter whose city did end winning the 2016 games, were also in attendance. But questions remain, and so far the White House hasn't responded. The most obvious is whether President Obama, given all the other problems that the nation was facing at the beginning of October 2009, would have taken the time to travel to Denmark if it wasn't for Chicago. Would the POTUS have campaigned as hard for New York City or Los Angeles? Of course, as we have seen the president likes campaigning and traveling, and this trip allowed him to do both.

Given the debates raging at home over health care, and with the president deciding on the issue of troops to Afghanistan, it still seems an odd choice. Chicago was already very well represented, as the city's Mayor Richard M. Daley went to Copenhagen, along with TV talk show host Oprah Winfrey, whose syndicated TV show is taped in the Windy City. Really, with Oprah on board did the city of Chicago need Obama? Oprah helped Obama get the White House, wasn't that enough of a glowing recommendation that if she couldn't do it, no one could?

In the end the city didn't even get past the first round. It was eliminated faster than a Jamaican bobsled team or Eric Moussambani, the swimmer from Equatorial Guinea who had never seen an Olympic regulation-length swimming pool before![7] Moussambani, who had the worst time ever in the 100-meter freestyle, of course lost, but he was expected to lose and lose badly. Obama came home defeated, and this was something he wasn't used to, at least prior to his run for the White House. Spin control worked overtime, and the pundits found a way to note Obama's defeat without calling it such.

This is because often times those adopting the Third Way of politics look beyond winning and losing. As with their third way of politics they try to find a third way besides winning and losing, but there can be no doubt that this effort was a major failure.

However, no sooner did Obama return home than the media and the pundits worked overtime to say it wasn't such a bad thing. This is because nearly half of the city's residents didn't even want their hometown to be the 2016 host city. Even before the dust had settled Salon.com reported, "Chicago's Olympic bid has divided the city right down the middle."[8]

Pushing for such a major event when only half the city was really in favor seems like an odd thing to do, but then again consider that the health care debate essentially divided the nation as well and that didn't stop proto-Fascists in the House and Senate from pushing the bill. But in the case of Chicago was more at work? Personal vanity perhaps? Salon.com's Edward McClelland further states that the 2016 Chicago Olympics could have been the city's biggest moment since the Columbian Exposition of 1893, an event that announced Chicago's arrival as a great American city. "A Chicago Olympics, opened by a Chicago president, would make us a world-class city," at least in the mind of Mayor Daley.[9]

Furthermore, it could wash away the Second City label, and more importantly the specter of Al Capone. "Around the U.S., Capone has long ceased being the face of the city. But there are still foreigners who hear the word 'Chicago' and think of a pinstriped gangster in a double-breasted suit, carrying a violin case."[10] It isn't hard to see that these issues could be close to Obama's heart, and that he'd drop what he was doing to campaign for his adopted hometown. After all, as we've pointed out, travel and campaigning are also close to his heart.

Besides the seemingly similar passion for the Olympics by Hitler and Obama, the United States has in recent years become obsessed with sports and fitness. Beginning long before the rise of the Nazis, the Germans had their own fascination with sports - and as we've touched upon this went back to the Olympics, where Berlin was chosen to host the 1916 Olympic games. As these games were canceled, the Olympics finally headed to Berlin in 1936, but by this time the Germans under the Nazis had become very focused on sport and fitness.

So much so that the nation formed the Deutscher Reichsbund für Leibesübungen (DRL), or German League of the Reich for Physical Exercise, later also known as the Nationalsozialistischer Reichsbund für Leibesübungen (NSRL). To the Nazis physical fitness was part of the indoctrination process that helped mold followers. "The better an athlete was an athlete, the less he was allowed individualism and the more he was cast as an allegorical, ideological battler. This was more true in Nazi Germany than any other country. Activity in preparation for the Berlin games and the reverberating effects of the outstanding performance of German athletes made sports a national cause."[11]

The DRL was first established in Nazi Germany in July of 1934, and it soon became the official sports governing body of the Third Reich, and it lasted until late 1938, when Hitler ordered its name changed to the NSRL, which also meant that the organization was placed under party control. Virtually all sports fell under the control of this highly influential group, so much so that when the Nazis were defeated, even this group was dismantled as the nation underwent its De-nazification.

It is hard not to see a passion with sports in America, but this passion is also worldwide. Nearly every nation throughout time has rooted for the home team, and booed and hissed its opponents. But it is worth looking at how the Nazis took this to new levels, and in many ways these same tactics have been used in the United States.

Part of this approach under the Nazis was to build those deemed ethnically superior, and Hitler's obsession with this belief in Aryan superiority is well documented. One motivation was clearly that the Nazis were bent on domination over Europe and needed physically fit individuals, but there is more to it as well. "Nazi society was based on the fundamental premise, according to one theoretician, that the minimally educated person who was physically healthy and possessed solid character filled with unencumbered decisiveness and willpower was more valuable to the community than a highly educated weakling."[12] Thus the nation under Hitler imposed fitness activities that were based on German social principles, and even in play members of the Hitler Youth (Hitler Jugend or HJ) focused on fitness to determine leadership, essentially a quasi-leadership through strength position. "Those who took the lead in games became leaders of HJ units as a matter of course. Command and obedience in one situation transferred automatically to others."[13]

Sports also helped meld the classes into one unit. One's socio-economic background isn't important in a sporting event. Performance and natural leadership are paramount, not pedigree.

Sports is one of the few areas of life where the wealthy and poor compete on a level playing field. The Nazis didn't want to create a classless society like the Communists did, but they expected all strata of society to work together for the good of the Volk.

The irony with this approach is that it put too much emphasis on the physical, and clearly at the expense of the mental. Who was to build Germany's new super weapons if the society focused too greatly on the physical? Clearly this was a shortcoming of the program, but one problem with Fascist leaders is that they often look to short term fixes for current problems, whether it is in regards to economic stimulus or physical stimulus among the less than fit. For the Nazis it proved to be a moot point, because their troops proved to be no more superior in caliber to those of the United States or the Soviet Union.

The United States essentially adopted a similar approach that has existed since the early Cold War era. This of course is the President's Council on Physical Fitness and Sports, which publishes fitness guidelines for all Americans. This group is now part of the Office of Public Health and Science, a sub-department of the United States Department of Health and Human Services.[14]

This organization, founded by President Dwight D. Eisenhower who had served as Supreme Allied Commander during the Second World War, was meant to encourage American children to be active and healthy. The Council was formed in 1956 after it was found that American youths were less physically fit than those of European nations. In 1963 President John F. Kennedy changed the title to President's Council on Physical Fitness to highlight that this council was directed at all Americans. Of course the Council never encouraged fitness over education, and given that obesity has become a problem in the United States it is worth noting that the idea of fitness is probably a good idea.

The question is whether we're going to be forced into fitness. Mission: Readiness, Military Leaders for Kids, a group that claims to be nonprofit, bi-partisan and is led by senior retired military leaders, released a report in November of 2009 that found that nearly 75 percent of young Americans would be unable to serve in the military.[15] The reasons included because they fail to graduate high school, engage in criminal activity or are physically or mentally unfit. Although the group claims to be bi-partisan, it is worth noting that General Wesley Clark heads up this organization, and that Clark had previously been a Democratic candidate for president. More complex to this issue is that U.S. Secretary of Education Arne Duncan joined with Mission: Readiness in releasing the study titled "Ready, Willing and Unable to Serve."[16]

While there would be those in the more liberal circles in Washington who might be pleased to find that so many of America's youth are unable to serve in the military, given that the nation is embroiled in two wars, now is not the time to face such a crisis. We may face a future where no one is fit enough to wear the uniforms. The problem is that while this report may in actual fact shed light on the issue, its solution is essentially narrow. The report calls for a greater emphasis on early childhood education, which still doesn't solve the other issues, namely fitness and criminal activity.

For now we'll focus on the issue of fitness, which is again a very slippery slope. There is no doubt that Americans have developed some extremely unhealthy lifestyle habits, but the solutions that are routinely thrown about are "sin taxes" and mandatory changes to diet. Left-leaning groups such as the Center for Science in the Public Interest regularly get the thumbs up from left-leaning politicos, and this group, which has been around since 1971 has basically declared war on "bad food."

Founded in 1971 by Michael Jacobson, Ph.D., the Center for Science in the Public Interest has transformed from a grassroots player to a major organization that now publishes the largest-circulation health newsletter in North America (Nutrition Action Healthletter).[17] The group states on its website that its goal is to:

- Get junk foods out of schools nationwide

- Rid the food supply of partially hydrogenated oil, the source of artificial trans fat that promotes heart disease

- Reduce sodium in processed and restaurant foods

- Improve food safety laws and reduce the incidence of food borne illness

- Advocate for more healthy, plant-based, environmentally-friendly diets

- Ensure accurate and honest labeling on food packages

- Require basic nutrition labeling on chain-restaurants' menus and menu boards

- Provide responsible information about the benefits and risks of agricultural biotechnology

- Obtain greater federal funding for alcohol-abuse prevention policies

- Expose industry influence over the scientific process and in government policy-making[18]

What the group's website is less than open about is that Jacobson co-founded the group with "two co-workers from Ralph Nader's Center for the Study of Responsive Law."[19] According to ActivistCash.com, a project from the Center for Consumer Freedom (a group that looks at anti-consumer activist groups and their funding) Jacobson is a vegetarian and sits on the national board of the animal-rights group "Great American Meatout." While there is nothing wrong with being a vegetarian (and as a matter of full disclosure one of the authors of this book is also a vegetarian) one has to question whether Jacobson's militant approach is truly in the consumer's best interest. ActivistCash.com alleges that Jacobson will not tolerate any of his employees eating so-called "bad" foods at work, and that Jacobson attempted to remove the office coffee machine, until one-third of the employees threatened to quit.[20] Would it be fair to call Jacobson a "food Nazi?" Possibly, but the problem is that this group is regularly quoted by the mainstream media, and as mentioned publishes one of the nation's most popular newsletters on nutrition.

And in some ways maybe calling Jacobson a "food Nazi" is a compliment. After all, it is clear that the true Nazis of Germany were also fanatical about food and what they ate. "Nazi nutritionists stressed the importance of a diet free of petrochemical dyes and preservatives; Nazi health activists stressed the virtues of whole-grain bread and foods high in vitamins and fiber. Many Nazis were environmentalists, many were vegetarians."[21]

While it is widely known that Hitler was a vegetarian, so was SS leader Heinrich Himmler, also a noted animal lover, who yet had no problem ordering millions of people to be killed. He further used slave labor at Dachau to grow various herbs that the SS sold for profit.

The pair were attracted to "homeopathic cures, and staunchly opposed to vivisection and cruelty to animals. Himmler even established experimental organic farms to grow herbs for SS medicinal purposes. At times, Hitler could sound like a veritable Green utopian."[22]

But of course the Nazis were not the only ones who were fanatical about health. As we have discussed the CSPI offered a take that would certainly seem similar. And while it is absolutely true that a great deal of the Nazi's views were later proven wrong - not the least of which was their notion of racial superiority - but so much of their beliefs were based on what today we would call junk science. Could the same be true of groups like the CSPI? Groups that have far too much influence with our government?

Consider that this group has waged war on the bad stuff? One example is that the CSPI is to a large part instrumental in removing trans fats from many American's diets. According to the group, this is a major step forward:

> "The amount of trans fat being put in our food has declined by more than 50 percent since about 2005! The end is in sight, with both food manufacturers and chain restaurants switching from the most harmful fat of all—the partially hydrogenated oil that is the source of artificial trans fat—to healthier oils. The 'end' will be the virtual elimination of trans fat from our food supply, saving roughly 50,000 lives per year! This web page provides information about the health consequences of trans fat."[23]

But isn't the CSPI partially responsible? After all the CSPI went after partially hydrogenated oils, which were replaced by trans fatS. Indeed, according to *The Wall Street Journal*, "twenty years ago, Mr. Jacobson's CSPI launched a public relations blitz against fast food joints for using palm oil to cook fries. The group claimed victory when restaurants started using partially hydrogenated oil instead. In 1988, a CSPI newsletter declared that 'the charges against trans fat just don't hold up. And by extension, hydrogenated oils seem relatively innocent.' Today, Mr. Jacobson is claiming trans fats kill 30,000 people a year."[24]

How the times change. Compare the above quote from Jacobson (now) regarding trans fats, and a statement from his newsletter back in 1988 (then):

> "Despite the rumors, there is little good evidence that trans fats cause any more harm than other fats. Though new questions can always be raised, some of the standard accusations can be laid to rest."[25]

What should have been laid to rest was anyone actually believing Jacobson or his "healthletter." But instead the CSPI has launched a crusade against food, and it might not seem like a big deal, but among those who believed Jacobson on the trans fat issue in recent years was New York City Mayor Michael Bloomberg. Today it is against the law for restaurants to serve foods that contain trans fats. And that is just the tip of the iceberg on this matter.

Cambridge, Mass., Stamford, Conn., Philadelphia, Penn. and several counties outside New York City, as well as the entire state of California now have a ban of trans fat. And all in the name of better health. With the passage of the health care bill that was signed into law in March 2010, there will likely be more changes that will directly affect consumers; especially those who like to consume fast food on occasion. "The health care law requires chain restaurants that have more than 20 locations to display calorie information next to the food item on the standard menu. The Food and Drug Administration has the task of establishing more specific regulations and determining when these changes go into effect." [26]

We can't put the blame for all of this on Obama - certainly not the local legislation - but as we've stressed repeatedly, there are many cobble stones in America's road to fascism, and here is yet another example. Given that Obama does have a Health Czar, Nancy-Ann DeParle, who is officially the Counselor to the President and Director of the White House Office of Health Reform, in addition to the Department of Health and Human Services (HHS), it is hard not to think that DeParle's duties could include getting - or could it be - forcing Americans to eat healthier? Time and time again we hear that this war on unhealthy eating is a national concern, but is it really? Isn't it a matter of "one's right to choose?" When it comes to healthy eating the matter of the social good is addressed. The idea of healthy eating again was something that was widely popular in Germany under the Nazis, and "nutritionists mounted a frontal attack on Germans' excessive consumption of meat, sweets, and fat, and argued for a return to 'more natural' foods such as cereals, fresh fruits, and vegetables."[27]

Could we see a slogan in the works? Maybe one could even be borrowed from the original Nazis?

>Your body belongs to the nation!

>Your body belongs to the Führer!

>Your have the duty to be healthy!

>Food is not a private matter!

>*Nazi slogans*[28]

So what is to stop the POTUS from appointing yet another czar, such as a "Food Czar" to oversee the diets of Americans, or extending DeParle's duties to include food and diet? While this could in fact have many benefits, the problem is that diet remains a science that evolves over time. Consider that children who grew up in the 1970s likely were offered a vastly different "food pyramid" than is offered today. In the 1990's we were told to eat low fat high carbohydrate diets until it was discovered that this led to an increase in diabetes type 2. Margarine was good and butter bad but this was turned upside down with butter being good and margarine bad.

In truth, here is where we can thank our progressive presidents for steering us in the wrong direction. The United States USDA first published dietary food guide called "Food for Young Children" under Woodrow Wilson in 1916. Under a later progressive, Franklin D. Roosevelt, this was revised, first as a "basic seven" food groups and then to make it less confusing, in 1943 to the "basic four," which included milk, meats, fruits and vegetables. So confusing was the issue of diet that in 1941 FDR called for a National Nutrition Conference, and this is the first time that the USDA introduced the Recommend Dietary Allowances (RDA) for Americans to follow.[29]

The basic seven that became the basic four was then changed again in the 1970s, under the advice of author and nutritionist Caroline Hunt when a fifth group was added that included fats, sugars and alcohol. The new group also moved meat and milk together, along with vegetables and fruits, and also added cereals.[30] So clearly we see that the opinion on what we should be eating has changed over time, and this has created a cottage industry devoted to diets, alternative diets and endless debate. But that is actually good. It allows people to consider various options, and to make their own mind on what is right for them. But the fact that some cities and even the State of California are restricting what we choose to eat is certainly just another stone on the road.

Some would possibly say the same thing about America's prohibition against tobacco, which ironically continues just as the debate over legalization of marijuana continues to rise. As with many other issues, the use of tobacco is one that divides the nation just as much as politics, and more so is a topic of debate that widely crosses party lines. There are those who say that it is a personal choice, and those who want to be nowhere near the stuff.

This is a debate waged by the two authors of this book, but for now we look at it as an issue from another perspective, one that can be used for political gains. Tobacco products are now heavily taxed by states and even some cities. It is worth noting that New York City and Chicago have two of the highest taxes,[31] the latter noteworthy as President Obama, a reported heavy smoker, is from the Windy City.

Forced Fitness and Health Under Fascism

Levels of government put restrictions on where and who may smoke, and tax tobacco because it is unhealthy. At the same time taxes generated from its purchase have become an import aspect of government coffers and making tobacco illegal would create a large hole in many state budgets.

Today smoking is of course banned on airplanes, in nearly every American airport - except for special places - and many states now ban smoking in restaurants and bars. This has been equated, at least by the tobacco lobby and by heavy smokers, as a "Nazi tactic." The irony is that it was actually a real Nazi tactic.

It is well established that Hitler did not smoke, and did not like those around him to smoke. But less well known is that the Nazis under Hitler had established the world's first anti-smoking campaign. It also was the Germans who were the first to find a link between tobacco use and cancer. But this link was found long before the Nazis came to power. The Germans were first to hold an international congress of cancer research, which was held in Frankfurt and Heidelberg in 1906, and the nation was also first to establish a permanent journal devoted exclusively to cancer research. In 1928 "Germans also apparently were the first to suggest that secondhand smoke might be a cause of lung cancer."[32]

Under the Nazis smoking was banned in many places, including the party offices and waiting rooms, but the German's ban of tobacco goes back centuries. It might seem odd to Americans to learn this fact, given that until Congress passed the Public Health Cigarette Smoking Act, which banned the advertising of cigarettes on television and radio in April of 1970, it was common to see commercials on TV for tobacco products. But on January 1, 1971 Virginia Slims was the last cigarette commercial to air on TV, at 11:59pm during a break for NBC's *The Tonight Show*.[33]

For the Germans opposition to tobacco could be in their DNA, as the earliest recorded opposition dates back to the Thirty Years War (1618-1648), when "the yellow leaf was introduced into Germany by Dutch and English soldiers."[34] There were soon smoking bans in many of the German states, and these lasted until 1848, a year that saw widespread revolutions across Europe. "Nazi philosophers would later use this coincidence to argue that liberalism spurred the uptake of corrupting vices like alcohol and tobacco - that absolute states had had a more reasonable approach to such matters."[35]

By the time of the Nazis, the tactics against tobacco had greatly increased. "In 1939, the Gesundheitsführer, Leonardo Conti, set up the Bureau Against the Dangers of Alcohol and Tobacco, two of the most deadly consumer poisons."[36] So do we see a similarity to the Food and Drug Administration's Center for Tobacco Products? Dr. Lawrence Deyton, who is being called the nation's first anti-smoking czar by the media was appointed to his position in July of 2009, and he now heads this newly created department, which under his direction is charted with writing new rules for the so-far unregulated tobacco industry. The center was created as part of anti-smoking legislation passed under Congress and signed into law by President Obama in June, 2009 with three goals: to reduce youth smoking rates, to reduce the over all toll of tobacco-related disease and to provide the public with information about the ingredients of tobacco products and their health effects. This law still bars the FDA from regulating tobacco farmers or their products however.[37] (As an aside: It is interesting to note that the EPA can regulate CO_2 gas, which every animal on earth exhales, but the FDA can't touch tobacco.)

For the Nazis the smoking ban was very strong, but several factors stood in the way. By the late 1930s smoking actually increased in Germany at a greater rate than in other European nations, notably France. Smoking it seems may have functioned as "resistance" against the government. The Nazis also backed off from a total ban of cigarettes, wary of how unsuccessful the American prohibition against alcohol had been, and with the outbreak of war, the nation had bigger fish to fry. Likewise, many notable Nazis, including Joseph Goebbels, were heavy smokers. Regardless of these factors, it is believed that the Nazi tobacco bans were not ever effectively enforced.[38] It will be interesting to see what bite the FDA's Center for Tobacco Products has under Dr. Deyton.

Chapter Seven
Eco-Fascism and the Green Takeover

One of the biggest lies spread about conservatives is that they don't care about the environment, and this opinion isn't one shared just by American liberals.

"If you care for the environment and want action on global warming, don't vote Conservative"

- Bruce Cox, executive director of Greenpeace Canada [1]

Even those who think they know a "conservative" from a "liberal" seem to believe that conservatives essentially hate the environment, and the only "green" they care about is in the color of the dollars that can be made from raping the land. In an essay for *The Independent Review*, Stephen M. Colarelli writes:

> "When it comes to the environment, however, liberals are conservative, and conservatives are liberal. Conservatives oppose preservation of the environment. They believe that the environment should be exploited for economic ends. Developers— usually Republicans—complain about regulations that slow their drainage of wetlands to develop golf courses and build condominiums. Logging executives and workers— usually political conservatives—complain that they should be able to 'harvest' forests as they see fit. Western ranchers and mining executives complain that new regulations requiring them to pay market rates to lease federal land will drive them out of business. Conservatives favor 'management' of the natural environment. They speak about 'wise use' or 'multiple use.' The environment exists for humankind to dominate and to bend to its will."[2]

Talk about seeing the world in black and white! If Colarelli is to be believed, then Republicans and conservatives are looking to exploit the world's resources and the entire environment for nothing but financial gain - not that a liberal would ever dare do such a thing (more on that in a bit). However, is this really a fair picture of conservatives? If this were the case, why is it that the big cities - the areas with the most development - are usually hotbeds of liberals, or at least those who vote Democrat, whilst the rural areas tend to more conservative and often vote Republican?

More importantly consider the voting patterns in this country for the past several elections, and it shows that the Democratic base is in the more heavily built-up East Coast of the United States, as well as the West Coast. Could it be that the liberals in these areas seem to think that the entire country is this built up and thus developed? Or could it be that the biggest supporters of the so-called "green" movement are so far to the left that even the center looks distant?

RingWingNews.com sums up this point extremely well:

"Unfortunately, most environmental activists today tend to be radical luddites for whom economic considerations are practically irrelevant. We're talking about people who try to stop almost every new power plant from being built, who oppose drilling a desolate Alaska wasteland laden with oil because they fear it might upset the caribou in the region, and who'd happily drive the US economy into a depression by supporting the Kyoto Accord [sic]. Conservatives want clean water, clean air, and a clean planet as much as the average person. However, unlike radical environmentalists, we're not purists. Conservatives have a sense of proportion, and we're not willing to drive America's standard of living back 50 years for some unnoticeable environmental gain. So in effect, conservatives are pro-environment, we're just moderates about it compared to the zealots in the environmentalism movement."[3]

It is also somewhat ironic that many of the policies of the "green" movement aren't all that far removed from past Fascists, such as the Nazis in Germany. To understand this we must look at the history as well. As with the German's emphasis on nutrition and tobacco, the Nazis merely borrowed and thus built on past traditions. In the case of the environment, it goes back to two 19th century figures: Ernst Moritz Arndt and Wilhelm Heinrich Riehl, the former being the earliest example of 'ecological' thinking in the modern sense.

As early as 1815 in an "article *On the Care and Conservation of Forests*, written at the dawn of the industrialization in Central Europe," he railed against shortsighted exploitation of woodlands and soil. However, Arndt's environmentalism was also inextricably bound with xenophobic nationalism.[4]

Riehl took this a step further, with his book *The Natural History of the German People as a Foundation of German Social Politics*, which essentially suggested that the geographical factors as well as social conditions defined the German culture. While he was criticized for his rather unprofessional and subjective generalizations, these criticisms weren't enough to stop him from being influential to the Nazis. Riehl had further stressed, "The fast pace of industrialization and urbanization toward the end of the nineteenth century caused unease."[5]

These teachings clearly served as the basis of the environmental movement during the Nazi era, when Hitler's government passed the "Reich's Nature Protection Law of 1935." This was passed with the support of Reich Chancellor Rudolf Hess, who has been seen as the most important supporter of the Nazi's so-called "green wing." Hess was of course Hitler's most devoted personal deputy, and was second in line after Herman Göring to succeed Hitler. Interestingly some of Hess's personal choices might not seem that far removed from some of today's extreme liberals.

"An inveterate nature lover as well as a devout Steinerite (followers of Rudolf Steiner's teachings), Hess insisted on a strictly biodynamic diet - not even Hitler's rigorous vegetarian standards were good enough for him - and accepted only homeopathic medicines."[6] Under Hess's backing numerous environmentalist legislation was approved, which included those that protected animal and plant species, called for reforestation programs and even blocked industrial development.

There is some irony that Hitler would later call for a complete "scorched earth" of Germany as the Allies and Soviet forces closed in on the mad dictator in 1945. However, this was a policy that was never actually carried out.[7]

The same cannot be said of many "green" policies in the United States, while global warming, also known as climate change, has become one of the biggest issues facing any politician in the United States today. Worse still is that this has been used as a talking point by liberals and the far left to continually attack the right almost non-stop, regardless at times whether the facts support the cause or not.

It is far beyond the scope of this book to address whether global warming/climate change is real, or whether it is manmade or a natural phenomenon. There are countless books that support climate change and countless books that debunk it. Whether you believe in the science or dispute it is not the issue in regards to the road to fascism in America, it is how the issue of global warming is being used.

First, the mainstream media in the United States, instead of trying to present just the facts, often editorializes the story about climate change, suggesting that it is necessary to seek urgent action, regardless of the cost, or regardless of what the voice of opposition has to say. Next, the issue is so big that the media and those on the left are using it as a way to suggest that the right wing is dangerous for not believing that global warming or climate change is real. While we'll discuss the "enemy within" in greater detail in an upcoming chapter, the issue of "global warming deniers" is something that we need to address.

Even when evidence has come up, such as the so-called "Climategate" e-mails that question the science of whether global warming is real, this is usually dismissed. Among the worst offenders of this is former Vice President Al Gore, who won a Nobel Peace Prize for his efforts to "combat global warming" in 2007 as well as an Academy Award for his documentary *An Inconvenient Truth*. Gore told MSNBC "that GOP leadership is in a 'global warming denier posture' that is fueling a partisan divide nationwide on climate change."[8] The inconvenient truth with this statement is that Mr. Gore made this statement when the Upper Midwest and the Eastern Coast of the United States was suffering through some of the worst winter December weather in recent memory.

It is interesting to note that the term "global warming denier" is based on the term "holocaust denier." Neo-Nazis and radical Islamists deny the historic truth that six million plus European Jews were intentionally murdered by the Third Reich. Anyone who questions the science of global warming is painted as just as radical and dangerous as those who question the Jewish holocaust.

Gore was responding to a *Washington Post* editorial by former Vice President candidate Sarah Palin, in which she wrote:

> "'Climate-gate,' as the e-mails and other documents from the Climate Research Unit at the University of East Anglia have become known, exposes a highly politicized scientific circle -- the same circle whose work underlies efforts at the Copenhagen climate change conference. The agenda-driven policies being pushed in Copenhagen won't change the weather, but they would change our economy for the worse."[9]

The issue here is that in November 2009 e-mails were hacked from a server used by the Climatic Research Unit (CRU) of the University of East Anglia (UEA) in Norwich, Arizona. These e-mails reportedly suggested that climate scientists may have withheld information, interfered with peer-review and even deleted raw data to prevent it from being reviewed under the Freedom of Information Act, while also manipulating existing data to make a stronger case for global warming. However, instead of reviewing these facts, some on the left took aim at the hackers, not what they revealed.

Senator Barbara Boxer, the lead Democrat on the Senate Environment and Public Works Committee stated that the focus should be on the hackers specifically. "You call it 'Climategate;' I call it 'e-mail-theft-gate.'"[10] This in turn has lead to new conspiracy theories about who might have been behind the very theft. As reported in *The Daily Telegraph* in Great Britain, this could even be a threat worthy of something out of a James Bond film, namely the work of the Russian Secret Service:

> "Russia, a major oil exporter, may be trying to undermine calls to reduce carbon emissions ahead of the Copenhagen summit on global warming. The CRU emails included

remarks which some claim show scientists had manipulated the figures to make them fit the theory that humans are causing global warming."[11]

One problem with this theory of course is that whoever was responsible for the hacking had to have some insight on what to look for - thus suggesting that this might have been "an inside job." More disturbing and more ominous is the fact that these findings are not only being dismissed but also that anyone who now questions this is labeled a "denier."

But we must also consider not only the "science" but also who is saying this. According to *USA Today* (December 7, 2006), "Public records reveal that as Gore lectures Americans on excessive consumption, he and his wife Tipper live in two properties: a 10,000-square-foot, 20-room, eight-bathroom home in Nashville, and a 4,000-square-foot home in Arlington, Va. (He also has a third home in Carthage, Tenn.) For someone rallying the planet to pursue a path of extreme personal sacrifice, Gore requires little from himself."[12]

Not only does Gore not practice what he preaches, but in some cases he doesn't listen to anything resembling science. Take this quote from his November 12, 2009 appearance on *The Tonight Show With Conan O'Brien*:

> "People think about geothermal energy - when they think about it at all - in terms of the hot water bubbling up in some places, but two kilometers or so down in most places there are these incredibly hot rocks, 'cause the interior of the earth is extremely hot, several million degrees, and the crust of the earth is hot."[13]

At several million degrees that would mean that the inside of the Earth is hotter than the surface of the sun, and this is nowhere near the temperatures provided by the "Ask a Scientist" website that is part of the Office of Science for the Department of Energy. According to this site, the temperature is far lower

> "There is no way to measure the temperature at the Earth's core directly. We know from mines and drill holes that,

near the surface of the Earth, the temperature increases by about 1 degree Fahrenheit for every 60 feet in depth. If this temperature increase continued to the center of the Earth, the Earth's core would be 100,000 degrees Celsius! But nobody believes the Earth is that hot; the temperature increase must slow down with depth and the core is probably about 3000 to 5000 degrees Celsius. This estimate of the temperature is derived from theoretical modeling and laboratory experiments. This work is very difficult (and speculative) since nobody can reproduce in a laboratory the high temperatures and pressures that exist in the core. Also it is not known exactly what the core is made of."[14]

At 5000 Celsius that would still be less than 10,000 degrees Fahrenheit, quite a ways off from the "several million degrees" that Gore said on TV. This could of course be dismissed as a mere slip of the tongue and an off the cuff remark that was a mistake, or was it just another example of bad science? Yet either way, it had practically no pickup in the mainstream press, and Gore was never called to defend this statement. Imagine if President Bush or Governor Palin had made such a remark in this political climate?

And before we completely move on from this issue, consider that Al Gore won a Nobel Prize (and Academy Award) for his environmental studies. This isn't just a case of a child mixing up thousands and millions; this is someone who lobbies, and speaks and tries to change U.S. environmental and energy policies. We would have at least expected Mr. Gore to make a statement to correct what he had said, but then again, maybe he believed that the temperatures inside the Earth were really millions of degrees. As Mr. Gore avoids any confrontation on the debate, it is really hard to know for sure.

So to recap, we have Gore, a man who says there is an agenda - "GOP leadership is in a 'global warming denier posture'" - doesn't practice what he preaches, is awarded for his work despite these facts, and has all but created a new religion around something opponents have labeled junk science. The problem is not that Mr. Gore might do some good in the process. No one would stop the efforts for a cleaner Earth, alternative energy, and most importantly freedom from dependence on foreign oil.

The problem is that the cure could be worse than the disease. One suggested alternative is the so-called cap and trade, a policy that on closer review truly sounds like something the Nazis might have done.

> "Under a cap-and-trade program, the government sets an overall cap on the level of CO2 emissions the United States economy would put into the atmosphere by a certain date. This cap would define the absolute maximum amount of CO2 that could be emitted in the United States. Over time this cap would be reduced, resulting in fewer CO2 emissions and higher CO2 emission costs. Each business would receive, either through issuance or auction, tradable allowances equal to their maximum allowable level of CO2 emissions. Those firms that can reduce their emissions more cheaply and efficiently could sell their unused allowances to others who would otherwise have to pay more to comply."[15]

This would create a new tax on the aforementioned emissions, thus raising the cost of doing business, and it would then create a new market where the trade portion of "cap and trade" would have to be monitored and regulated. Another problem is that cap and trade might only affect larger businesses, and while this is good news to all the small and medium-sized businesses out there, together they're likely to produce a lot of carbon, thus making cap and trade ineffective. How ineffective exactly? "Only 1.3 percent of facilities in manufacturing industries emit more than 25,000 tons of carbon dioxide per year and would be regulated under cap-and-trade bills being considered in the house and senate, a Duke University study concludes."[16]

However, while the green sector is no doubt trying to reassure small and medium-sized businesses, there are other reports that suggest this could be bad for everyone, at least in the wallet. Cap and trade detractors say this could hurt the overall economy. According to the report "The Adverse Economic Impacts of Cap-and-

Trade Regulations," from Arduin, Laffer & Moore Econometrics (September 2007):

> "Cap-and-trade regulations would likely impose a large cost on the U.S. economy. The U.S. Energy Information Agency (EIA) estimates that overall economic growth could decline by up to 4.2 percent if a cap-and-trade system were implemented to achieve the Kyoto Protocol targets (7% below 1990 GHGs by 2008-2012). The costs to reach the ultimate goal of some GHG control proponents (e.g., reducing GHGs to 80% below 1990 levels by 2050) would be significantly greater. However, these estimates assume that the government will auction off the rights to emit greenhouse gases as opposed to simply giving these rights away, which is the approach often discussed in the U.S. and what has actually been implemented in Europe."[17]

The remaining problem with cap and trade is that this is something America would undertake, whilst many parts of the world - notably the developing nations - would not adhere to these standards. Thus we would further increase our business costs, while allowing nations such as India and China to operate without similar restrictions. That seems like bad business all around.

More worrisome is that the president could impose these standards even if Congress does not pass the cap and trade legislation. One way that this almost happened was by allowing the Environmental Protection Agency's "Endangerment Finding" to open the door to regulate so-called greenhouse gas emissions, on the ground that global warming is hazardous to human health. Put another way, by using the power of the EPA, the president could regulate those gasses - such as Carbon Dioxide - without a single vote being cast in Congress. Rudolf Hess could only have wished for such power!

What exactly did the EPA have in mind? Here it is in the EPA's own words:

> "On December 7, 2009, the Administrator signed two distinct findings regarding greenhouse gases under section 202(a) of the Clean Air Act:

- Endangerment Finding: The Administrator finds that the current and projected concentrations of the six key well-mixed greenhouse gases--carbon dioxide (CO_2), methane (CH_4), nitrous oxide (N_2O), hydrofluorocarbons (HFCs), perfluorocarbons (PFCs), and sulfur hexafluoride (SF_6)--in the atmosphere threaten the public health and welfare of current and future generations.

- Cause or Contribute Finding: The Administrator finds that the combined emissions of these well-mixed greenhouse gases from new motor vehicles and new motor vehicle engines contribute to the greenhouse gas pollution which threatens public health and welfare."[18]

The irony is that this builds on legislation that most would agree was helpful. In the 1970s the government passed the Clean Air Act, and while this, and "the subsequent Clean Water Act, were criticized at the time as being too bureaucratic and onerous for businesses to comply, there's no doubt that our air and water are cleaner today as a result. The National Environmental Policy Act in 1970 authorized the creation of the EPA as an independent agency to monitor and issue specific rules on pollutants, and the EPA has done so, relatively free of political interference, in the ensuing years."[19]

However, while the agency has done much good, and despite the fact that the "green" movement has made it seem so, conservatives are not out to dismantle the EPA. But nor did anyone, including the government in the 1970s, intend to give the EPA this level of power.

As Kimberley A. Strassel of *The Wall Street Journal* writes, "From the start, the Obama team has wielded the EPA action as a club, warning Congress that if it did not come up with cap-and-trade legislation the EPA would act on its own - and in a far more blunt fashion than Congress preferred."[20] Thus if Congress didn't pass this legislation, the EPA would do it anyway. Is that democracy? Again, Rudolf Hess would be envious to have this much power!

Chapter Eight
Small Matters, Big Steps: The Fascist Way

In chapter five we looked at the various promises that President Obama has not kept, and we offered an overview of some of the issues he has not addressed. Now we must examine what exactly the 44th President of the United States has accomplished, and here again we find some notable parallels with past Fascist leaders. For Fascists don't really rule the land, and despite this notion of strong-arm militants who control everything and the stereotypes of dictators that do it all, the truth is much different.

While the Soviet Union's Josef Stalin was indeed such a man, the same isn't true of Adolf Hitler, Benito Mussolini, Francesco Franco or even Barack Hussein Obama. These are the type of men who make long speeches, campaign even after taking power and let the real rule of the land fall to their massively inflated government. We've touched upon this already, so again it comes back to what exactly do these men do? It might be best summed up that they sweat the little things. This is certainly true of Obama, who wants to be briefed on everything, and we're not just talking about the larger issues of the economy and the wars in Iraq and Afghanistan.

"In a White House ritual new with this administration, the president gathers with his advisers every weekday morning for an Oval Office update and debate on the economy. The breadth of topics is wide, from the under-employed to childhood obesity, and Mr. Obama often dives into the minutiae."[1] This might not seem like a problem, except that in the case of these leaders, it is more what they haven't done than what they've actually accomplished. In other words, a good leader doesn't sweat the little things at the expense of the larger issues.

Given that from the time he was elected in November until he took office in January the country sank deeper into recession, the auto industry was facing a meltdown and things were bleak. But what did the office of the President Elect focus upon? In a letter to Congressional leaders, John Podesta, co-chairman of Obama's presidential transition team, urged that the February 17, 2009 conversion date for the planned switch to all-digital broadcast television be extended. Obama's team warned, "that the TVs of millions of Americans could lose their pictures."[2] Numerous reasons were given including the fact that the government failed to educate the public, and that it was to help better prepare individuals, notably the elderly, the poor and those living in rural areas. Thus was born the *DTV Delay Act*, which changed the mandatory analog cutoff date to June 12, which finally saw the end of the old analog TV standard.[3] The issue is why did President Elect Obama's team take the time to address this seemingly insignificant matter? Was this a case of truly sweating the small stuff?

It does have the appearance. The FCC actually issued a mandate in early 2007 that by the end of 2009 all analog signals would be turned off, and began a campaign to prepare TV viewers for the transition. More importantly, this is not the first time that TV standards have changed in America. According to the FCC, it took 12 years for 10 percent of US households to get color television sets. But since the first digital televisions became available in the late 1990s, 32 percent of American homes have adopted them. That is largely due to surging demand for HDTV programming, because 80 percent of the digital sets deliver a high-definition picture.[4]

The difference with the switch from black and white to color was less of an issue, because black and white TVs could still receive the channels broadcast in color. With the switch from analog to digital, the TVs would not receive a picture unless they received the programming through a cable box or had a set top box if they were using rabbit ears. Additionally, there were those who opted not to use cable who had to install a roof-top antenna and still get a converter box to continue to use their own sets. However, all sets currently being sold in early 2009 were most certainly able to receive the DTV signal. The delay was clearly about that small majority that hadn't prepared for the switch.

So exactly how many people were even going to be affected had the transition gone forward? According to a press release from The Nielsen Company, the organization that tracks ratings and the number of viewers watching TV, as of January 22, 2009 about 5.7

percent of U.S. households, or roughly 6.5 million homes, were unprepared for the switch. That had actually been an improvement of more than 1.3 million homes since Nielsen reported readiness status at the end of December 2008.[5]

Not everyone was in agreement with the president, and leading the loyal opposition to the debate that waged in Congress was Rep. Joe L. Barton (R-Texas), who offered his opinion, "I guarantee you, no matter when you set the date - Feb. 17, June 12, July the Fourth, Valentine's Day - there are going to be some people that aren't ready."[6]

The point again is whether the president, his team or really anyone in the government needed to focus on the issue of the DTV transition, especially given that there had been ample warning. But there is the larger issue that this is just a single example of Obama's fascistic micromanagement style, one that has been called "paradoxical" by *The Wall Street Journal*. Furthermore, the paper wrote, "He has pushed an ambitious agenda that would involve remaking large parts of the economy, in such an extensive way that he has drawn opposition even from Democrats worried about injecting the government too far into the economy and pushing taxes and spending too high. And yet, even while championing the ambitious agenda, say presidential aides, Mr. Obama has shown last-minute caution on many fronts."[7]

One of those fronts is in light bulbs, perhaps because the image of a light bulb over one's head in cartoons suggests a brilliant though. President Obama has been called brilliant so many times by liberals in the media and from his adoring followers that perhaps he believes there is a light bulb over his head in many people's minds, and thus he feels compelled to create a better bulb. But this is not just any light bulb. "President Obama announced tougher energy efficiency requirements for certain types of fluorescent and incandescent light,"[8] which is just the latest step in the president's push to reducing the nation's energy use.

The question here is that given the number of czars and other offices, why is the president pushing for these particular light bulbs, especially given that compact fluorescent light (CFL) bulbs are considered by some to be a stopgap to newer technology. Likewise, the bulbs contain mercury, a substance that can be dangerous should the bulb be broken, and even receive a warning on the government's own Energy Star website. "Like any other product containing potentially hazardous materials that you use in your home, CFLs come with some special instructions."[9]

While it is true that the Energy Department has not updated the efficiency requirement of the light bulbs "since they were established by Congress in 1992," and furthermore "the department was supposed to update the requirement in 1997"[10] this hasn't happened. The problem however is that Obama would take the time to handle this now, offering this brilliant insight, "Now I know light bulbs may not seem sexy, but this simple action holds enormous promise because seven percent of all the energy consumed in America is used to light our homes and our businesses."[11]

Getting past the fact that the POTUS is handling an issue of light bulbs - which begs the joke "how many presidents does it take to change the light bulbs of America" - we must ask whether this president has done his homework on the issue. Beyond the mercury content of the CFLs, the fact is that Obama said nothing about tomorrow's technology. CFLs are not new. These have been around for a while, and as we've touched upon, these are, and always have been a stopgap. The irony is that many environmentalists jumped on the bandwagon, Energy Star has jumped on the bandwagon and others followed suit. In fairness the push to move to CFLs came under former President George W. Bush, but that was when eventual replacement technology was still being developed.

CFLs are one of those technologies we should have skipped, but the green movement couldn't wait for the next big thing and pushed a dead-end technology. But as we've seen eco-Nazis such as the Center for Science in the Public Interest push their own agenda. Whereas the push to trans fats happened with the best of intentions, so too did the push for CFLs. The point that must be made is why is Obama on board? And why hasn't he at least uttered the letters "LED?"

"To put it simply, LED light bulbs will eventually be what we use to replace incandescent bulbs – CFLs are merely a stopgap measure. LED bulbs are made out of clusters of light emitting diodes – you've seen them in use in countless places, but perhaps most commonly as the small indicator lights on electronic devices. LEDs use very little energy for the amount of light they produce."[12]

So why was there no mention of the LEDs by the POTUS? We can only assume the numerous czars and officials just simply didn't pay attention to this technology. Maybe the president should have called a "summit," something he's already started to do for other topics.

The first of course was the "Beer Summit," which took place on July 31, 2009 on the White House Lawn. This brouhaha was meant to cool simmering race relations after Boston area police officer, Sgt. James Crowley was accused of racial profiling for his part in a misunderstanding involving Harvard professor and "race-relations expert" Henry Gates Jr. This resulted in Crowley arresting Gates for disorderly conduct after police responded to a report of a possible burglary at the professor's Boston-area home. The charges were eventually dropped, but Obama quickly became involved - as he is a friend of Gates - and stated that police in Cambridge, Massachusetts, "acted stupidly."

The result was a photo opportunity, which included both President Obama and for reasons never fully explained Vice President Biden, both in shirt sleeves, joined by Crowley and Gates sitting around a table having a cold beer. What exactly did this accomplish, and what was its purpose? Does the leader of the free world really need to be taking time out for a meeting of this kind, and more importantly did it really do anything for race relations in the United States? Likewise, why was Joe Biden there, or is it just a case that the Veep can't pass up a photo opportunity or free beer – but for the record, Biden reportedly drank a non-alcoholic Buckler.[13]

And if the purpose of the meeting was to address race relations, what did it do for the American beer industry? NPR's Liz Halloran offered this opinion: "Any national exposure for beer is good — there is no such thing as bad publicity at this point in the game."[14] But was it good for American beer makers? While each of the attendees was offered his respective favorite beer, the fact is that this summit at the White House was hardly an American affair - at least when you examine the products that were served.

"The problem is that all three beers (not including Biden's non-alcoholic choice) are products of foreign companies. Red Stripe is brewed by London-based Diageo PLC. Blue Moon is sold by a joint venture in which London-based SABMiller has a majority stake."[15] Even Obama's personal choice of Bud Light has foreign entanglements. Bud Light is a beer that NPR called "a 'lawn mower' beer, perfect for after mowing the lawn or when you get home from work. It's one step up from a nice, tall glass of ice water and generally one of the lightest pale lagers made in the United States."[16] It is now made by Anseuser-Busch InBev NV, a Belgian-Brazilian company.

In the end the summit came and went. Again we ask, what was its point? It gave decent PR to three foreign owned companies, let the president roll up his sleeves to look like the everyman, and brought the veep along for the ride. But did it solve anything? About the only thing it might have done was give the mainstream news a chance to break from the month-long reporting on the death of pop singer Michael Jackson. Beyond that, it was a feel good event, and possibly defused a major gaffe by President Obama. This is perhaps the greatest irony in the whole situation. While the media devoted time to note the beers that were drunk - or to be drunk as the case may be - very few in the mainstream media noted that the president's off-the-cuff remark was quite stupid. As a small matter, let's examine exactly what the POTUS said:

> "I don't know – not having been there and not seeing all the facts – what role race played in that, but I think it's fair to say, number one, any of us would be pretty angry; number two that the Cambridge police acted stupidly in arresting somebody when there was already proof that they were in their own home," Obama said in response to a question from the Chicago Sun-Times's Lynn Sweet.[17]

The facts have been well established: Gates was locked out of his own house, a neighbor called the police, who responded to the report of a burglary, and Gates and Crowley became belligerent with each other. Why does any of this matter to the POTUS? Only because as Obama had said that Gates was a friend, and even admitted he might be biased about the situation. So is it not uncalled for that the POTUS then said "the Cambridge police acted stupidly," but clearly it is also established that Obama, a man the media has reportedly said is an eloquent speaker does his best work when in front of a teleprompter. Perhaps this is why the talking heads in the media fawn over the man; after all they're the ones who also are most comfortable in front of a teleprompter.

But more importantly, this is a trait that is typical of Fascist rulers. Hitler and Mussolini were both renowned for their ability to give speeches, to win over the crowds. But when pressed on issues, and asked questions to which they were unprepared, the answers were not quite so well expressed either. Could this be that charismatic leaders need to be prepared with just enough of the optimal settings to make their point? That much is debatable, just as is the final outcome of the "beer summit."

Despite Obama's attempts to be the "common man" and his supposedly all-American upbringing, he certainly shows that he's not exactly trying to get away from the trappings of office. A notable example is one of the most lavish White House State Dinners that we've seen in a long time (which we will cover in a bit), but also his wording of what is "his" versus the American peoples.

Said the new president in February,2009, "Hey guys, what do you think of my -- this spiffy ride here?" to a group of reporters traveling with him on the presidential plane.

Likewise, in an interview with *Newsweek* magazine in May of 2009, President Obama actually referred to the White House, a building owned by every citizen of the United States, as his house, and even admitted handily that he was indeed akin to Star Trek's highly logical Mr. Spock:

> "Now, movies I've been doing OK [with] because it turns out we got this nice theater on the ground floor of my house... So Star Trek, we saw this weekend, which I thought was good. Everybody was saying I was Spock, so I figured I

should check it out and—[*the president makes the Vulcan salute with his hand*]."[19]

The most truly logical man, even one with Fascist leanings wouldn't dare consider the White House or the Presidential Plane to actually be his. While we maybe making much out of this, consider that Hitler did consider the "Amerika" to be his personal train. Could this be a case where Obama, or at least the proto-Fascist part of him really thinks these are his? Or are these just words that were ill chosen? Given that President George W. Bush was routinely criticized for every gaffe, Obama - the eloquent speaker - seems to get a pass time and time again. The question here is why the bar is set so low for any of Obama's accomplishments and deeds, while it seemed so much higher for his predecessor?

This is notable in the next summit the White House hosted in 2009. While the president spent much of the year traveling and/or campaigning, either to meet foreign leaders in a so-called progress of "nation" building - much like the aforementioned President-Elect Herbert Hoover in 1928 - or to reassure Americans that help was on the way, there was the "White House Jobs Summit."

The summit was held held on December 2, 2009, as America faced the highest unemployment numbers since 1983, and which had steadily risen from 7.6 percent in January to 10.2 percent in October. The event included around 135 leaders from every sector of the economy, including government, labor, academia, non-profits and business of all sizes. "Obama acknowledged the skepticism that the summit would produce tangible results."[20] And just as telling was who was not involved in the summit.

"Missing from a partial list of attendees released by the White House are the self-proclaimed voices of business - the U.S. Chamber of Commerce and the National Federation of Independent Business - both of which have been critical of Mr. Obama's proposed health care overhaul."[21] In the end the summit was little more than a meet and greet with the president, and it was clearly an attempt to show that the president was at least concerned with the economic picture.

Here we must ask why this happened so late, and why so little was done. Of course the coverage in the media was nearly

Small Matters, Big Steps: The Fascist Way

completely overshadowed by yet another celebrity news item - this time involving professional golfer Tiger Woods' car accident and allegations of infidelity - as well as the so-called White House party crashers for Obama's first state dinner. It seemed that the media was more concerned with two people who weren't actually invited to the White House, than it was in those 135 individuals who came to talk about jobs.

While we've already highlighted previously that the same liberal media that gushed over Obama's January 2009 inauguration had previously had voices of dissent that called for former President George W. Bush to cancel both the 2001 and 2005 inauguration. The former for reasons of economic downturn and the latter because of the ongoing wars in Iraq and Afghanistan. Again, no such calls for cancellations were made in January 2009, nor was there much to be made that Obama's first state dinner was larger than any held by George W. Bush, who typically invited fewer than 200, while former President Bill Clinton had dinners with as many as 700.[22]

Obama didn't try to outdo Clinton, at least not yet, but the Associated Press noted that the 338-person guest list for the State Dinner for Indian Prime Minister Manmohan Singh "was a study in contrasts, mixing wonky Washington, Hollywood talent, prominent members of the Indian community in the U.S. and Obama friends, family and campaign donors."[23] So large was the party however, that it wouldn't fit in the traditional state dinning room at the White House, and a tent was erected instead. It reportedly sprouted on the South Lawn and completely hid the South Portico and the first floor of the executive mansion from view.[24] Yet hardly any dissent for such a lavish event, one held just prior to the aforementioned White House Job Summit, as unemployment was again at its highest level since 1983. It is almost ironic that someone didn't suggest that erecting the tent actually put people back to work!

However, Obama may also be on track in one regard to be more like "former President George W. Bush, who would never be taken for the most social president, hosted just six state dinners in his eight years in office, compared to 29 state dinners during the Clinton administration."[25]

The news of this first state dinner would have likely been forgotten were it not for the Internet social media website that is known as Facebook.com. Less than a day after the event and long after the media seemed to forget about the actual indulgence of the event, the news hit that in addition to the 338 persons on the guest list two additional people attended the party. Tareq and Michaele Salahi showed up to the highly exclusive event without an invite, somehow managed to get past several Secret Service checkpoints, despite not being on a guest list, and were able to meet the president and the Indian prime minister on the receiving line. Their story is that they never heard a voice mail from earlier in the day that advised them that they did not make the guest list. This was the account of the story that the Salahis gave to a Pentagon official who had tried to get them invited, and which was obtained by The Associated Press.[26]

What is fascinating is not the fact that the Salahis were able to get into the White House, but the fact that the White House worked overtime on damage control. The Associated Press quoted President Obama, "the system didn't work the way it was supposed to,"[27] but is that good enough? He said in a joint interview with *USA Today* and the *Detroit Free Press*, "I could not have more confidence in the Secret Service." But instead of anyone throwing themselves on their swords for this breach, the White House is otherwise staying quiet, whilst letting the Secret Service take all the blame. [28]

Secret Service Director Mark Sullivan faced a "firing squad of lawmakers determined to find out how the vaunted Secret Service could allow uninvited guests into the White House"[29] while speaking to the House Homeland Security Committee in early December 2009. Sullivan said that he had put three Secret Service officers on a paid leave for the incident, and he was asked by the committee to share out some of the blame for this security lapse.

What is shocking is that the Salahis refused to testify, perhaps because they were actually invited in this case. When the Salahis finally did show up to face a grilling from the Committee in January 2010, both evoked the fifth amendment repeatedly. However, while we might make light of that fact, what is not clear is why Social Secretary Desiree Rogers, reportedly a friend of the president and

Mrs. Obama, also refused to testify. The White House evoked executive privilege, with press secretary Robert Gibbs noting "I think you know that based on separation of powers, staff here don't go to testify in front of Congress. She will not be testifying in front of Congress."[30]

As Ms. Rogers was asked and not subpoenaed she faced no criminal charges, and there is the legal ruling from the Supreme Court in 1974 that stated in *United States v. Nixon*, that presidents maintain a "valid need for protection of communications between high government officials and those who advise and assist them in the performance of their manifold duties."[31]

So what is the White House hiding? A long list of presidential advisors has actually testified in recent years, even after the 1974 ruling. As *Time Magazine* points out "much of the testimony in recent decades has resulted from major congressional investigations, including the 1970s Watergate break-in and the 1990s Whitewater land deal. In the eight years of the Clinton Administration, dozens of presidential advisors testified before Congress."[32]

After all, shouldn't some of the blame for this lapse in security fall on the office of the Social Secretary? Why would the White House evoke executive privilege? That's something that those on the House Homeland Security Committee clearly wanted to know too, including Rep. Charles Dent (R-Penn.) who said, "I'm very impressed by your willingness to take responsibility for this incident. We always expect the Secret Service to take a bullet for the president; we don't expect the Secret Service to take a bullet for the president's staff."[33]

Among those passing the buck was White House Deputy Chief of Staff Jim Messina, who had reviewed the incident according to ABC News, and which Gibbs said looked "at whether we were doing enough to complement the work that the brave men and women do at the Secret Service."[34] The answer seemed to be no, and Messina further posted a blog on the White House website noting:

> "After reviewing our actions, it is clear that the White House did not do everything we could have done to assist the United States Secret Service in ensuring that only invited guests

enter the complex. White House staff were walking back and forth outside between the check points helping guests and were available to the Secret Service throughout the evening, but clearly we can do more, and we will do more."[35]

The issue here is that this still puts much of the blame on the Secret Service, and almost suggests that these highly trained men and women are supposed to be the presidential bouncers, concierge and bodyguards all in one. Even the most obnoxious Hollywood insider has multiple people that do specific duties. The Secret Service's role should be to protect the president and guests, not to be the keeper of the guest list! While no doubt the agents allowed for a breach in security, it seems Obama forgot that these aren't his personal bodyguards akin to the Praetorian Guards of ancient Rome.

This was clear as the issue continued to unfold, when President Obama responded to questions on TV's *60 Minutes*, and was quoted as saying, "I was unhappy with everybody who was involved in the process. And so, it was a screw-up. It won't happen again."[36] This is just another action that suggests how disingenuous this president really is, as it is the job for the Secret Service to take a bullet for him, and it is his Social Secretary's job to manage the invites and check the guest list. But Obama also shows how he further sweats the little things by adding, "What I know is what everybody knows, which is that these people should not have gotten through the gate."[37] Shouldn't who gets through the gates at a party be the concern of Ms. Rogers and her staff? Without her bumbling this would never have happened, and while there is no doubt that the Secret Service did "screw up," it still seems that essentially Obama has suggested that the Secret Service take a bullet for his wife's friend!

The issue is who else will the president expect to take a bullet. As he begins to send more troops to a war in Afghanistan - albeit it with already somehow setting an exit date, as if a military campaign is a carton of milk with an expiration date - it is clear that Obama isn't caught up just in the small matters. But these examples of the small matters show that the president over thinks, considers, reconsiders and likely second-guesses himself.

What we must hope is that the proto-Fascist in President Obama doesn't try to take the lead and micromanage any war effort. That would have very bad results, especially as the tactical genius of true Fascists such as Mussolini and Hitler speaks for itself. This is not just about the unfortunate deaths of our young men and women that this level of indecision or just plain bad decision could cause, but the very security of our country, and the future of Western civilization.

Chapter Nine
The Business of Fascism

In early December 2009 General Motors chief "Fritz Henderson was given the bullet by the group's board, led by chairman Ed Whitacre, after just eight months in the job."[1] Henderson had reportedly "flunked" a 100-day review of his performance since GM emerged from chapter 11 bankruptcy protection, and he was just one of several executives who either resigned, or were given their walking papers in a company bloodbath-like cleanout.

Henderson had replaced GM chairman and CEO Rick Wagoner earlier in the year, after the White House pushed out Wagoner. President Obama has ousted Wagoner and even "instructed" Chrysler to form a partnership with Italian automaker Fiat as conditions for receiving government aid.[2] This came about just weeks after Obama had taken office, and followed some questionable decisions on the heads of the Big Three American automakers.

2008 had not been a good year for the American auto industry, due in no small part to record high gasoline prices in the summer of that year. The global economic crisis that followed left two of America's auto companies on the brink of disaster and the heads of these companies unwisely opted to fly to Washington looking for a handout. After public and media outcries over corporate jets the companies did a U-turn and put spin control in overdrive, with the heads of the companies each driving to the nation's capital in the latest hybrid or extremely energy efficient vehicles. These PR stunts were nothing more, but the government was poised to offer bailouts, just as it was in the process of doing for the nation's banks, which were also highly affected by the worst economic downturn since the Great Depression of the 1930s.

So far there have been no great public works projects that are indicative of the New Deal, but the government has been spending money at an alarming rate, and leveraging the future with bonds. Although much has been made about these bailout packages, which have been questioned on both sides of the aisle, and these could be debated in length, the purpose of this book is not to question

The Business of Fascism

each and every one of Obama's strategies, bur rather to indicate and address those that have the sinister trappings of fascism. For while Mr. Obama may have said otherwise when giving aid to the auto companies, the United States government now finds itself in the auto business, and his choice of words are also reminiscent of the deeds that transpired during the 1930s.

> "I don't want to run auto companies, I'm not an auto engineer. I don't know how to create an affordable, well-designed plug-in hybrid. But I know that, if the Japanese can design an affordable, well-designed hybrid, then, doggone it, the American people should be able to do the same. So my job is to ask the auto industry: Why is it you guys can't do this?"

We would like to ask Mr. Obama why he thinks that this is his job at all, but as we have already seen, it is really hard for proto-Fascists not to get caught up in these small matters. The small matter is not that the government bailed out the auto industry, but rather that Obama has - without any experience designing cars as he has stated - demanded the direction that the American auto industry takes going forward! Eva Rodriguez in an op-ed piece for *The Washington Post* sums up this problem quite well:

> "There's nothing wrong with Chrysler and GM building fuel-efficient green cars -- if they can make money. I'd have no problem whatsoever if one of them manufactured a pink, snout-grilled mini-car that ran on manure -- as long as it proved profitable. (I wouldn't buy one, mind you, but I'd smile and wave as you drove by.)
>
> "My goal as a taxpayer is to see that these companies earn enough so that they return my tax dollars as soon as possible. And what if green cars aren't the way to go? What if market research and consumer surveys show that as long as gas costs only $2 a gallon, U.S. drivers will stick with the true road hogs, our SUVs? And what if CEO Obama doesn't like these answers because they don't jibe with his goal of reducing greenhouse gases?"[3]

So what's wrong with the leader of the nation telling its automakers to build a small, affordable car for the masses? Nothing at all, but here again is where Obama's words sound like they've been lifted from the Great Depression, and it wasn't progressive President Franklin Roosevelt who called for this automobile, it was German Chancellor Adolf Hitler with the "People's Car" or Volkswagen.

To understand this much, we must understand the history of the German auto industry. If it is true that America has a love affair with the car, so too it must be said of Germany, the land that could be credited with practically inventing the automobile. For the record, we do stress "practically" because various nations attempt to claim being the original inventors, but the point remains that Carl Benz - whose name should be recognizable as part of Mercedes Benz - generally is credited with taking the concept and having the vision to believe that an internal combustion engine could be used to power a horseless carriage.[4]

The Germans had had a sizeable auto industry before the Nazis had come to power, but the Great Depression essentially devastated Germany's auto industry. There had been 86 automakers in Germany in the 1920s, and many of these even managed to survive the era of hyperinflation, but by the 1930s there were only a dozen. The Nazis under Hitler looked to bail out the Germany auto industry with a policy known as Motorisierung, which was a sweeping transport policy that was meant to raise the people's standard of living. This included the vast highway building that resulted in the autobahn as well as the Volkswagen project to design and construct a car for the common man.[5]

The surviving companies in Germany formed the core group that led the nation out of the Depression. This was not least because of the special way that the National Socialist policy of resolutely promoting the motorization of German society, but also because of the "need" for the nation to rearm. "The regime, in fact Hitler himself, urged the automotive industry to take on the Fordist challenge and jointly develop and produce a Volkswagen, a people's car, that would sustain mass motorization as Ford's Model T had done."[6]

The Business of Fascism

Here it is easy to compare Hitler's call for a people's car with that of Obama's urging for American automakers to step up and create the car he thinks the people want. There are differences of course, because while Germany maybe as car crazy as the United States today - with both nations being among the largest producers of automobiles - it took this jumpstart by Hitler to get the German automakers in full gear. Today the result is that the automobile industry is among the largest employers in the Germany, and it has more than 29 percent of market share (source OICA, 2002) in Europe.

But this all began in 1935 when a "German engineer named Ferdinand Porsche created his best design. His car was called the *Volkswagen*, which means 'people's car' in German. Many years later, Porsche made his own famous sports cars. The Volkswagen was an unusual design. It was small and round, and its engine was in the back, where most cars had trunks. The engine was cooled by air, so it did not need a radiator. The headlights looked like two big eyes. Some people thought the car looked like a bug - like a beetle!"[7]

However, before Porsche's design or Hitler's vision was realized, the government had to overcome the fact that the industry stubbornly resisted, so much so that the government finally acted in 1938 by founding the VW Factory.[8] What is worth considering is that Obama hasn't so much forced the U.S. government to make fuel-efficient hybrids (yet), but instead has taken a step even further than Hitler had with the German auto industry. As we have addressed, Obama all but ordered Chrysler to merge with Italy's Fiat, and fired Wagoner from GM. Is this not exactly what Mussolini had meant by corporatism, the merger of the state and corporate power? Under Mussolini's Fascist vision the idea was that the government tells the corporation what to do - being that it is in the best interest of the country and its people.

Obama has essentially ordered Chrysler what to do, but as we shall soon see, it isn't even clear it is in the best interest of that company, let alone the country. Could this be a situation where the POTUS had a good idea but managed it badly? Was this a case where Obama possibly was sweating the small stuff, without really grasping the bigger picture?

It is also clear that it had not been a smooth ride for Obama in other aspects of the auto sector either. In July of 2009, Steven Rattner, head of the Obama's administration's auto task force, resigned. While he had been praised for his efforts to restructure GM and Chrysler, the "Auto Czar" came under a cloud of investigation from an influence peddling scandal in New York, which resulted in Rattner resigning from his posts. He was replaced by former steelworkers' official Ron Bloom.[9]

Unlike many who move on to something different, Rattner stayed present, and even offered his take on the government's handling of the auto bailout in a piece he wrote for *Fortune* magazine. It included some very telling details:

> "Everyone knew Detroit's reputation for insular, slow-moving cultures. Even by that low standard, I was shocked by the stunningly poor management that we found, particularly at GM, where we encountered, among other things, perhaps the weakest finance operation any of us had ever seen in a major company."[10]

More telling is what Rattner had to say about the state of Chrysler:

> "Badly run after Daimler bought it in 1998, Chrysler had been sold nine years later at the peak of private equity mania to Cerberus Capital Management. Larded up with debt, hollowed out by years of mismanagement, Chrysler under Cerberus never had a chance. We marveled, for example, that Chrysler did not have a single car that was recommended by *Consumer Reports*."[11]

So given that Daimler left the company in such a bad position, why would the road ahead be better with another foreign backseat driver? If Chrysler was so badly run by Daimler, why would a deal with Fiat even be in the U.S. automaker's best interest?

Forbes' Jerry Flint asked the same question ("Is Fiat Helping Chrysler - Or Fiat?"), noting that "Fiat's proposal for Chrysler appear more to be aimed at helping Fiat rather than at saving Chrysler. That, at least, is the impression from looking at the information that has leaked out before the Italian company's formal announcement of its plan."[12] Fiat had not had an American presence in decades, but a deal with Chrysler meant the company could have access to a North American plant to build its own cars, and for Chrysler it meant… not as much, except killing other potential partnerships such as one to build pickup trucks for Nissan. For an American president with small and affordable cars, however, Fiat might seem like the better move, even if the American market wasn't interested.

As the economy still struggled in the fall of 2009, former U.S. President Bush urged Obama to get out of the auto business, even if Obama had said previously he didn't want to be there in the first place. Bush argued that only private companies could spark an economic rebound, stating that government has "to get out of the private sector, and therefore I hope our government gets out of the autos and the financials in which they have a stake."[13]

It would be easy for Obama to pass the blame for the economic meltdown on the former administration, but considering that Obama did say, "I don't want to run auto companies," it isn't hard to ask the question, then why are you doing so now? Another question that has been asked is why the U.S. government lent money and essentially bailed out the banks, which in turn was good for the banking industry but didn't do much to help Main Street?

Even here there have been some significant misunderstandings. Many opponents of former President George W. Bush put the economic meltdown at his feet, but have praised Obama's efforts. While there is nothing ominously fascistic about any of this, it needs to be cleared up. The TARP fund - Troubled Assets Relief Program - was a program created by the United States government to purchase assets and equity from financial institutions to give a boost to the financial sector, and it was a major part of the government's efforts to address the subprime mortgage crisis of 2008. Clearly this was done under Bush's watch, and Bush took heat that Wall Street was given the money whilst Main Street suffered.

But by the end of 2009, the loans - and at the core that's what these were: loans - were being repaid. According to the *Financial*

Times in early December 2009, some $175 billion would be repaid by the end of that year, while even the once struggling Citigroup was working to return its $20 billion in outstanding funds that it took during the crisis.[14]

What Bush's opponents and Obama's supporters have failed to address is that the Obama administration essentially overstretched the original purpose of the TARP, and this included deploying tens of billions of dollars to the auto industry. As of December 2009, the debate on job creation remained, with the government split on where money for new programs would come from - some suggesting this should be from the $787 billion stimulus program, rather than TARP.[15]

The debate over stimulus, job creation and economic recovery raged even before Obama took office in January 2009 and it continued throughout the year. Strangely when it came to stimulus, instead of trying to ignore similarities with the Nazis, some in the mainstream media embraced it. *The New York Times* noted that Germany escaped the Great Depression faster than other nations:

> "More than any other country, Germany — Nazi Germany — then set out on a serious stimulus program. The government built up the military, expanded the autobahn, put up stadiums for the 1936 Berlin Olympics and built monuments to the Nazi Party across Munich and Berlin."[16]

As we have previously seen the efficiency of the Nazis is hard to question, even when we must question their motives. Even in the post-war years there were those who would argue that Germany under the Nazis had tried to do some good. "Of all the Third Reich's seductive repertoire, the construction of the autobahn remained one of the most potent devices. For years after the war, many Germans would admit that their love of Hitler was irrational, that they were held captive by black magic. In the midst of their self-defense, they would suddenly say: 'and what about the autobahn?' The autobahn network built under Hitler was proof of a 'good' National Socialism, of a forward-looking system that had non-evil goals."[17]

The cost of Hitler's social and military spending during the pre-war years nearly bankrupted Germany. Vast amounts of money were

The Business of Fascism

borrowed and it was estimated that by the end of 1941, three-fifths of all annual revenue would go towards interest payments on the national debt. The only way Nazi Germany was able to continue to appear prosperous was by waging war with its neighbors and stealing their wealth to prop up Hitler's regime.[18]

There is no doubt that even the Nazis did some good, and that any Fascist may believe they are in fact doing good. What we must question however is where those means will take us. What are the ends to these means? We have seen how the Nazis essentially increased the size of the government, and to stimulate the economy dozens of organizations were created, with the Berlin government essentially taking control over practically all facets of life in Germany by the outbreak of World War II.

This included the Nazi's efforts to combat unemployment, which saw the establishment of the Reichsarbeitsdienst (or RAD, Reich Labour Service). This organization was formed in 1934 as the official state labor service under the Nazis. "Originally, the institution was an instrument in the fight against unemployment at the end of the Weimar Republic."[19]

As we have previously seen many of the policies taking place under the progressive President Franklin Roosevelt had similarities with those of the Nazis, and this included the Civilian Conservation Corps (CCC), which was a New Deal public works relief program. Whereas national labor service was introduced in Germany in 1931, the United States did not take this step initially. However, "in 1933, both the National Socialists regime and the New Deal saw a labor service as a partial answer to the worldwide economic crisis."[20] The Nazis adopted what was in place, creating the RAD, while the United States, under a newly elected president, created the CCC. The purpose was to provide aid relief to the unemployed, while implementing a natural resource conservation program as well."

We have addressed these similarities previously, yet it is further worth considering that several times it has been suggested that President Obama could possibly create a new program based on the CCC, and do so with government funding. "Congress could provide money for new public-sector jobs to clean up parks, along the lines of the Civilian Conservation Corps of the 1930s. Obama told *USA Today* he would like to keep this approach modest, along the lines of summer-jobs programs for teenagers."[21]

The concern is where this goes next. Part of the greater Nazi effort under the RAD included the Deutsche Arbeitsfront (DAF or German Labour Front), which became essentially the National Socialist trade union, replacing the various Weimar Republic trade unions. "After their seizure of power the Nazis moved to coordinate labor by destroying the trade unions on May 2, 1933, and establishing the German Labor Front (DAF) four days later. German workers did not resist the destruction of their unions. By the fall of 1933, the German Labor Front had taken on a new appearance. It was now defined as the organization for all working peoples regardless of economic or social position."[22]

The purpose was supposedly to create a productive community. But under bad management - or with bad work ethic it could have been a disaster - the result was that wages were set by the DAF, but it also meant that dismissals were made difficult. Under the Nazis the DAF was really meant to educate all working Germans "to support the National Socialist state."[23] For Germans they traded job security for loyalty. Could an American president do the same thing?

Chapter Ten
Fascism at the Community Level

When looking back at past Fascist movements, notably those of Fascist Italy and Nazi Germany, it is hard not to focus on the massive size of the governments that were created. Nazi Germany for one created a state within a state, but we must remember that this movement began in a beer hall with a handful of followers. Likewise, Mussolini began his political career as a newspaper editor.

As we have touched upon, Barack Obama took a similar path. But what we haven't addressed yet is how the United States has also had a long (and at times shady) history of quasi-Fascist movements at the community level. Over time these groups have grown from small grass roots organizations to powerful lobbies. While that in itself really is not the issue, what is more of a problem is that these groups often use government money to fund their nefarious political agenda.

One such group was likely unknown to the average American until the 2008 Presidential campaign, and that of course was ACORN, a group we will discuss shortly in length.

But to understand this group, we must first examine the 2008 election. More so than any other election in the history of the United States community level organizations helped elect the POTUS. And while these groups are considered "community level," the truth is that under the Obama team these small groups became part of the very machine he publicly spoke out against!

"In some ways, the Obama campaign learned from the mistakes of the past. It hired hundreds of organizers from labor unions, community and environmental organizations, and religious groups. They, in turn, recruited tens of thousands of volunteers and trained them in the skills of community organizing. They used door knocking, small house meetings, cell phones, and the Internet to motivate and energize supports."[1]

These included not only ACORN, but also groups such as MoveOn.org and the Sierra Club - the latter one officially claims to be non-partisan, although the group does note that it supports pro-environmental candidates for elected office.[2] While it is no secret that the nonprofit MoveOn.org is essentially a left-wing political action committee that pushes the cause of Democratic candidates, ACORN has long remained a shadowy organization that was only brought into the spot light as Obama took the center stage.

Here is the official "About ACORN" from its website:

> "ACORN is the nation's largest grassroots community organization of low- and moderate-income people with over 400,000 member families organized into more than 1,200 neighborhood chapters in about 75 cities across the country. Since 1970, ACORN has been building community organizations that are committed to social and economic justice, and won victories on thousands of issues of concern to our members, through direct action, negotiation, legislative advocacy and voter participation. ACORN helps those who have historically been locked out become powerful players in our democratic system."[3]

The group has long claimed to bring people together, and in a 1995 publication, written for ACORN's 25th anniversary, the group's "philosophy" of togetherness was reaffirmed:

> "From the beginning, when it brought together Black and white [sic], welfare and working poor, ACORN defied expectations of what a community organization could be. It pioneered multi- racial and multi-issue organizing, led the way in electoral organizing, and branched into innovative housing development, community media and labor organizing."[4]

This sounds good, but what exactly does community-organizing mean? In some ways it sounds familiar and not in a very good way. This sense of community was strongly emphasized by past Fascist regimes. "The seduction of Nazism was its appeal to community, its attempt to restore via an all-powerful state a sense of belonging to those lost in modern society. Modernization, industrialization, and secularization sowed doubt and alienation among the masses. The Nazis promised to make people feel they belonged to something

Fascism at the Community Level

larger themselves."[5] Doesn't that seem a lot like what these community and grassroots organizations are trying to do?

Social and economic justice, two cornerstones of ACORN, is a soft sounding way to say redistribution of wealth and affirmative action. This is a socialist belief that says the achievers of society, those who earn a high wage for their labor and intellect, owe the less fortunate and underachievers monetary compensation. ACORN and similar groups want economic and social fairness but to achieve this they have to take from someone else. The more a nation moves towards economic equality the less freedom there is for the individual to exercise. Your money is your freedom and if the government takes it away to give to someone else, you become more of a servant to the government, not a citizen thereof.

We could also dismiss ACORN as just another not-so-subtle left-wing leaning group, were it not for the endless controversies that have come to light in recent months. In July 2008 *The New York Times* reported that Dale Rathke, brother of Wade Rathke, the founder of ACORN, was found to have embezzled nearly $1 million from the group.[6] Dale Rathke reportedly made about $948,000 in improper credit card charges in 1999 and 2000, however this was eventually handled as an internal matter. The Rathke family and a donor eventually repaid the money, and charges were never filed, yet the matter isn't fully resolved. The group's national headquarters in New Orleans was raided in November 2009 as part of a Louisiana state investigation into further accusations of embezzlement and tax fraud.[7]

Readers may recall that these events may seem eerily similar to those of Fritz Julius Kuhn of the German American Bund, who we discussed in chapter three. Kuhn's charges of embezzling were overlooked by his group as well, suggesting that inappropriate appropriations of money in Fascist and quasi-Fascist groups is just par for the course.

In the case of ACORN, embezzling was the least of the group's troubles it seems. Videotapes were released in the summer of 2009 that "showed two people posing as a pimp and a prostitute seeking advice on tax evasion at Acorn offices. The responses given by the

ACORN workers in the tapes led Congress and state governments to cut financing for the organization."[8]

Much of this would be worth looking past, were it not for the fact that Obama has close ties to this group. Since becoming President, Obama has forgotten his ties to the group, just like he never heard racist or anti-American preaching from the Rev. Wright, even thought being a member of the Wright congregation for 20 years. In fact, he seems willing to feed the group to wolves if it becomes politically expedient. According to ABC News: "the President said that ACORN 'deserves to be investigated' in light of the 'inappropriate' video that's gone viral, he did not endorse recent votes in Congress to cut off federal funding for the community group."[9]

Here is a transcript of the full exchange from the ABC News website (September 20, 2009):

STEPHANOPOULOS: How about the funding for ACORN?

OBAMA: You know, if -- frankly, it's not really something I've followed closely. I didn't even know that ACORN was getting a whole lot of federal money.

STEPHANOPOULOS: Both the Senate and the House have voted to cut it off.

OBAMA: You know, what I know is, is that what I saw on that video was certainly inappropriate and deserves to be investigated.

STEPHANOPOULOS: So you're not committing to -- to cut off the federal funding?

OBAMA: George, this is not the biggest issue facing the country. It's not something I'm paying a lot of attention to.[10]

While we won't comment (much) on the casual tone of Obama's concerning this issue, it is interesting to note that the most eloquent public speaker since the Roman orator Cicero ends a sentence in a preposition. While this poor use of grammar isn't a high crime or misdemeanor, when Bush made language gaffs it became fodder for late night laughs. Could this be a further sign that without a teleprompter Obama really isn't the orator for the ages?

But beyond his choice of words, we must ask how it is that Obama didn't know ACORN was "getting a whole lot of federal money." Can we really believe that the community organizer Obama never realized where the money came from? But as we've seen, Obama typically likes to disavow problems if he can't blame others.

To this we say, maybe he should take a point from the fictional Jack Ryan, protagonist of Tom Clancy's novels, who offers his President the line that instead of denying he should leave the media with nowhere to go. Instead of Obama offering the "I didn't know line," he should have responded, "they've been getting a lot of federal funding and this is clearly time they are cut off!"

Regardless of whether Obama knew that this group was getting money from the federal government, the damage is done - both to Obama's reputation and to the organization as a whole. So much so that ACORN may not be able to survive. Already the California branch has split from the group, and will be reorganized as Alliance for Californians for Community Empowerment, or ACCE. The group claims that it will have no legal, financial or structural ties to ACORN, and promises stricter controls over its finances.[11] In March of 2010 ACORN also closed up shop in Maryland with no plans to rebrand the group under a different name. This was a move that was also made by several ACORN affiliates across the country. [12] With this we expect that ACORN will have lost of its power to do potential harm, but we doubt that this scandal-ridden group will manage to avoid headlines. In fact, ACORN might not exactly be buried for good. ACORN Housing does indeed live on. This group, which was rebranded as Affordable Housing Centers of America (AHCOA), retains the same board of directors and maintains its headquarters in Chicago. Likewise, while ACORN maybe gone in Baltimore (and other cities), AHCOA plans to live on. "According to Alyson Chadwick, communications director for AHCOA, ACORN Housing was never a subsidiary of the larger ACORN organization and had begun reorganizing a new identity for itself in 2008." [13]

This may not seem all that relevant, but consider the various Fascist and quasi-Fascist groups that we discussed earlier in this book. Names changed often, but the motives remained the same - often with the same people in power pulling the strings. Thus AHCOA could be seen pulling the same strings that ACORN once pulled.

One area where we expect to see more in the way of news is in another widely misunderstood power base of American politics - that being the labor unions. Typically, the role of unions has long been misunderstood. This is in part because of the relationship that the Nazis had with unions. After coming to power the Nazis essentially took over what the labor unions controlled. "All assets, presses, and offices of Socialist unions were seized and many leaders arrested. Confused, fatalistic, without their leadership, and caught off guard by this swift action, workers offered no resistance. Other unions acquiesced thereafter by voluntarily submitting to a Nazi takeover of their institutions."[14]

We don't expect to see a similar takeover - at least not yet. But one reason for this is that labor unions in Germany were strongly divided by party lines during the chaotic days of the Weimar Republic, whereas labor unions have typically been far more partisan in the United States, almost always throwing their support to Democratic candidates. Politics they say makes strange bedfellows, and the liberal Fascist agenda still manages to draw endorsements from labor unions despite the wealth and hypocrisy of powerful Democrats. Some of it is mind boggling, such as how many labor unions supported Senator John Kerry's bid for the White House in 2004. How could labor endorse a near billionaire, but yet they did.

Democrat Speaker of the House, Nancy Pelosi gets support from unions and has even received the Cesar Chavez Award from the United Farm Workers Union. But Pelosi and her husband own vineyards and a winery in Napa that are non-union. She is also part owner in a resort hotel and restaurant chain. The hotel and restaurants employ over 1150, all non-union jobs. And yet Pelosi has received more money from Hotel and Restaurant Employees unions than any other member of congress in recent times.[15] Pelosi has moved the

Fascism at the Community Level

unions from being a bedfellow to a lap dog. They continue to ignore her hypocrisy as long as she throws the occasional bone.

Thus unions have been friendly to Barack Obama as well - even the United Mine Workers of America endorsed Obama for President, despite his defeats in the primaries in coal-producing states.[16]

Just days before the election an Obama interview with *The San Francisco Chronicle* came to light, in which the candidate said, "So if somebody wants to build a coal-powered plant, they can. It's just that it will bankrupt them because they're going to be charged a huge sum for all that greenhouse gas that's being emitted."[17] Despite this ominous statement, the United Mine Workers of America reiterated its May 21, 2008 endorsement of Obama one day before the general election.

Thus it really isn't a surprise that Obama, as well as the left wing in Congress have been quick to turnaround and offer special perks to union members. Except they call it a compromise. This was over the so-called Senate backed plan to include a "Cadillac tax" on some health care plans in the proposed Obamacare. The White House and labor unions reached a deal on revising the tax on high-cost insurance plans, "which was criticized by labor unions and some Democrats who said it would hit middle-class families and union members who gave up higher wages for better health benefits."[18]

The issue here is why does the POTUS debate this with unions, except for the fact that Democrats typically seek these powerful endorsements. Why is the issue about - as Reuters suggests in the above quote - "union members" rather than average Americans?

Obama campaigned on fairness, even stating he would raise the capital gains tax even though that would cause a drop in federal revenue because it was "fair" to do so. How is it that it is fair for non-union members to pay a tax that union members are exempt from? Non-union employees also negotiate for wages and benefits and may forego a larger wage for health care benefits. The 14th Amendment says all American's get equal protection under the law. Does the Obama compromise with the unions mean that all American's are equal but union members are more equal than the rest?

The fact remains, even as the authors write this book, that few issues have so divided the country as the issue of health care. It is one that the liberal leaning media called "too important" as the race for "Teddy Kennedy's seat in the Senate" was being decided. But what strikes us as odd is the fact that it really seems that Obama the man could probably have done a better job helping people as a community organizer than he has as President.

This is certainly clear, as the labor picture remained bleak in early 2010. According to *The Washington Post* which reported in mid-January 2010:

> "Unemployment for African Americans is projected to reach a 25-year high this year, according to a study released Thursday by an economic think tank, with the national rate soaring to 17.2 percent and the rates in five states exceeding 20 percent."[19]

For African-Americans hope might be all that many have left, because this probably wasn't the change they were hoping for under Obama. So maybe Obama should go back to being a community organizer, but what exactly did he do as a "community organizer?"

Before Obama was even a candidate *The Nation* ran a story in April of 2007 on the then Senator Obama, which explains how after graduating from Columbia University in 1985, Barak Obama decided to become a community organizer. Obama went to work for Jerry Kellman, an organizer working on the South Side of Chicago, who was looking for someone to help with the new Developing Communities Project, which focused on black city neighborhoods. "Despite some meaningful victories, the work of Obama - and hundreds of other organizers - did not transform the South Side or restore lost industries. But it did change the young man who became the junior senator from Illinois in 2004, and it provides clues to his worldview as he bids for the Democratic presidential nomination."[20]

But the real problem now is that too often it seems that Obama continues to believe his skills as a community organizer carry over to the Oval Office, and as his time in that office has shown, they don't! Byron York, Chief Political Correspondent for *The Washington Examiner* offered his own take on why Obama the

President shouldn't be drawing experience from his community organizing past:

> "Obama the organizer spent most of his time teaching community members how to put pressure on the city government, or on various wealthy corporations, to give them money. Obama's organizers could be confrontational, or they could be conciliatory - Obama favored the latter - but the whole idea was to make powerful people feel guilty, or embarrassed, or annoyed enough to give them things.
>
> "Obama, born in 1961, felt that he missed the great days of the civil rights movement. Becoming an organizer was the next-best thing he could find. But his successes were small; he wanted to redistribute wealth and resources on a large scale, and he could only accomplish so much by protesting outside the housing project management office. That was the reason he ultimately left organizing to go to law school and run for public office."[21]

What is remarkable is that following a meteoric rise; Obama has now shown signs of burning up like a meteor entering the atmosphere. After a year on the job CBS News reported:

> "Obama has suffered the steepest decline in job approval of any first year president since they started keeping such data: in most surveys, he is barely at, or under fifty per cent."[22]

It could be that after a year under Obama, many Americans were waking up to his true colors of hope and change. And while this is a good sign for the near future, the concern remains on what this one-time community organizer can do to help make it easier for future proto-Fascists down the road.

It is also important to note that setbacks are nothing new for Fascists either. A crisis remains a surefire way for power to be seized, and while the poll numbers have turned, the allure of fascistic charisma remains in these troubled times. This makes it all the easier for the Great Leader to point out that the dangers and enemies - whether they be internal, external or simply imagined.

Chapter Eleven
The Enemy Within

One fact that is undeniable about fascism is that it sees enemies everywhere. During former President George W. Bush's term in office many on the left, including American author and political consultant Naomi Wolf, argued that the United States was taking the necessary steps for a Fascist take over of the country. However, as we have discussed, elections were held and the United States saw the democratic and peaceful transfer of power.

This does not mean we are out of the woods. The point again is that past presidents, as well as past members of congress, and even Supreme Court justices have helped build the foundation of America's road to fascism. In fact, the rallying cries today, under the proto-Fascists in power, are much more in-line with past Fascist movements. Again, as we have touched upon fascism is not a movement from the far right, but ironically this has become the new enemy, the internal enemy. Fascists view this enemy within as the greatest danger. But is it a real danger, or just a loyal opposition? For those now in power there is no question, and this is exactly to note that Fascists need this opposition, which they never see as loyal.

"Enemies were central to the anxieties that helped inflame the fascist imagination. Fascists saw enemies within the nation as well as outside. Foreign states were familiar enemies... internal enemies grew luxuriantly in number and variety in the mental landscape as the ideal of the homogeneous national state made the difference more suspect."[1] Consider that with the liberal talking heads in the media, from Michael Moore to Bill Maher to Ed Schulz, and how after the election of Barack Obama, and with control of the House and the Senate, there was a fear from the "Republicans" and "the right-wing." These are the internal enemies, the ones who will stand in the way of freedom and the American way - at least according to those liberals, who suddenly were shocked that anyone would say something nasty about this great president.

Never mind that there had been eight years of name-calling, mudslinging and endless questioning of former President Bush.

What had once been labeled "patriotic" had become "treason" or even "racist." A word comes to mind, ironic.

This irony can be seen in many ways, including Ms. Wolf's "Fascist America, In 10 Easy Steps."[2] While she certainly believed that Bush was culpable in driving down the road to fascism, the current administration under President Obama is heading straight down the same road and at an alarming speed. We shall take a look at each of these steps.

1. Invoke a terrifying internal and external enemy.

While it would be easy to see that Bush did invoke a terrifying external enemy, the fact remains that terrorists attacked the United States on September 11, 2001. This was not a false flag act - despite what any conspiracy buffs might believe - nor was it an event that the government used to seize power. But where was the "internal" enemy with Bush? *The Patriot Act* has hardly made Americans the enemies! Consider that since President Obama has taken office the media has again begun to pay attention to "militias" and so-called "home grown terrorists." We'll get to those, but if these were such a threat why has so little been mentioned of them for so long? Could it be that the power of the white supremacist movement was broken? And what about the "Tea Baggers" and other opponents of Obama? Why are they covered with such distain?

These are questions that we'll look at more in detail as well. Likewise, this isn't to say that Mr. Obama faces no external threat. In addition to the ongoing wars in Afghanistan and Iraq, the nation continues to face the greatest threat to mankind… ever! That of course would be global warming or climate change, which we have already discussed in great length. The debate on this topic rages, and shows no sign of going away. It has, in essence, become so big that it is truly that great external threat. One that could allow the president and the government to change laws to "save mankind." What bigger external threat could you possibly ask for if you were trying for a Fascist takeover of the United States?

2. Create a Gulag.

Here Ms. Wolf clearly means this to be Gitmo, or Guantnamo Bay, which we have discussed. But as we also covered, Gitmo was positioned far from American soil, and no American citizens have been sent there. There have been no reports on Gitmo that suggest the detainees have been engaged in forced labor, like the prisoners in Stalin's Gulag system.

However, President Obama has called for the closing of the prison at the military base, and the establishment of a replacement on American soil. Wouldn't that be the real gulag?

3. Develop a thug caste

Under President Bush there was no domestic Republican Army, but yet President Obama has previously called on a National Service Bill. Wouldn't this be a "thug caste?" There have been reports that union members who support the president have shown up at Tea Party rallies to counter-protest the protesters. Are these thugs for Obama?

4. Set up an internal surveillance system

While there has been increased internal surveillance, it isn't as if President Obama has set about to dismantle any of it. More importantly he carried on past administration policies, including appointing a "Border Czar" while adding a "Terrorism Czar" into the mix.

5. Harass Citizens' Groups

Can we really believe that the "Tea Baggers" or the "militias" aren't being watched very closely? Aren't these too citizens' groups? And aren't they protected under the constitution as with any other group?

6. Engage in arbitrary detention and release

Was there ever really a policy of arbitrary detention? Ms. Wolf seems to imply that this was standard with Bush, but as *The Wall Street Journal* reported in May 2009, "The Obama administration's efforts to craft what it calls a 'preventive detention' plan for suspected terrorists will face constitutional challenges similar to those raised against the Bush administration's policies. Some detainees held at Guantanamo Bay, Cuba, are deemed too dangerous to release and may not be able to be put on trial, creating a quandary that President Barack Obama said Thursday poses 'the toughest issue we will face.'"[3] Clearly this indicates that Obama has at least the same plans as to detention as Bush, and whether any of this is really "arbitrary" in the matter of national security is open to debate.

7. Target key individuals

As we covered in the previous chapter, didn't Obama essentially fire, or at least call for the resignation of Rick Wagoner, CEO of GM? Although Obama did not target any individual specifically, he did say that the Cambridge Police acted "stupidly," a point we have also previously covered.

Likewise, the proto-Fascist followers of Obama - including the aforementioned talking heads - have endlessly targeted Sarah Palin. The argument there might be that she is fair game, but she is just one of several Republicans that have been declared "dangerous" by Obama's faithful. Speaking on Headline News' *Showbiz Tonight* TV personality and convicted felon Martha Stewart said that she believed Palin was dangerous.[4] Considering the influence that people like Stewart or Oprah Winfrey wield we have to ask what is the real danger, and who else might be "targeted?"

8. Control the press

We'll cover this point in greater detail, but suffice it to say that just a consideration of the "Fairness Doctrine" and the White House's handling of whether Fox News was a legitimate news organization goes a long way to show that some proto-Fascists are already looking to control the free press in the United States.

There has also been a call by some politicians that the government needs to bailout newspapers like *The New York Times* because of falling subscriptions. With government money comes government strings. Will Obama become the puppet master of the free press?

9. Dissent equals treason

At this point it could be argued that we're going around in circles. The same proto-Fascists that argued that Bush was bad were up in arms about any dissent over Obama. And this is something we'll address more in detail

10. Suspend the rule of law

Again, we must argue that if former President Bush, and former Vice President Dick Cheney were indeed Fascists, and had suspended the rule of law, then why are they not in power now? Why were there elections in 2008, and why did the power transfer democratically to President Obama? Because George W. Bush for all his failings was not a Fascist, nor was he a proto-Fascist, but we must watch carefully to see if any efforts are made by Obama to suspend the rule of law going forward.

Article I, Section 9, of the Constitution does give the president the power to suspend Habeas Corpus "in Cases of Rebellion or Invasion the public Safety may require it." At what point do terrorist attacks become an invasion and protests become a rebellion?

As a look at this list shows, it is very easy to offer examples that suggest that the country could still very much be headed down the road of fascism, and that even if Mr. Bush played a role as navigator it is clear that Mr. Obama is now in the driver's seat.

Throughout this book we have also tried to present comparisons with past Fascist movements, notably those of Mussolini in Italy as well as Hitler's Nazi Germany. In this chapter we won't go into the comparisons, and for a number of reasons. Hitler's and the Nazis' crimes are well documented, as are Mussolini's, and additionally it is beyond the scope of this book to chronicle each case-by-case example. Suffice it to say that we know past Fascists looked towards an internal threat to solidify power, which eventually became absolute power. So far the United States of America has avoided this consolidation of power, but again, as we have shown various progressives, liberals and even conservatives have laid the groundwork.

The Enemy Within

However, what is happening with this country now is the most worrisome, with numerous threats to our liberty. The irony is that depending on whom you talk to the threat could be very different. While the United States is now involved in two foreign wars, and faces continued threats from overseas' countries, including Iran, there is renewed interest in the internal threat.

In the spring of 2009 the Department of Homeland Security released a report that warns against the possibility of violence by unnamed "right-wing extremists," who might be concerned with issues ranging from illegal immigration to restrictions on firearms. The report went on to suggest that returning war veterans could be of particular threat.[5] This report was titled "Right-wing Extremism: Current Economic and Political Climate Fueling Resurgence in Radicalization and Recruitment," and was dated April 7. It suggested that there were not any indicated plans to carry out violent acts![6]

By June 2009, less than six months after Obama had taken office, the media and other organizations had appeared to jump on this bandwagon. CNN's Anderson Cooper wrote in his blog in June, "The Southern Poverty Law Center's Director of Research, Heidi Beirich, says Obama's election and the country's subsequent move to the left in politics has started putting air in the balloon of the anti-government movement."[7]

The Southern Poverty Law Center, a group that has tracked organizations such as the Ku Klux Klan for decades, also has suddenly seen new threats, noting that the ring-wing militia movement in the United States is growing and that this could spawn violence. In August 2009, the group released a report titled "The Second Wave: Return of the Militias."[8] The report had some interesting language too:

> "They're back. Almost a decade after largely disappearing from public view, right-wing militias, ideologically driven tax defiers and sovereign citizens are appearing in large numbers around the country."

> "A key difference this time is that the federal government — the entity that almost the entire radical right views as its primary enemy — is headed by a black man. That, coupled

> with high levels of non-white immigration and a decline in the percentage of whites overall in America, has helped to racialize the Patriot movement, which in the past was not primarily motivated by race hate."[9]
>
> "Authorities around the country are reporting a worrying uptick in Patriot activities and propaganda. 'This is the most significant growth we've seen in 10 to 12 years,' says one. 'All it's lacking is a spark. I think it's only a matter of time before you see threats and violence.'"[9]

Whilst it is true that prior to September 11, 2001, a homegrown terrorist, Timothy McVeigh, committed the worst example of terrorism perpetrated in the United States, the release of this report and the "surge" in media interest in militias and other focus on domestic groups still casts an ominous shadow. The great threat to America isn't the terrorists that attacked America on September 11, or have declared Jihad; it is the homegrown threat that has gotten the lion's share of attention.

Why have there been no similar reports released on other domestic threats, such as Islamic sleeper cells or other Islamic radicals? The interesting point here is that the so-called "war on terror," essentially ended under Obama, and now the threats are from these right-wing groups. This seems to be an extreme about face.

Here too we must bring up another interesting point. The timing of this report is curious too, as it came out while Obama and the Democrats in Congress work to push their health care agenda. The mainstream media, and key Democrats have continued to warn of threats from the right-wing in government. Thus it could be argued that there is guilt by association. Any politician who declares him or herself to be "right-wing" suddenly could be cast with the so-called "right-wing extremists," at least in the eyes of the public.

In the eyes of the media it is another thing entirely. Following the passage of health care reform the media devoted no small amount of time to alleged, and so-called attacks, threats of violence and other incidents against Democratic lawmakers. Yet mostly absent were threats of violence against conservatives during this time.

The Enemy Within

President Bush was called many names, with protestors carrying signs that labeled the former president a terrorist and a war criminal. During Bush's eight years in office it was practically considered patriotic to question the government - to the point of borrowing the line from the science fiction comic book and later movie *V for Vendetta*:

"People should not be afraid of their governments. Governments should be afraid of their people." [10]

Many liberals also embraced this refrain. In a 2005 video montage, various self-professed Democrats are heard spouting such classic lines as "I don't know if the elections are working," and "us Democrats are going to get up in arms. [11] We'll have to come out and kill someone I guess." But was this just harmless ranting? Probably.

After all, no one rose up. But more importantly power wasn't held absolutely by President Bush or Vice President Cheney, and free elections were in fact held in 2008. But today it is a different story entirely, at least in how the media continues to report on it. Any ranting or raving by the Tea Party movement, or any group opposed to the left wing or President Obama is suddenly labeled dangerous and subversive, and certainly racist.

So much so that cable news outlet MSNBC ran a special "documentary" in the spring of 2010, which was hosted by liberal talking head Chris Matthews. Titled "Rise of the New Right," it covered fringe groups and anyone that sounded bad (or was it good) on camera.

But did anyone believe the show? It made numerous outrageous claims, such as "Rush Limbaugh's references to the 'Obama regime,' but neglects to mention that several liberals - including MSNBC's Ed Schultz - and Matthews himself referred to the 'Bush regime.' He recounts threats made against Democratic members of Congress after the passage of health care reform, but neglects to mention a death threat made against Republican Rep. Eric Cantor." [12]

We can consider this an extreme look at so-called extremists. Yet, there has also been no attempt to re-classify the extremists as just extremists. As we have discussed, the extremist movements

America's Road to Fascism

that could be rightfully considered Fascist in nature, or at least tend to embrace some facets of fascism are not right-wing. Yet, time and time again the two are tied, or perhaps intertwined, together. Meanwhile the media and the government have tried to separate Islam from extremism.

In a speech at Cairo University President Obama said, "Islam must be based on what Islam is, not what it isn't."[13] Why is the same standard not applied to the so-called right-wing extremists? This discrediting of the right will likely continue, and so will the media spin on it.

The irony with the fear of militias is that Obama's call for volunteerism and civilian service has been seen by some as a stepping-stone to an SS style private army for the president. While it is unlikely it would go so far, the *Edward M. Kennedy Serve America Act* (also known as the *Generations Invigorating Volunteerism and Education Act, GIVE Act*) could create 175,000 "new service opportunities" under the AmeriCorps, bring the number of participants in the national volunteer program to 250,000. "Some critics on the right suggest that the president's push for national service goes too far, and the recent congressional steps toward expanding the federal role in volunteerism and 'civilian service' smacks of a larger agenda. They point to a campaign speech the president made last July (2008) in which he suggested national security could be entrusted to a civilian force."[14]

Whether this could turn out to be a private army, akin to Hitler's SS, is still debatable. But this group could certainly fit with Naomi Wolf's contention of a "thug caste," at least if there is political indoctrination involved. Could the AmeriCorps turn into an Obama Youth? We're also reminded of Rep. Paul Broun (R-Georgia) and his warnings that during the campaign Obama called for "'a civilian national security force that's just as powerful, just as strong, just as well-funded' as the military." That is certainly one fear, even if it is a remote possibility. Yet, even it isn't a full blown private corps, it does have the inkling of inching us closer to the sort of allegiance to the president directly. From the Serve.gov website:

"United We Serve - The President is calling on all Americans to participate in our nation's recovery and renewal by serving in our communities. There are many ways to get involved. America's new foundation will be one community at a time - and it starts with you."[15]

This is also not the only type of allegiance we've seen. While there was the aforementioned "I Pledge" video from celebrities this was done by consenting adults, who clearly think - or at least should be able to think for themselves. Unfortunately the same can't be said for many children, who are essentially being indoctrinated into supporting the POTUS as part of public school programs. One such example included a chant performed by students of Lincoln Bassett Middle School in New Haven, Connecticut. In a chilling video the school children are led by a teacher saying that they can "be anything I want to be. I am an Obama scholar." [16]

This is disturbing because the truth is that Obama has nothing to do with the educational system of Connecticut. Children should be encouraged to be "anything" they want to be, but they shouldn't offer praise to the POTUS in the process. This instead seems to be a way of making faithful supporters, akin to the Hitler Youth for Obama. Could this be the roots of an SS-like organization loyal directly to the President?

It will also be telling to see how much is made in the near future about the aforementioned White House party crashers and the failings of the Secret Service. Here again is where a myth has been perpetrated and continues to spread; that being that President Obama - being the first African-American elected to the highest office - is somehow at a greater threat level than past presidents. The question is whether there is actually any truth to these concerns.

This even made international headlines in August 2009. "Since Mr. Obama took office, the rate of threats against the president has increased 400 per cent from the 3,000 a year or so under President George W. Bush, according to Ronald Kessler, author of *In the President's Secret Service*."[17] This is certainly a disturbing fact, and one that would give credence to the growing concern of so-called "right-wing extremists." This number was widely circulated, with many news organizations reporting the figure. This included a high profile story in *The Boston Globe*: "Secret Service strained as leaders face more threats."[18] Thus from August through October and beyond the story had legs and it ran, and ran. The only problem is that this number is a myth.

In fact, Mark Sullivan of the Secret Service, whom we previously covered in chapter nine on the White House party crashers, shed some light whilst testifying to Congress about that incident. "The threats are not up," and Sullivan added that the Secret Service receives about the same amount of threats against Obama as they did for the last two presidents.[19]

This brings up another point, and that is why the President of the United States gets this level of security, which is clearly greater than most other world leaders. A look at the history is all that is really needed to answer that question. Four presidents, including Abraham Lincoln, James A. Garfield, William McKinley and John F. Kennedy have been assassinated while in office, and there have been attempts against 13 other presidents, including the most recent seven to hold the office.

The United States Secret Service is thus tasked to protect the POTUS, and while the agency was originally founded in 1865 as a branch of the U.S. Treasury Department to combat counterfeiting, since the assassination of President McKinley in 1901 this has been its second mission. In addition to the misunderstanding of whom the Secret Service protects - the list includes (but is not limited to) the president, vice president, the president-elect, vice president-elect, the immediate families of the above individuals, former presidents and their spouses, children of former presidents, visiting heads of state, major presidential/vice presidential candidates and their spouses during the election season - there is now confusion as how long this protection continues. It is worth noting that President Bill Clinton will be the last former president who is actually protected during the rest of his lifetime. In 1997, Congress enacted legislation (Public Law 103-329) that now limits Secret Service protection for former presidents to 10 years after leaving office.[20] It will be interesting to note whether such protection will be extended when - and some might say IF - Mr. Obama leaves office.

Thus it is not surprising that some in the liberal media have actually questioned whether the Secret Service should take an oath specifically to Obama. Liberal radio talk show host Ed Schulz actually suggested as much, saying that he should have "like-minded people around" him.[21] The irony in all this of course is that so far, at least in respect to the party crashers, Obama has essentially let the Secret Service take a bullet for the staff!

This also brings us to another significant facet of the "enemy within." Since even before Mr. Obama was elected in November 2008, there have been those on the far right who have spoken up against his policies, and those of the extreme left. These include numerous talk show hosts, such as Rush Limbaugh, Sean Hannity and Bill O'Reilly. This is not the first time that conservative radio hosts have seen a spike in popularity, and during the eight years of President Bill Clinton's term in office, AM radio saw a significant resurgence. The power of this medium has been so great for the right wing that many on the left have called to silence the radio.

The history of the Fairness Doctrine goes back to 1949, when the United States Federal Communication Commission established this regulation, "which required broadcasters to provide fair-and-balanced programming on the public airwaves. When one viewpoint was expressed on the radio, equal airtime had to be offered to those who disagreed. The doctrine was repealed in 1987 on the grounds that it was no longer necessary because of the diversity of voices being heard in the media marketplace... and that such regulation might well be unconstitutional."[22]

Today there are calls to reinstate the Fairness Doctrine, despite as we have just suggested that doing so might even be unconstitutional. Here we see that this could be considered a way of silencing the press, one of the 10 steps towards fascism suggested earlier in this chapter by Ms. Wolf. Additionally, for a point of record, the Fairness Doctrine should not be confused with Equal Time, which applies only to political candidates.

Despite whether the Fairness Doctrine is constitutional or not also seems not to matter to some liberal commentators, such as Steve Almond of *The Boston Globe*, who wrote:

> "Because talk radio's business model is predicated on silencing all opposing viewpoints. If Rush Limbaugh and his ilk were forced to engage in a reasonable debate, rather than ad hominems, they would forfeit the moral surety - and the seductive rage - that is the central appeal of all demagogues."[23]

The irony here is that *The Boston Globe* could arguably be seen as an extremely left wing leaning newspaper, one that regularly endorsed Democrats in elections, including Barack Obama for president, which it did on October 13, 2008.[24] Whilst this was an editorial rather than news, why couldn't Mr. Almond see that essentially what talk show hosts are doing could also be seen as akin to editorials? Why should these programs be forced to offer opposing viewpoints? How is it possible to offer all the viewpoints of any subject in a three or four hour radio show?

And more importantly how would Air America fit into this mix? The progressive talk radio network, which aired programming from Montel Williams and Ron Reagan, was available on more than 50 stations across the country and also online.[25] How would this fit into a formula that called for opposing viewpoints? Perhaps the ratings would actually have gone up!

Since it was launched in 2004 Air America - the now defunct Air America - had routinely struggled to find both an audience and cash to run the network. Regardless of the reasons, the fact is that it seems that liberal radio just isn't good business, and one argument could be made is that it would be unfair to radio stations to enforce the Fairness Doctrine as it could spell the doom of AM radio in the United States. We will get to the silencing of the opposition, but let us also consider the business ramifications.

> "So the argument that more ownership diversity would create more opportunity for liberal radio talk show hosts is partially accurate. They would also have to generate big ratings to remain on these stations, and radio programmers around the

country question their ability to do that based on the low ratings of the all-liberal Air America... The ratings are not good. There isn't an obvious listener demand."[26]

We must next consider what exactly is meant by fair in the Fairness Doctrine? Isn't it fair to let stations air the programming they choose to air, especially if this is best for the bottom line? In the book *Regulating Broadcast Programming*, Thomas G. Krattenmaker and Lucas A. Powe sum this up better than most:

> "We do not believe Goldilocks would have stayed in the Three Bears' house for over forty years had she always found the porridge, chairs, and beds too hot or too cold, too big or too small, too hard or too soft. Fortunately the FCC also reached a similar conclusion, finding the Fairness Doctrine an ill-advised and inefficacious regulatory policy. Honoring the journalistic ethnic of thorough and balanced coverage is a noble goal. Legislating and enforcing such behavior, however, is at best a meaningless and futile gesture, at worst a counterproductive and unconstitutional act."[27]

Not all would agree with this, notably those who see that they would benefit from the Fairness Doctrine. Liberal loudmouth Ed Schultz is just one who has voiced an opinion that "socialism" would be somehow be "fair" for radio. In a rant following the passage of the health care reform bill, Schultz offered this tirade:

> "It is a cultural war that's taking place in America, you're exactly right. And it's being played out over the airwaves of America. And I hope the Democrats now turn to the Fairness Doctrine. It's time now for the Democrats to consider the Fairness Doctrine when you've got Rush Limbaugh out there saying, it's, we've got to defeat these bastards. He is now openly admitting that he is going to work against and campaign against the Republican, against the Democratic Party and campaign against Obama, and he is motivating people with the microphone and he's electioneering.
>
> "Keep on talking, Rushsky! Hell, maybe I'll get on 600 stations too, or how many you own or whatever. The fact is, look, it's not a level playing field when it comes to the audio culture of the country.

Ownership has its privileges. When you own, I will be honest, if I owned 500 stations, the Drugster wouldn't be on any of 'em. And that's just where it's at right now. But maybe we have reached the point where the Congress needs to equal it out. Equal out the audience." [28]

Is this actually socialism or just a case of sour grapes? Does Schultz really believe that this is "fair" or is it just his way to get some of Rush Limbaugh's audience? And what makes Schultz or anyone who supports the Fairness Doctrine really believe that the audiences will somehow "equal out" if equal time was given? Can you really regulate what people want to hear?

The battle over the Fairness Doctrine is not just about the silencing of the loyal opposition, but it is also part of what we've previously suggested is an attack on the right wing. Again, we have seen that the right wing is demonized again and again. The Anti-Defamation League even cited Fox News' Glenn Beck as the "most important mainstream media figure who has repeatedly helped to stoke the fires of anti-government anger."[29] So much for anti defaming!

Beck isn't the only talking head on the network who has come under fire either. Mara Liasson, National Public Radio's top political correspondent, was asked by executives at NPR to reconsider her appearances on Fox News because of what they perceived as the network's political bias. A case of the pot calling the kettle black indeed.

> "According to a source, Liasson was summoned in early October (2009) by NPR's executive editor for news, Dick Meyer, and the networks supervising senior Washington editor, Ron Elving. The NPR executives said they had concerns that Fox's programming had grown more partisan, and they asked Liasson to spend 30 days watching the network."[30]

This all came about following a showdown earlier in the fall of 2009 between the White House and Fox News. But the fight began much earlier. In June 2009, President Obama declared: "I've got one television station that is entirely devoted to attacking my administration."[31]

The issue heated up throughout the fall, when Anita Dunn, interim White House Communications Director, mounted an intense campaign against the entire Fox News Channel. As we have already covered in chapter five, noting that it was Joseph Goebbels, the Nazi propaganda minister who had said the role of the press "was that the people should 'think uniformly, react uniformly.'" To Dunn, it must have appeared as if this one news organization wasn't falling in-line. As we previously noted, it was Dunn who said to *The New York Times*, "we're going to treat them the way we would treat an opponent. As they are undertaking a war against Barack Obama and the White House, we don't need to pretend that this is the way that legitimate news organizations behave."

On Sunday, October 11, 2009, Dunn took this even further, when she appeared on CNN's *Reliable Sources*, where she made the following statement:

> "The reality of it is that Fox News often operates almost as either the research arm or the communications arm of the Republican Party. And it is not ideological... what I think is fair to say about Fox, and the way we view it, is that it is more of a wing of the Republican Party."[32]

Glenn Beck, among others, were able to have the last laugh. Beck was able to show footage of Dunn addressing a high school graduation ceremony in June 2009, where she described Mao Tse-tung and Mother Teresa as two of her "favorite political philosophers."[33] Fittingly, soon after Dunn was given her marching orders for a Long March much different from Mao's. Whilst he was eventually able to gain power in China, Dunn instead resigned from her post. However, as with others who were appointed to White House positions, Dunn has other ties to President Obama. Her husband, Robert Bauer, is Obama's personal attorney. The pair was considered the "power couple" in a *Newsweek* magazine article that looked at Obama's new Washington elite.[34]

The White House's enemies aren't limited to Fox News and the right wing talkers either. Within weeks of Obama taking office in January 2009 a new movement emerged in the United States, and suddenly "tea baggers" became part of the American lexicon. But we need to back up a second.

When Barack Obama was sworn in as president, there was a concern by some on the right that the Democrats (who also obviously controlled both houses in Congress with solid majorities) might think they had free rein to increase federal spending. This was proven somewhat true with the passage of the "stimulus" package, and thus was born the "tea party" movement, which was nothing more than a group of Americans invoking the spirit of the American Revolution, and notably the Boston Tea Party. Therefore April 15, 2009 - tax day - was chosen as a day of protests to call on three core values including fiscal responsibility, constitutionally limited government and finally free markets.[35]

Since that time the liberal media has made much of this movement, with some left wing talking heads even poking fun at the double meaning of "tea bagging," which can refer to a crude sexual act of dipping one's scrotum in the mouth or near the mouth of another individual - as you dip a tea bag in a cup of water. Crude indeed and unfortunate that the movement has been labeled "tea baggers," but when and how this happened is still open to debate. While the movement called for "tea parties" akin to the "Boston Tea Party," it seems that many in the media were calling those supporters "tea baggers" from the get go - suggesting that they had the double meaning in mind. This was debated so much by the media at the end of 2009 that it needs no attribution, and a Google search of the Internet would show countless websites now focused on whether "tea bagger" is in fact a pejorative term.

A greater and far more disturbing fact is how many on the left responded to the tea baggers. Even before the tea was (figuratively) brewed, liberal activist, comedian and former Air America personality Janeane Garofalo appeared on the April 15, 2009 edition of "Countdown" with MSNBC's Keith Olbermann to discuss the day's events. She essentially called the partygoers "a bunch of tea bagging rednecks" and argued that this wasn't a tax protest, but rather "this is about hating a black man in the White House. This is racism straight up."[36]

This opinion that the dissent wasn't about taxes or political issues but rather the color of President's Obama skin continued throughout the spring and summer of 2009, even making the news throughout the world. *The Daily Telegraph* in Great Britain picked up the story in September, five months after tax day:

> "Members of the Congressional Black Caucus are convinced that the antipathy of some critics is rooted in an unwillingness to stomach the fact that a black man occupies the White House. 'As far as African-Americans are concerned, we think most of it is,' Congressman Eddie Bernice Johnson of Texas told the Politico website. 'And we think it's very unfortunate. We as African-American people of course are very sensitive to it.'" [37]

The charges of racism were not the only ones that the tea baggers faced either. Over the same period as the issue of racism was debated, there were many protests that suggested Obama was a Nazi, a Fascist, akin to Hitler and one that even compared him to the Joker character from the latest *Batman* film. Of course it is hard for us to argue these points indiscriminately, especially as the point of this book is to make the very comparisons between Hitler and Obama, as well as Mussolini and other Fascists and proto-Fascists to Obama.

However, there is irony in the fact that many liberals tried to use this same argument about former President George W. Bush during his eight years in office. There were suggestions that doing so wasn't being respectful of the president or the office - despite the fact that it had been fine, even patriotic according to the likes of some such as Garofolo, to criticize Bush! To depict any president with a Hitler moustache and swastika diminishes the true horrors that the Nazis inflicted on others based on racial theory. The holocaust and other Nazi atrocities become cartoonish in the hands of a protestor.

It becomes even more ironic in fact that some of those making the statements that compared Obama to Hitler didn't even come from the actual right wing, but rather came from the supporters of a Democrat. In August 2009 Rep. Barney Frank (D-Mass.) was "greeted with shouts and boos at a town hall meeting on heath care," where protesters held up a pamphlet depicting the president with a Hitler moustache and comparing Obama to the Nazi leader. These weren't Republicans or other conservatives, but supporters of Lyndon LaRouche, who has been labeled as a "perennial independent political" by *The Washington Post*.[38]

However, Mr. LaRouche and his supporters consider themselves Democrats, and although it would be possible to write an entire book on LaRouche and his antics (there are already a few), we'll leave it by saying that clearly liberals were looking for an enemy from the right, and found that LaRouche's followers strangely fit the bill.

Along with global warming and climate change the proto-Fascists continue to look at the dangers from the "right wing," and as we have seen this is a many-tiered threat, and likely won't go away anytime soon. Missing from the equation still is that imminent threat that as Ms. Wolf points out could allow the president - whether it is Obama or another future proto-Fascist - to suspend the rule of law. In other words, we're not out of the woods yet.

Chapter Twelve
The External Enemy

Just as the internal enemy allows Fascists to solidify their power, external threats are used to hold this power. The most notorious examples are the Fascist governments of Hitler's Nazi Germany and Italy under Mussolini, as well as the quasi-Fascist government of Imperial Japan in the 1930s under Hideki Tojo. For these three leaders going to war to face foreign enemies was their downfall.

The Fascist leaders who endured over time, notably Salazar in Portugal and Franco in Spain, did not take part in foreign "adventures." In the case of Salazar neutrality in World War II was the best option. With distant colonies in Africa, Portugal would have had a hard time defending these from British and/or South African occupation, making siding with Nazi Germany extremely difficult. Siding with the Allies could have meant invasion - possibly through Fascist Spain. Thus Salazar wisely followed a path that was as straight down the middle of neutrality as possible.

Even before World War II broke out in 1939, "Salazar and Franco signed a treaty called informally the Iberian Pact. Under its terms, the two neighbors agreed that neither one would aid a country that attacked the other and that each would respect their 750-mile border... Franco and Salazar realized, Iberian neutrality depended almost entirely on the good will of both Britain and Germany."[1]

When World War II did break out with the German invasion of Poland in September 1939, Fascists states Spain and Portugal did sit on the sideline, as did Italy. Only when France was nearly defeated on the ground by Germany in June 1940 did Mussolini look to take advantage of the situation. It would be his downfall. Franco however is generally remembered in history for remaining on the sidelines, yet this isn't entirely accurate. On June 14, 1939, Franco exploited the situation the French were facing and sent 3,000 men across the Strait of Gibraltar to occupy the Moroccan port of Tangier. Franco further allowed for Germany to send a military team to consider a joint invasion of British held Gibraltar.[2]

In 1941, with Britain seemingly on its knees Hitler even visited Franco at the French-Spanish border to discuss Spain's entry into the war. Terms were never finalized, and Franco managed to politically outmaneuver Hitler - the latter typically the one who mastered the political dance. In the end Spain never entered the war, although Franco did allow workers to go to Germany. But Franco's greatest balancing act was with the Blue Division, a group of volunteers who eagerly went to join the German invasion of the Soviet Union. At one point Mussolini even tried to get the Spanish dictator to officially join the war, to which Franco asked Mussolini if he ever considered trying to get out of the conflict. According to Franco's take on the story, Mussolini responded, "if only I could, if only I could."[3]

Yet throughout the rest of Franco's rule of Spain he managed to rally against foreign threats while actually steering his nation from actual conflict. This can be contrasted with past American Presidents - notably Wilson and Franklin Roosevelt - who campaigned on the promise not to get caught up in foreign wars. Then shortly after their reelections America was dragged into the two world wars!

Thus it is interesting to consider Obama, who as a Senator spoke out against the war in Iraq, yet within a year of taking office as President, decided - after a protracted debate - to send 30,000 troops to Afghanistan. But it is easy for political promises not to be kept, and for Fascists and proto-Fascists to offer the line of being doves yet have the hearts of hawks. In the case of Obama, the authors don't actually think he is truly a hawk in the traditional sense. Unlike Mussolini or even moreover Hitler, Obama doesn't seem to be the type of man who dreams of a vast empire, nor does he evoke restoring some glorious past. This however is why Obama as the war president, and how he addresses conflict with our potential external enemies, is so dangerous.

Obama lacks the aggressiveness of Hitler or Mussolini, which could suggest that he would not slide into their downfall - yet, in their defense, both men managed to do very well considering the odds. Yet on the flip side Obama isn't the master of the diplomatic dance the way Franco was either. Whereas Obama maybe a former community organizer, Franco was a wartime leader and managed a balancing act that they don't teach even at Harvard Law School.

Thus Obama, without this ability to do the diplomatic dance - and bowing doesn't count - could be heading down the same road as President Lyndon Johnson, as he gets caught up in this generation's Vietnam. Previously in this book, it was mentioned that Obama missed out on the 1960s, and ironically he could end up repeating Johnson's biggest mistake - derailing all his ambitions of hope and change in the process. In the process he is adding to the road towards American fascism.

First, we must explore briefly the situation that is Afghanistan. The key word is "situation" because in truth Afghanistan is far more a situation than it has ever been a country. It is a land that has practically swallowed vast armies whole, and ironically the authors are not just referring to the most recent invasion by the Soviet Union, which began in 1979 and was one of the causes of the "Evil Empire's" downfall.

There is much blood in the sand of Afghanistan. Alexander the Great was one of the earliest to lead armies across its vast plains; and later its trails were crossed by the Mongol Horde on their way to the Middle East. But it was the United Kingdom that found itself embroiled in several conflicts in Afghanistan. During the 19th century this land in central Asia was ground zero in what has become known as the Great Game between Imperial Russia and the United Kingdom. This fact is typically lost on modern pundits, who all too often only look back to Russia's (or more accurately the Soviet Union's) adventure into this land.

Unlike what would later happen with the Soviets, the British managed to keep the nation in check - and by that we mean without allowing it to serve as a forward base for an invasion of the Jewel in the Crown of the British Empire, and that of course was India. But more importantly, while keeping Afghanistan in check the British never really became overwhelmed with the conflict. In fact, this could explain why it is essentially all but a forgotten war - or rather series of wars - when the history of the British Empire is considered. "If Afghanistan was to prove the graveyard of many a solider, it was

America's Road to Fascism

only one amongst many of the conflicts waged by Britain during Victoria's reign (1837-1901)."[4]

For the United States and President Obama Afghanistan is just one of two wars he inherited from former President George W. Bush. And ever since Bush called for a U.S. led invasion in October 2001, a month after the 9/11 attacks on the World Trade Center and the Pentagon, this conflict has been compared to the Soviet style invasion.

In truth Bush's strategy has been more reminiscent of the typical British invasion, which usually came about because of a governmental change that was suddenly unfriendly to Great Britain. This threatened India, and the British dispatched an army to set things right. This usually meant a small-scale invasion and a quick war, followed by some clean up. At times British forces remained to help with the task of what we would today call nation building. This contrasts the lengthy Soviet invasion that saw near constant fighting against rebel forces and insurgents, hence why it became known as the Soviet's Vietnam.

On the surface it could seem that the American strategy under Bush failed. It did not meet its objective of capturing Osama bin Laden, but in truth when we look at the bigger picture, this really was closer to victory and a success in many ways. The Taliban was overthrown; Al-Qaeda's was pushed out of its foothold.

However, the situation in Afghanistan remained (and remains even as the authors conclude this book) one that can best be described as hostile. But we should try to understand that this isn't at all the fault of the United States-led invasion, nor is it the fallout of our efforts in this land. The country has not been at peace in decades, and it is unlikely that even a large U.S. military presence will change this fact.

But Obama has made a mistake in efforts to move away from nation building. In speaking to CBS *Early Show*, White House Press Secretary Robert Gibbs offered this take:

> "This can't be nation-building. It can't be an open-ended, forever commitment.

"We're going to accelerate going after al Qaeda and its extremist allies."[5]

But wasn't one criticism of the Reagan-Bush era that not enough was done to actually nation build after the Soviet's pulled out of Afghanistan. The book and movie *Charlie Wilson's War* chronicles how the Democratic Texas Representative managed to supply aid to the Afghan rebels, which - depending on your take - hastened the fall of the Soviet Union. When the Soviets pulled out, the United States pulled the funds and thus allies of convenience became not so friendly, yet were trained with American dollars. The common view is that the CIA "turned an army of primitive tribesman into techno-holy warriors."[6]

Yet, it wasn't so simple. As had happened a generation earlier when President Jimmy Carter came to office, allies suddenly were cut off. As Carter turned his back on Iran and Nicaragua, President Bill Clinton moved "to place Pakistan on the list of state sponsors of terrorism for its support of Kashmiri freedom fighters. The Pakistan military had long been the surrogates for the CIA, and every Afghan and Arab mujahid came to believe that the Americans had betrayed the Pakistanis."[7]

As we have discussed in detail, politics and situations make for strange bedfellows and since 9/11 the view of Pakistan has of course changed, even if that nation's policies have not. This is not a condemnation but just a realistic fact.

What is more important to consider is Obama's policy in dealing with Afghanistan, and now how the role of U.S. troops is beginning to look more and more like the policy carried out by the Soviet Union. This is especially interesting, considering that Obama was awarded the Noble Peace Prize just days after announcing that he would send 30,000 troops to Afghanistan. Obama tried to explain this seemingly paradoxical situation:

"Still, we are at war, and I am responsible for the deployment of thousands of young Americans to battle in a distant land. Some will kill. Some will be killed. And so I come here with an acute sense of the cost of armed conflict - filled with difficult questions about the relationship between war and peace, and our effort to replace one with the other."[8]

It must weigh heavy on all leaders to send soldiers to war, and even past Fascists have noted that they want no young man or woman to die in battle. So we understand that this was not an easy decision for Obama to make, but we must question again his plans - including those that call for a scheduled pull out. While Gibbs may suggest that Obama doesn't want to be caught up in an "open-ended, forever commitment," how could any leader plan for the withdrawal of troops before they even arrive?

Actually, stranger things have happened with Fascist leaders. Hitler built models of Germania, the future envisioned rebuilding of Berlin, and Mussolini often saw victory before battles were even fought. Just as the Axis powers neared victory in North Africa in 1942 prior to the turning point at the Battle of El Alamein, "Mussolini flew over to North Africa, accompanied, in another airplane, by a white charger, on which he planned to make a triumphant entry into Cairo."[9]

In the case of Obama the goals are not nearly so lofty or grandiose. It is simply about bringing the troops home. Mark Sappenfield of *The Christian Science Monitor* laid it out in December 2009:

> "Obama's timeline involves deploying troops to Afghanistan as soon as next month, and then beginning to scale back the surge in July 2011. That timeline essentially gives the surge 12 months at full strength in Afghanistan at the earliest possible date."[10]

The problem with this strategy again is that it sets not only an unrealistic timetable, but leaves no room for other serious setbacks. Even before troops did arrive in mass, the situation has become an even more hostile one, and the question must be asked whether it is really doing any good. Is it possible to root out the enemy in this time - wouldn't they just hide or lay low until the United States pulls out, only to resurface again - and will it really leave the country in a reasonable state when we leave?

The External Enemy

Another problem compounding this issue is that it is becoming one of political debate, even by those with little or no understanding of how wars are fought. Ultra-left wing political action committee MoveOn.org offered this take soon after Obama announced he would be sending troops to Afghanistan:

> "The President just announced that he's sending 30,000 more troops to Afghanistan. Whatever they think of his decision, MoveOn members agree that we need a binding military exit strategy and firm benchmarks so we can bring our troops home safely and quickly.
>
> "The President doesn't want an open-ended commitment, but pro-war advocates are already pushing him to reverse course. So Congress has to make sure the President keeps his word that our commitment isn't open-ended."

This could almost be seen as borderline dangerous speech, as it makes a wartime strategy one of political agenda! Besides, are there really "pro-war advocates" who are calling for an open-ended war without end? If there are such people we challenge anyone at MoveOn.org to find them and bring them forward. What in fact those opposed to the timeline are suggesting is that it is merely impossible to set a timeline for waging war, and defeating an enemy as if it were an easily scheduled event.

We also said at the beginning of this chapter that wars can bring down Fascist leaders, and it could be that the war in Afghanistan helps bring down proto-Fascist Barak Obama. For his decision to be the Nobel Peace Prize winning, yet war time President has those who previously praised him finding that they're not exactly supporting the idea of war. Even before Obama made it official, Michael Moore, the controversial propaganda/faux filmmaker offered this take on his website (MichaelMoore.com):

> "Do you really want to be the new 'war president'? If you go to West Point tomorrow night and announce that you are increasing, rather than withdrawing, the troops in Afghanistan, you are the new war president. Pure and simple. And with that you will do the worst possible thing you could

do - destroy the hopes and dreams so many millions have placed in you. With just one speech tomorrow night you will turn a multitude of young people who were the backbone of your campaign into disillusioned cynics. You will teach them what they've always heard is true - that all politicians are alike. I simply can't believe you're about to do what they say you are going to do. Please say it isn't so."[11]

Given this "disillusioned" take, along with the election of Republican Scott Brown to the Senate - in "Ted Kennedy's seat" no less - it is clear that many are seeing President Obama's policies for what they really are, and this could hopefully steer us away from the road to fascism.

However, Afghanistan is not the only external enemy we face in the 21st century. While we will cover the global threat of Islamic Fascism - a threat linked to, but not entirely connected with Afghanistan - the other significant threat is one that is both economic and militaristic. That threat of course is China, a country that has seen a major economic surge in recent years.

It is beyond the scope of this work to discuss China's economic growth, except to note that China has lent the United States a great deal of money. This makes pressing China on key issues such as human rights, privacy and the environment extremely difficult - and why issues such as "global warming" are all the more complex. In that regard, how can the United States adhere to one standard of carbon dioxide production knowing full well that China will do whatever it sees best for China?

The more important issue here is that Barack Obama shows that his skills are those of a community organizer, and that again you cannot community organize the world. Worse still, Hillary Clinton heads the United States State Department without the usual background, and training required to even work in the State Department. She is a former Senator promoted up to Secretary of State, and it shows in her demands in January 2010 to China for unrestricted Internet access. Addressing a turf war involving search engine giant Google, which threatened to pull out of China, Clinton offered, "We look to the Chinese government to conduct a through and transparent review."[12]

It seems as if either Clinton or the mainstream media seem to forget about the history of China, and the impact it has had in shaping the nation. While Clinton, or Obama for that matter, can look to the Chinese government, most of these demands will fall on deaf ears. And here is where not understanding the past can have dangerous ramifications for us today.

Unlike much of South East Asia, Africa, South America or even North America, China was a land that was not technically colonized by Europeans. It was conquered by the Mongols (those people did get around as we've seen), and later was essentially occupied and ruled by the Manchurians, who were the final imperial dynasty (Qing Dynasty) until 1912. The final decades of this dynasty could easily be described as one of tragedy, the greatest of which could be the Opium Wars, which devastated China.

Both Britain and China regarded their respective cultures, civilizations and even way of life as infinitely superior to the other, so this brought on friction, each seeing the other as practically barbarians. Thus the war they fought was not merely limited to trade markets. "The cause of the Opium War has been attributed to the greed of the British merchants in China, but the real causes of the war were cultural rather than commercial."[13]

Regardless of the cause however, the war did cause much hardship to China. Not only did China and Great Britain fight two Opium Wars (1839-42, and 1856-60), with France and even the United States joining with the British, the end results were for China a nation gripped with a drug problem exponentially greater than any America has ever seen. Addiction reached the very top of society in China, even as China officially outlawed the drug in 1906, at which time "the Dowager Empress Cixi was herself an opium addict."[14]

This is all just a small part of the issue of European - as well as American and even Japanese - influence on China in the late 19th and early 20th century. At the end of the 19th century the nation had faced numerous crop failures, a plague of locusts and floods on the Yellow River - all of which may be familiar to Chinese residents who have faced recent earthquakes and floods. China was defeated by the Japanese in a humiliating war (1894-95), followed by various European powers "demanding" an open door policy in China. Germany seized Kiaochow and Tsingtao (where the Chinese brand of beer is still brewed today thanks to German colonialism), Russian demanded a lease on Port Arthur and Darien, France occupied Kwangchowwan and the British extended their hold on China with a lease on Wei-Hai-Wei. "Natural disasters had weakened the Chinese people and Western technology had lowered them to the point where they feared becoming merely servants to the intruding foreigners."[15]

None of this excuses the path that China has taken. Nor did its troubles end when the European powers left. China faced a decades long Civil War, interrupted only by invasion from Japan. This followed a Communist victory that brought Mao Tse-tung to power and featured decades where the nation could be described as moving backwards, if it really moved in any direction at all. Only in recent decades, as China embraces western models of business, is the nation moving forward again.

It most certainly remains an issue, but we must hope that we avoid a new Cold War with this seemingly resurgent super power. The irony is that while President Reagan called for Gorbachev to tear down the Berlin Wall, and then eventually outspent the Soviet Union to win that conflict, we don't see that Clinton's words - or Obama's overture's - will have the same resonates.

And here finally we see some irony. If Obama and the White House move away from nation building in Afghanistan, aren't we abandoning the Afghan people to the Middle Ages, where girls never go to school and women cannot go outside unless covered up? We call for better human rights in a country that is moving forward - yes, it has a long way to go but it is moving. But thousands of miles away we are focusing on destroying an enemy, destroying the land in the process and we already seem to have our exit date on the calendar.

Chapter Thirteen
Islamic Fascism

In past chapters we have devoted our attention to internal Fascist threats to the United States, as well as those external enemies. However, no book on the subject would be complete without discussing perhaps the greatest threat to the security of the United States in the 21st century - that being the threat from Islamic fascism. This is both an internal and external threat, and one that will likely only grow if left unchecked.

Before we delve too deeply, we must understand that this is not meant to be an assault on Islam or the Muslim faith. There is absolutely no doubt that the vast majority of Muslims worldwide are peace-loving people, who want only to live their lives and have no desires to do harm to the United States or its people. In no way are the authors attempting to present a bias against Islam, but rather it is our goal to specifically address the threat of the most extreme aspects of Islam, which of course could be labeled Islamic Fascism.

It is also necessary to stress that some would argue that there is no such thing as Islamic Fascism, or "Islamofascism." Eric Margolis, a contributing foreign editor for *Sun National Media Canada*, and author of *War at the Top of the World*, wrote:

> "The term 'Islamofascist' is utterly without meaning, but packed with emotional explosives. It is a propaganda creation worthy of Dr. Goebbels, and the latest expression of the big lie technique being used by neocons in Washington's propaganda war against its enemies in the Muslim World."[1]

Obviously, we must agree to disagree with Margolis on this point, but maybe this is a matter of semantics. After all, we hardly think that most conservatives would find his use of "neocons" to be complimentary, and in his usage it does seem pejorative.

With this point considered, there are obviously Muslim groups that don't care for the term either. Dr. Timothy R. Furnish, assistant professor of history at Georgia Perimeter College, and author of

Holiest Wars: Islamic Mahdis, their Jihads and Osama bin Laden, offers another side of the coin on the term "Islamic Fascism."

> "Predictably, the usual suspects—such as the Council on American-Islamic Relations—have been quick to condemn the usage of this term, accusing the President of 'equat[ing] the religion of peace with the ugliness of fascism.' Indeed, CAIR is half-right: Islam should NOT be identified with fascism—but not because it is inherently a peaceful ideology. Rather, the term 'Islamic fascism or 'Islamofascism' should be avoided because it's simply another way to let Islam off the hook."[2]

There are of course those who want to let Islam off the hook, Margolis included to some degree. In his argument against the term of "Islamic Fascism," he added:

> "The Muslim World is replete with brutal dictatorships, feudal monarchies, and corrupt military-run states, but none of these regimes, however deplorable, fits the standard definition of fascism. Most, in fact, are America's allies. Nor do underground Islamic militant groups ('terrorists' in western terminology). They are either focused on liberating land from foreign occupation, overthrowing 'un-Islamic' regimes, driving western influence from their region, or imposing theocracy based on early Islamic democracy."[3]

Again, is this a matter of semantics? In a way it is, but in another way Margolis does offer us a glimpse into the "Muslim World." In fact, this is where we would argue with Margolis that "a rose by any other name," still can look as red as the color so adored by the Nazis. In this we mean that he hits the nail on the head on one point, the point that is of the biggest concern to us: "imposing theocracy based on early Islamic democracy." Margolis, and others of his ilk, can't really be so naïve as to think that those spreading or "imposing" it intend that this theocracy will stay in the Muslim World.

The intent by many of these radical groups is clearly to bring this to the greater world! Liberating the lands from foreign occupation, something they've been fighting for since the Middle Ages, is just one step. The next is to spread this theocracy to every corner of the globe. The danger is not that they're doing it, but that we're letting them, and in many cases helping them!

To better understand this, we must take a step back. As we said at the beginning of the chapter, we do not believe this is the intention of every Muslim, but those extremists have taken the word of their prophet a bit further. To again quote President Obama, there is also a major lack of understanding of Islam - "Islam must be based on what Islam is, not what it isn't."[4]

What we can understand about Islam is that until the 7th century it did not exist. Yet, Muslims do not see this as a new religion, but rather see the prophet Muhammad as being the restorer of the monotheistic faith that included Adam, Abraham, Moses and Jesus. It was Muhammad (born 570 CE) who according to the tradition received the word of God, and preached to the people to convert them from their polytheistic ways. "Many aspects of Muhammad's message were conveyed in concepts and sometimes in words that were already familiar in Arabia. In part, this was what made Muhammad's message comprehensible to his first audience. The ideas of monotheism, a Last Judgment, heaven and hell, prophecy and revelations, and the emphasis on intense, even militant, piety were widespread in the Near Eastern scripturalist religions in the sixth century."[5]

Where Islam stands apart from other "new" religions that flowered from this region - notably Judaism and Christianity - is the widely held belief that Muhammad's word spread as much by the sword and spear as by the word of mouth alone. Say what you will about the pen being mightier than the sword, but in the 7th century the sword was better for spreading the word of God, or at least that remains the common opinion when discussing the Islamic conquests.

What is true is that within just a few hundred short years, the Islamic conquests stretched from modern Turkey, across North Africa and reached what is today modern day Spain. "This successful conquest and subsequent conversion of the Middle East and beyond has inevitably resulted in a variety of myths and prejudices throughout the ages. It is important to note that the conversion of the peoples of what are now the heartlands of the Islamic world was a largely peaceful process and was separate from the Arabs' military conquests of these same areas. Indeed, the conversion largely resulted from the example set by the early Muslim Arabs themselves and the activities of preachers, missionaries and merchants."[6] The more accurate depiction of these events is that the armies of Islam conquered the lands, while preachers and missionaries converted the people.

The counter to this argument is that anyone conquered would have no choice but to convert. And in a way, this is true. The conquered people of the Sassanian Empire, which was roughly located in what is today modern day Iran, followed the Zoroastrian religion, and were not initially "regarded as a 'People of the Book,' meaning that they were not adherents of a 'true' albeit 'corrupted' religion. Christians, on the other hand, were, like the Jews, a 'People of the Book' who shared the same God as Muslims. This commonality supposedly allowed the Byzantine Empire to survive for several centuries."[7]

Yet, in the end Constantinople did fall in 1453 CE to the Ottoman Turks, who converted to the Muslim faith, and countless other cities also were conquered by armies under the supposed will of Allah. This is a fact argued again and again by westerners, who look to make all of Islam appear as a violent religion bent on conquest. The contrast to this is that Christians often use the excuse of spreading the word of Jesus to somehow cleanse away the sins of the Spanish conquests of South America in the 16th century, the Europeans conquest of Africa in the 19th century or any other empire building. Onward Christian soldiers indeed, because even the armies of Nazi Germany wore belt buckles with the legend *Gott Mitt Uns* ("God With Us").[8]

Thus clearly Islam is neither without sin, nor alone in its sins. However, this is not a book that looks to praise or discredit any empire building based on religion. Rather, this is just an attempt to put this in context, or in religious terms, "let which religion is free from sin to cast the first stone" - because as it appears most believed they were righteous and thus cast many a stone. The point however, is that today the extremists in Islam are as dangerous as those aforementioned right-wing extremists that have the American media all worked up, and apparently need watching by the government.

Likewise, as we have already stressed previously, men who certainly were not Muslims committed the worst terrorist attack in the United States prior to September 11, 2001. However, that should not overshadow the fact that only some two years earlier it was Muslim terrorists who perpetrated the first attacks on the World Trade Center, and as we previously covered, carried out attacks on the U.S. embassies in Kenya and Tanzania in 1998 and the attack on the *U.S.S. Cole* in 2000. Thus the war on terrorism did not begin on Tuesday, September 11, 2001 when the first plane hit the World Trade Center - or even when its crew and passengers were taken hostage. This was a war that has been raging for years, decades even centuries. Yet we see that left leaning thinkers and authors such as Margolis try to somehow apologize for our actions.

Part of the time the blame is that we prop up Israel and the rest of the time is that we support supposed "bad regimes" in nations such as Saudi Arabia. Somehow, the logic on the left says, if we didn't support these wicked regimes Islam might at least not hate us so much. Could it be, as President George W. Bush said in the spring of 2006 that it is just that the extremists hate us because "they hate our way of life. They hate our freedom."[9]

When looking at the words of Osama bin Laden, in his "Letter to the American People," it isn't really hard to see that this hatred for our way of life is indeed real. However, some of his points are so far from the center that perhaps he might have been welcome with open arms during the climate summit held in Copenhagen, Denmark:

> "You have destroyed nature with your industrial waste and gasses more than any other nation in history. Despite this, you refuse to sign the Kyoto agreement so that you can secure the profit of your greedy companies and industries."[10]

While that passage might almost justify attacks on the United States, his anti-Western and more importantly anti-anything that isn't his brand of Islam make it clear that bin Laden is anything but a man of peace. He, and his followers, clearly would change America and the western world:

- "You are the nation who, rather than ruling by the Shariah of Allah in its Constitution and Laws, choose to invent your own laws as you will and desire. You separate religion from your policies.

- "You are a nation that permits acts of immorality, and you consider them to be pillars of personal freedom.

- "You are a nation that permits gambling in its all forms. The companies practice this as well, resulting in the investments becoming active and the criminals becoming rich.

- "You are a nation that exploits women like consumer products or advertising tools calling upon customers to purchase them."[11]

If it is to be believed that those are the real worlds of bin Laden, it is hard to argue that his goal is to at least change the Western way of life. The counterargument has been that these extremists merely want the West to leave the Middle East, and while it is beyond this book to discuss whether it would be possible to even do so, we should consider that even if bin Laden and his sort aren't calling for total conversion of the West, there are other groups that are doing just that.

Even the non-violent extremist can be seen as dangerous. One threat that the country is already experiencing is that many Muslims look to transform America through non-violent means, with the goal to introduce Shari'a or Islamic Law. To do so would require drastically more American Muslims, and "there are three possible means to increase Muslim numbers to achieve this dream: immigration, reproduction, and conversion. Sensing that overwhelming the country with immigrants would provoke a backlash and that reproduction will take a long time, Islamists focus most of their efforts on conversion."[12]

Thus a danger faced by the United States in the 21st century is in fact ironically from the will of its own people. Here we could say that if conversion works, then maybe truly it is "the will of Allah." More worrisome for those not wishing to convert is that many politicians in America practically fall over themselves with the stance that not all Muslims are bad - such as the quote from Obama that "Islam must be based on what Islam is, not what it isn't." The problem is that Obama is just among the most recent of leaders who are actually guilty of presenting not what Islam is, but what it isn't. During his visit to Egypt Obama offered these words in a speech from Cairo University:

> "It was Islam - at places like Al-Azhar - that carried the light of learning through so many centuries, paving the way for Europe's Renaissance and Enlightenment."[13]

This may be as big a myth as that of Islam being a non-stop militant force bent on world domination in the Middle Ages. Neither is accurate. Whilst Western Europe succumbed to a so-called "Dark Age" with the fall of the Roman Empire in the 5th century, it must be remembered that Islam didn't even come onto the scene until the 7th century. Moreover, Constantinople had been the beacon of learning and enlightenment for centuries, and Europe was in a major upswing by the High Middle Ages, beginning in the 10th century. Thus Islam's role in "paving the way for Europe's Renaissance" sounds nice, but it is far from factual.

"More telling still are Obama's historically inaccurate portrayals of Muslims as being at 'the forefront of innovation and education,' and his blaming colonialism and the Cold War for their falling behind. In fact, Muslims have not been at the forefront of anything since *ijtihad* (reason) was declared un-Islamic ten centuries ago and replaced by blind obedience to reactionary sharia dogma, which, in turn, ushered in a cultural and intellectual stagnation that is yet to be overcome. Indeed, the greatest Muslim minds over the centuries, from Averoes and Avicenna to Noble Prize physicist Abdus Salam, have invariably been persecuted and declared apostates by the guardians of Islamic orthodoxy."[14]

This apologetic stance doesn't note that it was Great Britain that essentially unified India - only to have it break upon their departure. The colonialism of Northern Africa by the Europeans only occurred in the second half of the 19th century, so it was hardly centuries of oppression by outsiders that kept these people in the dark. In fact, the Europeans in India, in Africa and in other previously independent Muslim lands brought progress and technology.

Likewise, the heart of the Islamic World - that being Arabia and the Middle East was dominated by the Ottoman Empire until the end of the First World War in 1918. The Ottoman Turks, as their predecessors the Seljuk Turks, had been early converts to Islam, thus it is ironic that Obama - or any critic for that matter - would fault colonialism on the decline of Islam. It could be further argued that some of the woes of Eastern Europe, namely in the Balkans, are the direct result of Ottoman conquests in that region, which began in the 14th century. During their rule of the Balkans the Ottomans were hardly the purveyors of learning, nor did they do much to preserve the classical past. "In 1803, the Ottoman Turks, who controlled Greece, could care less [sic] about Greek cultural treasures. They were happy to take a bribe from Englishman Lord Elgin to let him make off with the finest of ancient Greek statuary."[15] These include Parthenon statues that remain to this day in London.

Nor were the Ottoman Turks able to even keep a hold of the lands they ruled and by the 19th century the Ottomans were considered the "sick man of Europe."[16] During the First World War it was Muslim Arabs that rose up - and with the help of the British Army officer T.E. Lawrence (of "Lawrence of Arabia" fame) - the Turks were driven from the Arab lands. In fairness, these lands unfortunately for the local peoples who did the fighting, did not unify under a single Arab banner. Until the end of the Second World War, much of this land fell under French of British mandates, which is another way of saying "colony."

Yet, it is clear that throughout the period from the 7th Century to the 20th Century, there was an Islam empire very much present in the world. Thus, it should not "be forgotten that throughout most of its history, Islam has been a premier imperialist and colonialist power itself."[17]

More importantly it is also clear that Islam, having failed to "conquer" the world - at least at Constantinople in 717-8 CE,

Islamic Fascism

Poitiers (The Battle of Tours) in 732 CE, and then at Vienna (Sieges of Vienna) in 1529 CE and 1683 CE - was on a defensive stance for the past three and a half centuries. It has only been in the past several decades that Islam has been on a new offensive. This included efforts to drive out the Israelis from the Middle East, and here much has been made of the "nexus between Islam and fascism," as in that both have shown to be anti-Jewish.[18]

This is however not entirely accurate either, nor is it entirely a new phenomenon. In fact, Dr. Furnish argues that this has existed since the days of the Prophet. While the Jewish people were seen as being among "People of the Book," there is evidence that Islam also sought to destroy many of them. "The founder of Islam, Muhammad, ordered the Jewish tribe of Banu Qurayzah liquidated during the early Islamic community's sojourn in Medina, allegedly for conspiring against him and questioning his prophethood."[19]

More recently Muslims and true Nazis came together, when the latter embraced the Mufti of Jerusalem Amin al-Husayni. This wasn't so much for commonality, as it was for a pact against a common enemy. "Before 1940, neither the German Auswärtiges Amt (Foreign Office) nor the Mufti were prepared to begin cooperation. Germany was not ready to go beyond friendly statements and negligible financial support, because the Middle East was only of peripheral importance. Moreover, the Nazis viewed the Arabs with contempt."[20]

Al-Husayni's relationship dated to the late 1930s, but the outbreak of the Second World War changed the stakes, especially once Germany's Afrika Korps rolled across North Africa. "The Axis began giving generous subsidies to the Mufti in Baghdad, and Germans modified their racial theory of the Arabs, who were upgraded from a primitive people belonging to the lower races (though above Jews, gypsies, and blacks) to those possessing Nordic influences."[21]

It is also important to stress that while the Mufti did support the Germans, and that there were Muslim volunteers in the German forces - notably Bosnian volunteers from the Balkans - many Arab Muslims fought for the Allied forces. The Free French army was made up in part from volunteers from Algeria, Morocco and other

North African colonies. The courage and the dedication of these men cannot be understated.

However, Muslim Arab armies did fight the west during the Suez Crisis, and of course engaged in the decades long conflict with the Israelis. Understanding these various wars and the evolutions of the independent Muslim states requires a bit of background, which we will briefly cover. The Arab-Israeli conflict is much deeper of course than what can be said in this book. But for clarity we can say that this goes back to the later days of the Ottoman Empire, which as we stated ruled the lands that today make up modern day Israel. This was known by its name since Roman times, Palestine.

Before the dust even settled during the First World War, the British government issued the 'Balfour Declaration" in 1917, which essentially supported the establishment of a home for the Jewish people in Palestine. Twenty years would pass before a Royal Commission of Inquiry recommended the termination of the Palestine Mandate and the partition of Palestine into two states. These would include an Arab state that would be unified with Transjordan, and a Jewish state.

This followed a 1939 White Paper that restricted Jewish immigration to no more than 15,000 per year for five years, after which it would only occur with Arab consent. However, this didn't sit well with many Jewish people, and a Zionist conference was held in New York in 1942 to determine the future of Jewish Commonwealth. Following the Holocaust, and the end of World War II, an Anglo-American Commission of Inquiry then recommended that Palestine be open to 100,000 Jewish refugees. The British Foreign Secretary rejected this recommendation, and in 1947 the British referred the Palestine question to the UN. The United Nations Special Committee on Palestine recommended the end of the British Mandate and suggested the partition into an Arab state, a Jewish state and an international city of Jerusalem, all of which were to be linked in an economic union. One day before the end of the British Mandate of Palestine, on May 14, 1948 Israel declared its independence. The next day the armies of Egypt, Syria, Jordan and

Iraq, as well as well as some irregular troops from Lebanon invaded. Thus began the first Arab-Israeli War.[22]

There were several more wars over the next three decades, until Egypt and Israel signed peace accords at Camp David during President Jimmy Carter's administration in 1979. There followed a treaty with Jordan in 1994. These two nations are the only Arab League nations that have regular relations with Israel to this day.

Today however, Germany and Israel have normal relations. This began in 1950 when the two nations reached an agreement on reparations from the Holocaust and World War II, but normal diplomatic relations were not reached until 1965. The normalization process took time because some "politicians on the far right and left in Israel, who had always maintained that nothing had changed in Germany since Hitler, and that Israel should therefore have no relations at all with any Germans."[23] This is worth mentioning because it shows that there can be mutual understandings between people after horrible events in the past.

We have seen that the Germans have left behind their Nazi past, hopefully for good. Although there is a "Neo-Nazi" movement in Germany, the threat is not nearly as great as other Fascist threats. Prior to unification this was considered very insignificant. "The West German government viewed right-wing militants as a very small minority, many of whom committed individual acts of violence and therefore were classified as common criminals."[24] The movement picked up after the unification of East and West Germany, but by the mid-1990s it lost steam. "Neo-Nazi activities seemed to diminish precipitously during the latter part of 1994."[25] Again, this isn't to say this threat is completely gone, but it is clear that the greater threat may indeed be that of Islamic Fascism, which has shown no similar signs of decline.

This is especially true in Western Europe, which the Muslims failed to ever take by conquest but may now change through a type of counter assimilation. Instead of adopting the ways of their adopted new homes, many Muslims are calling for Shari'a as the law of the land - the Muslim law of the land in nations that have significantly small Muslim populations.

In October, in England, the Ahlus Sunnah wal Jamaah is just such a group, and its leader Anjem Choudary has called for the nation to adopt the Muslim laws, for the "flag of Allah" to fly over Downing Street, for all women to wear burkas and even public caning for drunkenness. Choudhary is also linked to Islam4UK, which reportedly "supported the 9/11 Twin Towers attack in the US."[26]

Conservatives in the U.K. have charged that the Labour government isn't doing enough to combat the likes of Choudhary. "Tory leader David Cameron said the Government was going soft on Muslim fanatics in Britain. He singled out the handing over of £113,000 of taxpayers' cash to two schools with links to extremists."[27] Clearly this isn't the U.K. of old that had battled various other Muslim fanatics such as Mahdi Muhammad Ahmad (who conquered the city of Khartoum in 1885), or his successor Abdullah al-Tasshi (who was defeated by the British at Omdurman in 1898).

We mention the "Mahdi" because he is a true fanatic in the most biblical sense. Whilst there is no actual mention of a "messiah" in the Koran, over time the messianic idea - which was so central to Judaism and Christianity - eventually sprouted in Islam as well. Usually these messiahs failed to gain much of a following. But for Mohammed Ahmed it was different, even if he wasn't one of the first 19th century Arabs to declare himself Mahdi (the prophesied redeemer of Islam who will appear at the end of times). However, Mohammed Ahmed had several things going for his claim. The most important is that he fit the prophesied version of the Mahdi perfectly. "The Mahdi would be a descendant of the Prophet. He would have the same name as the Prophet, and his father would be called Abduallah, like the Prophet's. He would be tall, balding, and have a brown Arab complexion, an aquiline nose, and a gap between his front teeth. He would appear at the end of century when Islam had fallen into corruption and weakness. He would spread Islam just as the Prophet had spread it, by military conquest of the enemies of Allah."[28]

As we previously warned about groups that wear a solid colored shirt, we must now warn against any Muslim named Muhammad who happens to have a gap in his teeth. The physical description bears an uncanny likeness to bin Laden of course, who also arrived at the end of a century when corruption could be seen throughout the Islamic World. Yet bin Laden didn't exactly take up the mantle of Mahdi.

And in truth bin Laden could be considered a moderate compared to the hard line of Mohammed Ahmed. Not only did the Mahdi centralize all the power of the area of the Sudan that he ruled, but he called upon his followers to hold true to the twin virtues of poverty and jihad. He cast out a thousand years of Islamic cultural development, instead creating a new society that was based on 7th century Arabia. "The only law was sharia in its crudest form. A man who called his fellow Muslim 'a dog, a pig, a Jew, a pimp, a dissolute, a thief, an adulterer, a fraudster, cursed, an infidel, a Christian or a homoesexual' received eight lashes and a week in prison, as did a man caught in possession of alcohol. Tobacco, the Turkish habit, was expunged from the face of the earth. A man caught smoking, chewing, or even taking snuff received eighty lashes. A man who donned the jibba but refused to pray would suffer eighty lashes, a week in prison, the confiscation of all assets, and if he was still alive after that, death."[29]

This may sound extreme, but consider that women had it even worse. Men were promised the reward with guarantee of heaven for taking part in jihad at least. "He punished women for their existence. At five years of age, a girl had to be fully veiled. She could not go outside 'unless strictly necessary.' She could not speak in public. She could not speak to a man unless she wore a veil. When she did speak, she must whisper."[30] Punishments could be handed down for so much as using obscenities, speaking with a loud voice or showing her hair.

Surely this would not be the world today. But in fact it is, and a part-time model was set to face a caning in Malaysia for merely drinking a beer in a hotel bar. Part-time model and mother of two, Kartika Sari Dewi Shukamo was arrested in 2007 during a raid in the beach town of Cherating. In Malaysia, clubs and lounges which serve alcohol are not required to check if customers are Muslims prior to serving them. However the nation's Muslim population (about two-thirds of its 28 million people) are governed by Islamic courts. Most alcohol offenders face a fine, but the law provides for a three-year prison term and caning. [31] At one point Shukamo had said that she would accept her punishment, which was to be six strokes of the cane, but as of April 1, 2010, the sentence was commuted.

She was told via a letter from the Pahang state Islamic department that notified her that the state's sultan had decided that she would be sparred from the canning. Instead Shukamo was ordered to do three weeks of community service. Her response was just as surprising, "I have very mixed feelings. I was shocked because this was unexpected." [32]

Clearly Shukamo broke a law, albeit a questionable law at that, and clearly she believed enough in her faith to accept her punishment, but is this a blind faith that is all too much like that of the followers of the Mahdi? To understand the issue, we must first look at Shukamo's stance on the issue. "The former model said she felt 'tortured' while waiting to be caned and now feels the punishment should have been carried out." [33]

It was also stressed that the caning would have been "different" from those issued to men, where "drug offenders, kidnappers and others are caned with a thick rattan stick on bare buttocks," [34] which can break the skin and leave lifelong scars. In Shukamo's case, it was widely noted that she would have *merely* faced a punishment delivered with her clothes on, and with a thin cane. To most Americans that would still fall into a category we've come to know as cruel and unusual.

Now Consider that Choudhary had said that people in England would receive lashes under Shari'a. How could America allow this type of corporal punishment, which is in direct conflict with the Constitution's VIII Amendment prohibition against "cruel and unusual punishment?" This brings us back to our earlier point that Islam must be based on what Islam is, not what it isn't.

The point must also be made that many Muslims would like to see Shari'a exist as it does in many supposedly "moderate" Muslim lands - such as Malaysia! Thus the laws might only apply to Muslims at first. "Most of Malaysia's 13 states are ruled by sultans who usually play a ceremonial role in governance but have the power to rule in Islamic matters." [35]

Again, this is not an attack on the religion as a whole, but the problem is that the apologists, including the proto-Fascists such as President Obama, and the mainstream media in America remain so caught up in not offending the average Muslim that they white-wash the religion's darker side. Thus those considering converting may not hear of these harsh laws regarding minor offenses.

Ever since former President George W. Bush uttered the words, "they hate us for our freedoms," there have been attempts by the liberal media to suggest otherwise. There has been a whitewash that practically defends the actions, suggesting that it isn't our freedoms. Case in point, a post by *Newsweek's* Katie Paul in her The Gaggle Blog:

"Let's just get it out of the way right off that bat that Al Qaeda madmen don't actually want to blast through bridges, skyscrapers, and subways in righteous protest of the First Amendment. It's mind-boggling that politicians still consider this nonsense an effective enough talking point as to employ it in their keynote speeches to national audiences." [36]

But it isn't just the fringe in the media that seemingly apologize to, and seemingly for, the actions of the so-called extremists. A White House aid practically wanted to say this isn't a "Muslim thing" at all. John Brennan, the president's top counterterrorism advisor actually noted that the concept of jihad was a "legitimate tenet of Islam," and he argued that the very term "jihadist" should NOT be used to describe America's enemies, nor should be described in "religious terms." [37] Brennan actually described the extremists as "victims of political, economic and social forces," but then argued that their tactics were not a jihad:

"Nor do we describe our enemy as 'jihadists' or 'Islamists' because jihad is a holy struggle, a legitimate tenet of Islam, meaning to purify oneself or one's community, and there is nothing holy or legitimate or Islamic about murdering innocent men, women and children." [38]

The enemy, the extremists, certainly see this as a jihad, and Brennan should realize that they see much more than just the Middle East as their "community." This is after all, exactly what Choudhary and others are talking about when they call for Islamic law in England, and eventually in the United States. To the extremists this is therefore a legitimate jihad, and is an actual holy war to them.

Here again is where bin Laden could be compared somewhat to the 19th century Madhi, as noted in a February 4, 2005 Congressional Research Service document:

"Bin Laden urged Muslims to find a leader to unite them and establish a 'pious caliphate' that would be governed by Islamic law and follow Islamic principles of finance and social conduct. Bin Laden repeatedly argued that Afghanistan had become a model Islamic state under his Taliban hosts and used religious rhetoric to solicit support for the Taliban and Al Qaeda." [39]

Thus it seems, the extremists - those who look to spread the faith, either through bullets or ballots - remain dangerous. Their tactics, as we have seen, are somewhat in keeping with those of past Fascist groups, including the Nazis in Germany. The irony is that in our efforts to win over the Muslim World, we may end up becoming part of it, whether we like it or not. And for this we must blame those such as Barack Hussein Obama, a man born to a Muslim father, and raised in a Muslim country. Whether President Obama is in fact a Muslim is not the issue, but it is his pandering to the Muslim World that is a problem. But finally, it is the fact that again, the Western World is lied to about Islam. Shouldn't Islam be based on what Islam is, not what it isn't?

Chapter Fourteen
The Road Ahead

Clearly the road ahead isn't going to be easy. As we have seen the road towards fascism is not one that most nations sought to take, or even expected to take. Instead the cobblestones were laid over time, making for a solid foundation on which the aspiring charismatic leader could build upon. From here the other elements were smoothed out, providing a smooth highway for the nation to move towards its destiny.

It is our duty to be diligent, to be aware and to ensure that this final destination is never reached. But whether it is Barack Obama who is the driving force, or just another passenger, it is undeniable that his polices are building on that foundation and making it all the easier for a future American leader to take America in a frightening direction.

This is clear in the most recent events that have transpired as we conclude this book. We find that President Obama continues to be disingenuous, as he responded to the Christmas Day attempted terrorist bombing of an airliner traveling from the Netherlands to Detroit. First, the President was slow to respond, as if it was an inconvenient truth that bad things would happen over his Christmas holiday to Hawaii - a trip the President rushed to make, even as Senators remained in Washington, D.C. until the last possible moment for a vote on healthcare.

First Obama took three days to even offer a statement publicly about the attempted attack on Northwest Airlines Flight 253, and much of his initial reaction was to publicly scold the United States intelligence community for the failures to "connect the dots." According to *The Los Angeles Times*:

> "This was a screw-up that could have been disastrous," Mr. Obama told the officials, White House officials said later. "We dodged a bullet, but just barely. It was averted by brave individuals, not because the system worked, and that is not acceptable."[1]

While Obama did not specify an individual or an agency, he never seemed to actually blame himself as part of the potentially disastrous "screw-up." Whereas past leaders, such as Harry S. Truman took the blame, and President Truman had his famous "The Buck Stops Here" sign on the desk in the Oval Office, Obama shows his true colors as the proto-Fascist who looks to point fingers and blame others for these failures.

What is notable about this incident is that it has emerged that Obama might have gotten prior warning, but saw no problem with jetting to the most distant part of the United States of America from Washington, D.C. for the holidays. According to *Newsweek* magazine, Obama indeed had prior warning, yet still took the time for his vacation:

> President Obama received a high-level briefing only three days before Christmas about possible holiday-period terrorist threats against the U.S., *NEWSWEEK* has learned. The briefing was centered on a written report, produced by U.S. intelligence agencies, titled "Key Homeland Threats," a senior U.S. official says.[2]

If former President George W. Bush had made a similar trip given the circumstances, the mainstream media would have picked up this story and it would have been fodder for weeks. But the fervor over it faded faster than many New Year's resolutions.

The media did however note, typically with distain, that this failed attack drew away the focus from health care reform. And previously Obama had remarked that he found that there were too many problems, and that this was in fact a problem for him! "I'd love if these problems were coming at us one at a time instead of five or six at a time. It's more than most Congresses and most presidents have to deal with in a lifetime. But we have been called to govern in extraordinary times."[3]

Consider that past Presidents such as Lincoln dealt with a Civil War, or FDR had the Great Depression and World War II, or that former President George W. Bush was faced with attacks on America, coupled with a recession at the same time, and later rising oil prices and the aftermath of a major natural disaster!

Could it be that the times aren't so extraordinary, and that perhaps Mr. Obama is just extra ordinary, and not up to the task at hand? This could certainly explain why Obama's numbers in the polls have fallen faster than any first-term POTUS.

But there are still nearly three years left to Obama's term in office. In this time he could surge ahead in the polls and get elected for a second term, or he could (as some conspiracy-minded types have suggested) "find a way" to cancel the 2012 elections and become a true Fascist dictator. While the authors don't believe the latter will actually happen, we do have some predictions as to what Barack Obama may do in the near future and over the rest of his term in office.

Continue to Play the Blame Game

Despite some pitfalls, President Obama has the support of the mainstream media and this could allow him to further blame Bush and Cheney for all the problems he is facing. In fact, Obama isn't just getting support from the media but actual encouragement to further blame former President Bush. In an op-ed piece, *The New York Times* Paul Krugman wrote:

> "Mr. Obama could have done the same — with, I'd argue, considerably more justice. He could have pointed out, repeatedly, that the continuing troubles of America's economy are the result of a financial crisis that developed under the Bush administration, and was at least in part the result of the Bush administration's refusal to regulate the banks."[4]

Was Krugman serious? Apparently he was. This an attitude that is shared repeatedly by the liberal left, because when in doubt, there is always someone else to blame. Failing that, as we have seen, it is easy enough to suggest that you didn't really expect to see these problems coming in waves. So where does the buck stop in today's government? Possibly wherever Obama can find someone to take the blame?

As we have seen, Obama blamed the Secret Service for not being better doormen during a state dinner, he blamed the intelligence community for failing to connect dots that perhaps he should have helped connect, and he even took the time to scold Democratic senators over health care reform. If we are to believe the media hype, Obama is the smartest man to have ever held the position of president. Surely he could teach the intelligence community some lessons on how to do their job. But jet setting around the world to apologize for America's perceived wrongs seems to have priority to American's safety.

Moving forward, we see no reason not to expect more of the same. The problem is that this isn't very presidential. While it might work for a community organizer, or a motivational speaker, it sends a message that there is the President's way or the highway. (And we don't mean shovel ready stimulus projects that aren't so shovel ready.) When something doesn't work it must be someone else's fault. There are many games played every day in Washington, but the blame game is one that should be left on the shelf, especially for a candidate who promised a new tone of cooperation in Washington.

Demonize Sectors of the Economy

Another part of the blame game is to go after the financial elite, suggesting that these are the people "who got us in this mess" and who deserve to hear the wrath of the American people. Thus the easiest targets for Obama will be those on Wall Street, and of course bankers.

As Doug Elliot, a Fellow at the Brookings Institution in Washington commented, "The politics on this is really quite easy. The public would be supportive of anything up to shooting and burning the bankers."[5] And Obama offered up the next best thing, suggesting that the largest banks in the country should be taxed, with the money making up a projected $117 billion shortfall in the government's financial crisis bailout fund.

This would be a levy of 15 basis points, or 0.15 percent, on the liabilities of large financial institutions. "The tax, which would require congressional approval, would last at least 10 years and generate about $90 billion over the decade, according to administration estimates. 'If these companies are in good enough shape to afford massive bonuses, they are surely in good enough shape to afford paying back every penny to taxpayers,' Obama said."[6]

"Give me back my legions," is just one statement that comes to mind when hearing Obama's words. Of course it wasn't a Fascist dictator who reportedly uttered those words, but rather the first Roman Emperor Augustus. Still, Obama demanding a tax is just as short sighted. While surely the banks can pay the tax more than Quintilius Varus could have returned the Roman Legions that were massacred in the late summer of 9 CE in a German forest on the Rhine, the point is that many bankers are now being ridiculed despite never taking a single government dime. As Charles Krauthammer, syndicated columnist, and Fox News contributor summed up on *Special Report with Bret Baier*:

> "This is being sold with incredible demagoguery as a payment. The president says I want my money back. In fact, the majority of banks have repaid. Some of the banks never received any of the TARP money, and some of them were forced into receiving it at the point of a gun in the Bush administration."[7]

Krauthammer further stressed that the "real delinquents" were not the banks, but rather bankrupt automakers Chrysler and GM, neither of which is "being asked to pay anything because of Democratic ties with Michigan and the UAW."[8]

Obama may have bossed around these automakers, as we've touched upon in earlier chapters, but suggesting a tax is another issue. In fact, what we are seeing is another example instead of Obama's abhorrence to capitalist success. The banks had a good year, started to turn matters around and the employees were duly rewarded, so Obama decided to tax this success. Fellow panelist on *Special Report with Bret Baier*, Juan Williams, news analyst for National Public Radio offered this insight on the matter:

> "He could just simply tax the bonuses. Maybe that's what he should be doing. But I think the anger that he was expressing today, and I think Charles is right when he calls it demagoguery, but it is the flavor of the moment in American politics. It is pure populism, it is anger at Wall Street."[9]

Is it really populism or fascism? In this case, it certainly feels like a bit of both. But it takes us back to the original point regarding the dangers expressed by Fascists of free market capitalism. And it must be remembered the corporations, including banks, don't pay taxes. They put this cost on their consumers. An extra cost by way of taxes will trickle down to the consumer, Jane and John Doe if you will.

Consider too that even before being elected Obama preached how he would reform health care. As this book nears completion health care remains an ongoing debate, but the entire health insurance industry has been demonized endlessly for not covering everybody.

Obama has offered warning signs and portents that the federal government could actually go bankrupt if health care reform isn't passed. But this is ridiculous rhetoric. The nation has survived for more than 235 years, two World Wars, a Civil War, threat of nuclear annihilation and a continued threat from global (and if you are to believe hype domestic) terrorists bent on our destruction - but somehow rising medical costs will bring the nation down? That's a doomsday theory worthy of the best 2012 theory, but it is exactly what Obama said, "Because if we don't do this, nobody argues with the fact that health care costs are going to consume the entire federal budget."[10]

Yet roughly half of Americans don't want this reform. Are they wrong, or misguided to think that the nation won't go bankrupt? Given the backroom deal making that went on straight up to the last minute, why would any American trust anything in this package? The answer is not an easy one to answer, but it is yet another point that we must be diligent in watching.

More importantly, when Obama says "nobody argues with the fact," then he should be asked to explain how the 40 Republican senators in Congress essentially said they didn't believe this fact. But as we've seen throughout this book, fear mongering is another way to obtain and maintain control by Fascists and their ilk.

What about that openness that was promised? Obama promised an open government and more recently offered that the health care debate would be shown on C-SPAN, yet it was not. Many past Fascists made major decisions behind closed doors as well. In this case at least Obama is not alone in his guilt, and Senator Majority Leader Harry Reid of Nevada and Speaker of the House Nancy Pelosi of California are not only complicit in his crime, but are also complacent in their roles!

"When leaders decided not to initiate a formal conference committee for reconciling differences between the House and Senate bills, Pelosi and Reid effectively blocked coverage by C-SPAN, which normally would televise conference committee deliberations on so critical an issue. C-SPAN has been demanding access, and rightly so. As C-SPAN CEO Brian Lamb wrote in a letter to the congressional leaders of both parties: 'Now that the process moves to the critical stage of reconciliation between the chambers, we respectfully request that you allow the public full access, through television, to legislation that will affect the lives of every single American.'"[11]

Considering how this issue has split America, and how roughly as many Americans oppose the passage of this legislation as support it, one would think this is a debate that should be broadcast. Yet, Reid and Polosi opted to pull the plug instead.

The irony here is that Obama was granted a win-win. He looked like the good guy for suggesting that, and even calling for the debate to be broadcast on C-SPAN, knowing full well that his henchmen in Congress could provide a media blackout.

Offer Safe Havens for Friends and Followers

As we've seen Obama is quick to tax the fat cats on Wall Street, but as we've touched upon in previous chapters, union members (with their Cadillac health care plans) have been safe from such taxation. How do other affluent people fit into this mix? Labeled a man of the people by many wealthy liberals, who tend to speak about the common man, he is anything but common - yet we still say he is extra ordinary.

Where do those movie stars and celebrities who swoon over Obama in their pledge videos fall in? We realize that many celebrities do indeed give back, as we've seen during the aftermath of the tragic earthquake that struck Haiti, as well as in other natural disasters.

The truth however, is that the likes of Michael Moore and Oprah Winfrey really never put their money where their mouth is, when it comes to giving back. While they do donate and give back, the percentage is vastly smaller considering their net wealth compared to the real average American. American's give more to charity than any other people on earth, but the high taxes promised by the Obama administration will strip this altruistic title from us.

But more importantly, how could these multi-millionaires support the core beliefs of Obama, and the concept of wealth redistribution, if they didn't really believe that they'd be above it? The answer here is simple. These people, as well as the sports superstars who make tens of millions of dollars a year, believe they are either inside a bubble or outside the entire system. And honestly, as past Fascist movements have shown, sadly they're probably right!

Where National Socialism and fascism differ from communism is that there typically remains an upper class of privileged individuals. These people are rewarded for their loyalty to the leader, and get to keep their wealth, while the rest of the system is turned on its head. In other words, *George Moviestar* gets to maintain his wealth, and aura of influence, but gets to see the little guy get a leg up at the expense of those who don't support the régime. In this world, for these Fascists and their celebrity friends, it is a win-win. The low people on the totem pole move up at the expense of hard working bankers, but the millionaire celebrities maintain a status quo. This is an elitist system that is typical in past Fascist regimes.

Take Economic Control

Since taking office Obama said he didn't want to be in the auto business, but as we have seen he is in the auto business. He has suggested (firmly) to the automakers the types of cars they should make, he pushed out former GM head Rick Wagoner, and even instructed that Chrysler look to Fiat for a partnership. Yet again, Obama made it clear he didn't want to be in the auto business.

Obama had also said he doesn't want to be in the banking business, but as we've just touched upon he doesn't like the way they're doing business, so he's looking at ways to change the rules.

And clearly Barack Obama wants to be in the health care business, as it would give the U.S. Government and the POTUS (in other words Obama) control of one-sixth of the U.S. economy. Writing for *The Washington Post*, Charles Krauthammer explains, "By essentially abolishing medical underwriting (actuarially based risk assessment) and replacing it with government fiat, Obamacare turns the health insurance companies into utilities, their every significant move dictated by government regulators."[12]

One way to make health care costs more manageable would be to limit payouts for medical negligence. Monetary compensation for negligence is supposed to make the person hurt whole. But punitive damages, which are meant to punish the wrong doer as a warning to others, adds to the costs of health care with little if any benefit to the public. But Obama and Democrats in general receive millions of dollars from the Trial Lawyers. And as every Trial Lawyer knows, there are two types of doctors; those who have been sued and those who are going to be sued.

But this isn't the only type of economic control that we must diligently watch from the POTUS. As we touched upon at the beginning of this book, many of Obama's tactics date to prior progressives, and here too Krauthammer outlines some of the direction Obama took in his first year in the Oval Office. "Obama unveiled the most radical (in American terms) ideological agenda since the New Deal: the fundamental restructuring of three pillars of American society - health care, education and energy."[13]

The energy policy, the center of which is the concept of cap and trade - a topic we previously covered in detail - would give unprecedented federal control of American industry and commerce to big government. Fortunately, it seems to be a dead issue as we go to print, but here we must consider the ever-present fear mongering of global warming, and how future climate summits could mark this issue's unwelcome return.

Create a Climate of Change

We must watch to make sure that Obama, nor others on the liberal fringe, do not push a climate change agenda. There is hope that perhaps it isn't the globe that is warming, but perhaps the anger regarding this falsehood.

One of the best things to come about from the Copenhagen Climate Summit wasn't that anything was actually done about the ominous "global warming" or climate change, but rather that the American mainstream media finally was able to take a clear shot at Nancy Pelosi. Of course, it would be hard for even the most diehard liberal magazine not to question the Congressional delegation's motives for going on what must be described as a pre-holiday getaway to Denmark. This made headlines in *The New York Post* even before the summit was wheels up in a story dated December 17, 2009:

> House Speaker Nancy Pelosi is leading a large delegation on at least two Air Force jets to Copenhagen for the climate summit - where participants harshly condemn the use of jet airplanes for the high amounts of CO2 they emit.
>
> "This may be the largest congressional delegation I have ever heard of," said a source at the 89th Air Wing stationed at Andrews Air Force Base of the trip to the UN summit, which is increasingly being criticized as a farce.[14]

Fortunately, with holiday cheer and terror warnings, the media didn't forget this story in the New Year either. CBS News, a news organization that had been typically playing softball politics with the liberal left, seemed to believe that even Pelosi and entourage went too far. The news organization offered this biting take on January 11, 2010:

> Few would argue with the U.S. having a presence at the Copenhagen Climate Summit. But wait until you hear what we found about how many in Congress got all-expense paid trips to Denmark on your dime.
>
> CBS investigative correspondent Sharyl Attkisson reports that cameras spotted House Speaker Nancy Pelosi at the summit. She called the shots on who got to go. House Majority Leader Steny Hoyer, and embattled Chairman of the Tax Committee Charles Rangel were also there.[15]

So to recap, Pelosi and others in Congress (a vast majority Democrats) fly to Copenhagen to discuss human production of CO_2, and in the process produce the very so-called "toxic" gas and do so on the taxpayers' dime? And in the end, the conference produced very little. In fact, one of the loudest voices calling for something to be done about climate change, publicly lamented that the summit accomplished almost nothing. "Billionaire investor George Soros said December's summit on climate change in Copenhagen was 'a failure' and that the event, after tremendous buildup 'delivered very little.'"[16]

As we move forward, we must watch for these sorts of outrageous actions, and call them out when they happen. However, part of the problem is that Obama has set a standard that makes it easy. He's on planes so much that trips like this one to Copenhagen may not seem too shameful.

Create More Double Standards

As 2010 began, we witnessed one of the most egregious examples of the liberal double standard in American politics. When it came out that Senator Harry Reid described in private then-Senator Barack Obama in a book on the 2008 political campaign as being able to appeal to white voters as he was "light skinned" and "with no Negro dialect, unless he wanted to have one," there was little backlash.[17] It was fodder for the late night comics, who of course naturally lead with news that *The Jay Leno Show* on NBC would be canceled, and Leno moved to the 11:30pm timeslot. Even for those who never miss a beat to lampoon politicians missed a beat or two to mock their own situation first and foremost.

What was actually far more laughable was the fallout. Prominent African-American leaders lined up, following President Obama's lead, to express the fact that they didn't find it all that offensive. When the media did cover this episode, it was downplayed, ironic considering that when conservatives have stuck their feet in their mouths there has been a much more vocal backlash. But the real tragedy is that Reid's comments were brushed off, whereas former Senate Majority Leader, Trent Lott of Mississippi found his career essentially dead after making a remark that seems just as harmless.

"In 2002, Democrats ripped former Senate Majority Leader Trent Lott (R-MS) after he made racially-tinged remarks at the 100th birthday party for the late Sen. Strom Thurmond (R-SC), who was once a segregationist. Republicans eventually booted Lott from his leadership post."[18]

Or consider that words one never even spoke can derail a career! Whilst it is true that when Rush Limbaugh was a commentator for ESPN, and resigned after reportedly saying, "I think what we've had here is a little social concern in the NFL. The media has been very desirous that a black quarterback do well,"[19] it was a statement that Limbaugh denies making that was widely quoted that cost him part ownership in an NFL franchise. Before we get to what Limbaugh allegedly said we should compare these two statements for good measure.

Limbaugh said that for the NFL, "It would very desirous that a black quarterback do well," and it cost him his job; while Reid implied that Obama would do well because he spoke "with no Negro dialect, unless he wanted to have one." At a glance it almost seems as if Limbaugh's words are no worse than Reid's. Of course the argument was moot because many times over it was reported that Reid's words weren't meant to be public. Apparently being insensitive about the man you think could capture the White House for your political party is fine, as long as it is in private!

But let's look at a deeper issue. Limbaugh attempted to buy a stake in the St. Louis Rams professional football franchise which was derailed when he was quoted as saying, "Slavery built the South. I'm not saying we should bring it back; I'm just saying it had it's [sic] merits. For one thing the streets were safer after dark."[20] The problem with this is that Limbaugh denies ever making the comment, and attempts to find a transcript failed to turn up the quote! But the damage was done; Limbaugh was turned down from buying the team. It just shows another double standard that exists in this country, where liberals often get a free pass.

And not only a free pass, but sometimes such comments made by a liberal means you get a spot that puts you a heartbeat away from the oval office. It was then Senator Joe Biden who offered the words about then candidate Barack Obama back in 2007, "I mean, you got the first mainstream African-American who is articulate and bright and clean and a nice-looking guy. I mean, that's a storybook, man."[21]

Doesn't this suggest that past African-Americans who ran for president, such as Rev. Jesse Jackson or Rev. Al Sharpton are somehow inarticulate, not bright, dirty and ugly? Yet, Biden made this comment prior to the primary season and was somehow picked to be the vice presidential candidate anyway. Here, we must wonder whether Biden was treated by the Democrats as the Republicans treated Teddy Roosevelt, as they packed him off to a position where he could do no harm.

As for the double standard, we do see that while gaffe-making Democrats get a pass, the loyal opposition in the media continues to get marginalized. The White House's war with Fox News did not end with Anita Dunn's leaving the post, as the new White House Communications Director Dan Pfeiffer offered his opinion in a blog to *The New York Times*. "I have the same view of Fox that Anita had, which is that Fox is not a traditional news organization," and explained, "They have a view. That point of view pervades the entire network both the opinion shows, like Glenn Beck and Bill O'Reilly, but also through the newscasts during the day," finally adding, "We don't feel an obligation to treat them like we would treat a CNN or an ABC or an NBC or a traditional news organization."[22]

Should we expect that other Obama-favoring news organizations, or those that continue to oppose Bush-era policies - notably MSNBC - would be treated as a traditional news organization? It certainly sounds that way to us.

These are some of the ways that Obama could continue to build a road that if not Fascist by intent could either lead to a future Fascist takeover of America, or worse destroy it. Fortunately, our founding fathers also built a foundation that ensures there are continued checks and balances, but it is our job to watch, listen and respond to what our government does. For if we fail that, then perhaps we deserve to actually live in a land ruled by Fascists.

What we now have is a nation that is very different from what our founding fathers could have expected. Besides the technological advances and the growth in landmass, we live in a nation where even an African-American (a term that wouldn't have even been understood in concept in 1776) could become President of the United States. This is remarkable, but contrary to what the liberal fringe might think, it isn't (as we said at the beginning of this book) the color of a man's skin but his character that is at question. It is whether this leader really has the best interests of the average American in mind.

But the power still lies with the average citizen, and perhaps as we look at our future candidates we must not be taken in merely by well-written speeches read off a teleprompter, offering the extremely ambiguous concepts of "hope" and "change." We must ask what is really meant by these words instead, and look at the deeds done by these men and women, the associations with those who evoke anti-American sentiments and whether they will lead us down a road to which no one truly would care to go.

It was Benjamin Franklin who was asked at the close of the Constitutional Convention in Philadelphia on September 18, 1787 what type of governments the delegates had formed. His answer was simple and to the point. "A republic, if you can keep it."[23] Let us hope we can indeed keep it.

About the Authors

Peter Suciu is a New York based freelance writer. His work has appeared in more than three-dozen magazines and websites including *Newsweek, Reader's Digest, Playboy, Military Heritage*, MSNBC.com, CNN.com and Forbes.com. He is the author of the history book *Military Sun Helmets of the World*, and has contributed to multiple *Armchair Reader* publications. For two and a half years Peter Suciu was a Web producer and editor for FoxNews.com, where he managed the websites for *The O'Reilly Factor, Hannity & Combs* and *Fox News Sunday*.

Peter is a member of the Company of Military Historians and in 2009 launched the media watchdog website Firearmstruth.com, which tracks media bias against firearms ownership. Peter Suciu holds a bachelor's degree in Broadcast and Cinematic Arts from Central Michigan University.

John Kullman holds a jurist doctorate from Thomas Cooley Law School and a dual bachelor degree in English and Speech, as well as a minor in History from Central Michigan University. He previously was employed with Halliburton and Long & Wetzel. He is the managing editor of Firearmstruth.com, and is an avid gun rights advocate.

Notes

Chapter One - The Myth of Fascism

1. Bosworth, R.J.B, *Mussolini's Italy: Life Under the Fascist Dictatorship, 1915-1945* (New York, Penguin, 2007) p.150
2. Griffith, Roger, *The Nature of Fascism* (New York, Routledge, 1993) p. 7
3. Heller, Steven, *The Swastika: Symbol Beyond Redemption?* (New York, Allworth Press, 2008) p. 4
4. Bosworth p. 123
5. Griffith p. 71
6. Griffith p. 89
7. Liebknecht, Wilhelm, "Our Recent Congress" (1896) Retrieved from: http://www.marxists.org/archive/liebknecht-w/1896/08/our-congress.htm.
8. Mussolini, Benito; Schnapp, Jeffery Thompson (ed.); Sears, Olivia E. (ed.); Stampino, Maria G. (ed.). "Address to the National Corporative Council (14 November 1933) and Senate Speech on the Bill Establishing the Corporations (abridged; 13 January 1934)". *A Primer of Italian Fascism*. (Lincoln, University of Nebraska Press, 2000) Pp. 158-159.
9. Mussolini, Benito; Schnapp, Jeffery Thompson (ed.); Sears, Olivia E. (ed.); Stampino, Maria G. (ed.). "Address to the National Corporative Council (14 November 1933) and Senate Speech on the Bill Establishing the Corporations (abridged; 13 January 1934)". A Primer of Italian Fascism. (Lincoln, University of Nebraska Press, 2000) Pp. 158.
10. Spicer, Kevin P, *Antisemitism, Christian Ambivalence, and the Holocaust*. (Indiana University Press, 2007) p. 136
11. Axworthy, Mark. *Third Axis Fourth Ally: Romanian Armed Forces in the European War, 1941-1945*. (London, Wellington House, 1995) p. 24
12. Axworthy p. 24
13. Brennan, James P. *Peronism and Argentina* (Wilmington, SR Books, 1998) p. 88
14. Paxton, Robert O. 2005. *Anatomy of Fascism*. (New York, Vintage, 2005) p. 190
15. Paxton p. 191
16. Gallagher, Tom, *Portugal A Twentieth-Century Interpretation* (Manchester University Press, 1983) p. 31
17. Neocleous, Mark, *Fascism (Concepts in Social Thought)* (University of Minnesota Press, 1997) p. 49
18. "11 Companies that Surprisingly Collaborated With the Nazis." 11 Points Web Site. Retrieved from: http://www.11points.com/News-Politics/11_Companies_That_Surprisingly_Collaborated_With_the_Nazis
19. Gregor, Neil, *Nazism* (New York, USA: Oxford University Press, 2000) p. 222
20. Burleigh, Michaelm, *The Third Reich: A New History* (New York, USA: Hill and Wang, 2000) p.77
21. Burleigh p.77

Notes

Chapter Two - The History of American Fascism Part I

1. Hedges, Chris, *American Fascist: The Christian Right and the War on America.* (New York, Free Press 2007) p. 21
2. Gross, Bertram, *Friendly Fascism: The New Face of Power in America.* (South End Press, 1999) p. 235
3. Curtis, Bryan. "D.W. Griffith in Black and White: Was the Birth of a Nation Director Really a Racist?" Salon.com, January 3, 2003. Retrieved from: http://www.slate.com/id/2076307/
4. Stokes, Melvyn, *D.W. Griffith's the Birth of a Nation: A History of the Most Controversial Motion Picture of All Time* (New York, The Oxford University Press, 2008) p. 10
5. Hurwitz, Michael, *D.W. Griffith's Film, The Birth of a Nation: The Film that Transformed America* (BookSurge Publishing, 2006) p. 91
6. Price, R.G. 2004. "Rise of American Fascism." RationalRevolution.net. May 15, 2004. Retrieved from: http://rationalrevolution.net/articles/rise_of_american_fascism.htm
7. Title 4, Chapter 1, Section 4, US Code, Retrieved from:http://uscode.house.gov/download/pls/04C1.txt
8. Schilling, Chelsea. "Is Obama's face on U.S. flag illegal?" WorldNetDaily. October 14, 2009. Retrieved from: http://www.wnd.com/index.php?pageId=112893
9. Malkin, Michelle. "I pledge to be of service to Barack Obama." Michelle Malkin Web Blog. September 2, 2009. Retrieved from: http://michellemalkin.com/2009/09/02/i-pledge-to-be-of-service-to-barack-obama/
10. US Immigration Support Web Site. Retrieved from: http://www.usimmigrationsupport.org/oath_of_allegiance.html
11. Fest, Joachim C, *Hitler* (Mariner Books, 2002) p. 465
12. Shirer, William L., *The Rise and Fall of the Third Reich: A History of Nazi Germany.* (New York, Simon & Schuster; 1st Touchstone edition, 1990) p. 227
13. Smith, Richard, "Making a Pledge of Allegiance is a Serious Matter" Cross Resources Web Site, August 6, 2009. Retrieved from: http://crossmin.org/index2.php?option=com_content&do_pdf=1&id=55
14. Lincoln Bicentennial Web Site. Retrieved from: http://www.lincolnbicentennial.gov/uploadedFiles/Lincolns_Life/Words_and_Speeches/Proclamation-of-Amnesty-and-Reconstruction.pdf
15. Cary, Lee. "Does the Supreme Court Still Sit." American Thinker Web Site. October 27, 2009. Retrieved from: http://www.americanthinker.com/printpage/?url=http://www.americanthinker.com/2009/10/does_the_supreme_court_still_s.html
16. *The New York Times*, "JUSTICES UPHOLD A TEACHERS' OATH; Back State Law Requiring a Constitutional Pledge." January 23, 1968. Retrieved from: http://select.nytimes.com/gst/abstract.html?res=F70D1FFF3E541A7

Notes

493C1AB178AD85F4C8685F9&scp=10&sq=new%20york%20state%20loyalty%20oath&st=cse

17. Lieberman, Jethro K, *A Practical Companion to the Constitution: How the Supreme Court Has Ruled on Issues from Abortion to Zoning, Updated and expanded Edition of The Evolving Constitution* (University of California Press, 1999) p. 292
18. Dubofsky, Melvyn, *We Shall Be All: A History of the Industrial Workers of the World* (abridged edition) (Working Class in American History). (Abridged Edition, University of Illinois Press, 2000) Pp. 185-187
19. Watson, Bruce, "Crackdown! When bombs terrorized America, the Attorney General launched the 'Palmer Raids.'" *Smithsonian Magazine*. February 2002. Retrieved from: http://www.smithsonianmag.com/people-places/redsquare.html
20. Gage, Beverly, *The Day Wall Street Exploded: A Story of America in its First Age of Terror.* (Oxford University Press, 2009)
21. Wade, Wyn Craig, *The Fiery Cross: The Ku Klux Klan in America* (Oxford University Press, 1998) p. 237
22. Wade, p. 249
23. Pestritto, Ronald J. and William J. Atto, *American Progressivism: A Readers.* (Lexington Books, 2008) p. 7
24. Pestriotto, p. 215
25. Pestritto, Ronald J., *Woodrow Wilson and the Roots of Modern Liberalism* (Rowman & Littlefield Publishers, Inc., 2005) p. 259
26. Weisman, Steven R., *The Great Tax Wars: Lincoln - Teddy Roosevelt - Wilson How the Income Tax Transformed America.* (New York, Simon & Shuster, 2004) p. 1
27. Clements, Kendrick A., *The Presidency of Woodrow Wilson* (University of Kansas, 1992) p. 153
28. Higham, John, *Strangers in Land Patterns of American Nativism, 1860-1925.* (Rutgers University Press, 2002) p. 211
29. Stone, Geoffrey R., *Perilous Times: Free Speech in Wartime from the Sedition Act of 1798 to the War on Terrorism.* (New York, W.W. Norton & Company, 2004) p. 153
30. Boot, Max, *The Savage Wars of Peace: Small Wars and the Rise of American Power* (Basic Books, 2002) p. 86
31. Leuchtenburg, William E., *Herbert Hoover: The American Presidents Series: The 31st President, 1929-1933* (Times Books, 2009) p. 55
32. Hawley, Ellis W., *Herbert Hoover as Secretary of Commerce: Studies in New Era Though and Practice* (Iowa State Press, 1982) p. 47
33. Leuchtenburg, p. 120
34. Leuchtenburg, p. 120
35. Friedrich, Otto, Hays Gorey and Ruth Mehrtens Galvin, "F.D.R.'s Disputed Legacy." *Time Magazine*. February 1, 1982. Retrieved from: http://www.time.com/time/magazine/article/0,9171,954983-4,00.html

Notes

36. Boaz, David, "Hitler, Mussolini, Roosevelt" Reason, October 2007 via The Cato Institute Web Site. Retrieved from: http://www.cato.org/pub_display.php?pub_id=8727
37. Sweeney, Michael S., *Secrets of Victory: The Office of Censorship and the American Press and Radio in World War II* (University of North Carolina Press, 2001) p. 247
38. Schlesinger, Arthur M., Jr., *The Coming of the New Deal, 1933-1935* (The Age of Roosevelt, Vol. 2) (Mariner Books, 2003) p. 89
39. Brands, H.W., *Traitor to His Class: The Privileged Life and Radical Presidency of Franklin Delano Roosevelt* (Anchor, 2009) p. 391
40. Goldberg, Jonah. *Liberal Fascism* (New York, Random House, Inc., 2008) p. 132
41. Goldberg, p. 129
42. Schlesigner, p. 153
43. A.L.A. SCHECHTER POULTRY CORPORATION v. UNITED STATES, 295 U.S. 495 (1935) 295 U.S. 495, Retrieved from: http://caselaw.lp.findlaw.com/scripts/getcase.pl?court=US&vol=295&invol=495
44. Algeo, Matthew, *Last Team Standing: How the Pittsburgh Steelers and Philadelphia Eagles - The "Steagles" - Saved Pro Football During World War II* (Da Capo Press, 2007) p. 14
45. U.S. Constitution Online. Retrieved from: http://www.usconstitution.net/const.html
46. Thomas Jefferson: Reply to the Legislature of Vermont, 1807. ME 16:293. Retrieved from: http://etext.virginia.edu/jefferson/quotations/jeff1210.htm
47. U.S. Constitution Online. Retrieved from: http://www.usconstitution.net/const.html
48. Open Congress Web Site: Retrieved from: http://www.opencongress.org/bill/111-hj5/show

Chapter Three - The History of American Fascism Part II

1. Tolzmann, Don Heinrich, *German Immigration to America The First Wave* (Westminster, Maryland, Heritage Books, 2009) p. vi
2. Adam, Thomas, *Germany and the Americas: Culture, Politics, and History (Transatlantic Relations)* (ABC-CLICO, 2005) p. 15
3. Denk, Horst G.; Kenneth Rush, "The German-American Tricentennial: Three Hundred Years of German Immigration to America, 1683 - 1983; Final Report of the Presidential Commission for the German-American Tricentennial to the President and Congress of the United States". Presidential Commission for the German-American Tricentennial (1983). Retrieved from: http://usa.usembassy.de/etexts/ga-tricentennialreport.htm.
4. Wallace, Max, *The American Axis: Henry Ford, Charles Lindbergh, and the Rise of the Third Reich* (St. Martin's Griffin, 2004) p. 132
5. Wallace, p. 132
6. Wallace, p. 133

Notes

7. Grover, Warren, *Nazis in Newark*. (Transaction Publishers, 2003), Pp. 22-23
8. Grover, p. 217
9. Wallace, p. 133
10. Wade, Wyn Craig, *The Fiery Cross: The Ku Klux Klan in America* (Oxford University Press, 1998) p. 269
11. Wallace, p. 134
12. Grover, p. 259
13. Goldberg, p. 224
14. Levitas, Daniel, *The Terrorist Next Door: The Militia Movement and the Radical Right* (St. Martin's Griffin, 2004) p. 118
15. Grover, p. 270
16. Beekman, Scott, *William Dudley Pelley: A Life in Right-Wing Extremism And the Occult* (Syracuse, New York, USA: Syracuse University Press, 2005) p. 82
17. Martin, George Whitney, *The Red Shirt and the Cross of Savoy: The Story of Italy's Risorgimento, 1748-1871*. (Dodd Mead, 1969) p. 621
18. Beekman, Pp. 24-26
19. IMDB.com bio for William Dudley Pelley, Retrieved from: http://www.imdb.com/name/nm0671163/bio
20. Beekman, p. 4
21. Beekman, p. 137.
22. Beekman, p. 140
23. Beekman, p. 144
24. Simonelli, Frederick J, *American Fuehrer: George Lincoln Rockwell and the American Nazi Party* (Chicago, USA, University of Illinois Press 1997) p. 113
25. Simonelli, p. 44
26. Simonelli, p. 25
27. Schmaltz, William H., *Hate: George Lincoln Rockwell and the American Nazi Party* (Potomac Books, 2008) p. 57
28. Simonelli, p. 50
29. Kaplan, Jeffrey, *Encyclopedia of White Power: A Sourcebook on the Radical Right* (AltaMira Press, 2000) p. 153
30. Levitas, p. 291
31. Zeskind, Leonard, *Blood and Politics: The History of the White Nationalist Movement from the Margins to the Mainstream* (Farrar, Straus and Giroux, 2009) p. 58
32. Crespino, Joseph, *In search of another country: Mississippi and the conservative counterrevolution* (Princeton University Press, 2009) p. 123
33. Wade, p. 324
34. Lanier, Carlotta Walls and Lisa Frazier Page, *A Mighty Long Way: My Journey to Justice at Little Rock Central High School* (New York, One World/Ballantine, 2009) p. 91
35. Greenspan, Alan, *The Age of Turbulence: Adventures in a New World* (New York, Penguin, 2008) p. 246

Notes

36. Levitas, p. 493
37. Levitas, p. 354

Chapter Four - The Rise to Power of President Obama

1. Mostret, Mary. ConservativeTruth.org. Retrieved from http://www.conservativetruth.org/article.php?id=826
2. Mostret, Mary. ConservativeTruth.org
3. Retrieved from http://www.historyplace.com/worldwar2/riseofhitler/boyhood.htm
4. Corsi, Jerome. *The Obama Nation* (New York, Threshold Editions, 2008) p. 35
5. Corsi, p. 73
6. Corsi, P. 62 (From From Nickolas D. Kristf, "Obama: Man of the World," *New York Times*, March 6, 2007)
7. Kershaw, Ian. *Hitler: 1889-1935* (New York, W.W. Norton & Co., 2000) p. 14
8. FactCheck.org Web Site. September 25, 2008. Retrieved from http://www.factcheck.org/askfactcheck/how_many_times_did_obama_vote_present.html
9. Cashill, Jack. *American Thinker*. July 12, 2009. Retrieved from http://www.americanthinker.com/2009/07/who_wrote_audacity_of_hope_1.html
10. Heller, p. 3
11. Yue, Lorene and Brandon Glenn. "Chicago designers create Obama's logo." *Crane's Chicago Business*. February 22, 2007. Retrieved from http://www.chicagobusiness.com/cgi-bin/news.pl?id=23974
12. Ibid
13. Klein, Aaron. "American flag disappears from Obama campaign jet." WorldNetDaily. July 21, 2008. Retrieved from: http://www.wnd.com/?pageId=70236
14. "The Genius of the Obama Campaign Logo." HereComesTheScience.com. February 6, 2008. Retrieved from http://www.herecomesthescience.com/2008/02/06/the-genius-of-the-obama-campaign-logo/
15. FoxNews.com. "Woody Allen says President Obama should be granted dictatorial powers (seriously)." May 17, 2010. Retrieved from: http://entertainment.blogs.foxnews.com/2010/05/17/woody-allen-president-obama-dictator/#

Chapter Five - The Rule of Land Under President Obama and the Comparison to Fascism

1. Moore, Michael. "Pinch Me... A message from Michael Moore." MichaelMoore.com website. Retrieved from: http://www.michaelmoore.com/words/mikes-letter/pinch-me-a-message-from-michael-moore

Notes

2. Associated Press via *The Boston Globe*, "Prosecutors plan commission case in Cole bombing." November 20, 2009. Retrieved from: http://www.boston.com/news/nation/washington/articles/2009/11/20/prosecutors_plan_commission_case_in_cole_bombing/
3. Karash, Efraim, *The Iran-Iraq War 1980-1988 (Essential Histories)*. (Osprey Publishing, 2002) p. 73
4. Shirer, William, *The Rise and Fall of the Third Reich* (Simon & Schuster, 1st Touchstone Edition, 1990) p. 270
5. Lozowick, Yaacov and Haim Watzman (translator), *Hitler's Bureaucrats: The Nazi Security Police and the Banality of Evil* (Continuum, 2005) p. 180
6. Aued, Blake. "Broun warns of dictatorship." *The Athens Banner-Herald*. September 3, 2009. Retrieved from: http://www.onlineathens.com/stories/090309/new_489061975.shtml
7. Burleigh, p. 207
8. Burleigh, p. 209
9. Stelter, Brian. "Fox's Volley With Obama Intensifying." *The New York Times*. October 11, 2009. Retrieved from: http://www.nytimes.com/2009/10/12/business/media/12fox.html
10. Burleigh, p. 209
11. WhiteHouse.gov Web Site. Retrieved from: http://www.whitehouse.gov/administration/cabinet
12. Newton-Small, Jay. Time Magazine. October 22, 2009. Retrieved from: http://www.time.com/time/politics/article/0,8599,1931626,00.html
13. King Jr., Neil. "Role of White House Czars Sparks Battle." *The Wall Street Journal*. September 11, 2009. Retrieved from: http://online.wsj.com/article/SB125261851127501015.html
14. Beck, Glenn. List of Obama Czar. Glennbeck.com. Retrieved from: http://www.glennbeck.com/content/articles/article/198/29391/
15. Pitts, Edward Lee. "Czarist Rule." Worldmag.com. November 9, 2009. Retrieved from: http://www.worldmag.com/articles/16019
16. Moore, Michael Scott. "Insanity on the Spree." *Spiegel International*. March 20, 2008. Retrieved from:http://www.spiegel.de/international/germany/0,1518,540558,00.html
17. Gilbert, Martin. *Churchill: A Life*, (Holt Paperbacks, 1992) p. 248
18. Kershaw, Ian. *Hitler, 1889-1936*. (W.W. Norton & Co, 2000), p. 363
19. Sheppard, Noel. "SNL Skewers Obama: So Far I've Accomplished Nothing! Nada!" Newsbusters.org website. October 4, 2009. Retrieved from: http://newsbusters.org/blogs/noel-sheppard/2009/10/04/snl-skewers-obama-so-far-ive-done-nothing-president
20. The Huffington Post. "CNN Fact Checks SNL Sketch Detailing Obama's Failures." October 6, 2009. http://www.huffingtonpost.com/2009/10/06/cnn-fact-checks-snl-sketc_n_310841.html
21. Wolf, Richard. "Obama says he's just getting warmed up." *USA Today*. October 29, 2009. Retrieved from: http://www.usatoday.com/news/washington/2009-10-28-obama-promises_N.htm#table

Notes

22. Associated Press via *The Boston Globe*. "Offices Unlikely to offer H1N1 shots." September 17, 2009. Retrieved from: http://www.boston.com/business/healthcare/articles/2009/09/17/offices_unlikely_to_offer_h1n1_shots/
23. White House Blog. Whitehouse.gov. Retrieved from: http://www.whitehouse.gov/blog/change_has_come_to_whitehouse-gov/
24. Harper, Jim. "A Flagging Obama Transparency Effort." Cato @ Library. April 9, 2009. Retrieved from: http://www.cato-at-liberty.org/2009/04/09/a-flagging-obama-transparency-effort/
25. Harper
26. Boot, Max, p. 132

Chapter Six - Forced Fitness and Health Under Fascism

1. Arnold, Peter. 1983, *The Olympic Games: Athens 1896 to Los Angeles 1984* (London: Optimum Books, 1983), p. 66
2. Trimborn, Jürgen, *Leni Riefenstahl: a life*. (New York: Faber & Faber, 2007), p. 132
3. Arnold, p. 71
4. Arnold, p. 72
5. Walters, Guy, *Berlin Games: How the Nazis Stole the Olympic Dream* (New York: Harper Perennial, 207) p.201
6. Schaap, Jeremy, *Triumph: The Untold Story of Jesse Owens and Hitler's Olympics* (New York: Mariner Books, 2007) p. 211
7. Videovat.com. Retrieved from: http://www.videovat.com/videos/17730/Eric-Moussambani-Worst-Olympic-Swimming-Performance-Ever.aspx
8. McCelland, Edward. "Why Chicago Didn't Want the Olympics." Salon.com. Retrieved from: http://www.salon.com/news/feature/2009/10/02/chicago_olympics/index.html
9. McCelland
10. McCelland
11. Rempel, Gerhard, *Hitler's Children: The Hitler Youth and the SS* (University of North Carolina Press, 1990) p. 180
12. Rempel, p. 176
13. Rempel, p. 176
14. The President's Council on Physical Fitness and Sports. http://www.fitness.gov/
15. Mission: Readiness Web Site. http://www.missionreadiness.org/
16. Mission: Readiness website. November 2009 "Ready, Willing and Unable to Serve." Retrieved from: http://cdn.missionreadiness.org/NATEE1109.pdf
17. Center for Science in the Public Interest Web Site. Retrieved from: http://www.cspinet.org/
18. CSPI Web Site. Retrieved from: http://www.cspinet.org/about/index.html
19. ActivistCash.com Web Site. Retrieved from: http://www.activistcash.com/biography.cfm/bid/1284

Notes

20. ActivistCash.com
21. Proctor, Robert N, *The Nazi War on Cancer* (Princeton University Press, 2000) p. 5
22. Staudenmaier, Peter. "Fascist Ecology: The 'Green Wing' of the Nazi Party and its Historical Antecedents." Spunk Library and AK Press Web. Retrieved from: http://www.spunk.org/texts/places/germany/sp001630/peter.html#bib32
23. CSPI Web Site. Retrieved from: http://www.cspinet.org/transfat/index.html
24. "The Bloomberg Diet: The nanny state reaches into the kitchen." *The Wall Street Journal*. December 9, 2006. Retrieved from: http://www.opinionjournal.com/weekend/hottopic/?id=110009366
25. Blume, Elaine. "The truth about trans: hydrogenated oils aren't guilty as charged - trans fats." Nutrition Action Healthletter, March, 1988. Retrieved from: http://findarticles.com/p/articles/mi_m0813/is_n2_v15/ai_6482599/
26. Park, Madison. "Health care reform also touches tanning beds, restaurant menus." CNN.com. March 24, 2010. Retrieved from: http://www.cnn.com/2010/HEALTH/03/23/health.reform.consumer.impact/index.html?hpt=T2
27. Proctor, p 120
28. Proctor, p. 120
29. Greene, Lisa D. The USDA Knows Best: The Food Pyramid. December 2002. Retrieved from: http://iml.jou.ufl.edu/projects/Fall02/Greene/index.htm
30. Greene
31. STATE CIGARETTE EXCISE TAX RATES & RANKINGS. Retrieved from: http://www.tobaccofreekids.org/research/factsheets/pdf/0097.pdf
32. Proctor, p. 18
33. TV Party Web Site. Retrieved from: http://www.tvparty.com/vaultcomcig.html
34. Proctor, p. 176
35. Proctor, p. 177
36. Davis, Derva, *The Secret History of the War on Cancer* (Basic Books, 2009) p. 53
37. Carroll, James R. "Tobacco czar maps new agency's path." Louisville Courier-Journal, November 9, 2009. Retrieved from: http://www.mda.state.md.us/article.php?i=22107
38. Proctor, p. 232

Chapter Seven - Eco-Fascism and the Green Takeover

1. Cox, Bruce. Green Peace Canada website. September 30, 2008. Retrieved from: http://www.greenpeace.org/canada/en/recent/dont-vote-conservative
2. Colarelli, Stephen M. "Conservatives Are Liberal, and Liberals Are Conservative - On the Environment." *The Independent Review*. Summer

Notes

2002. Retrieved from: http://www.independent.org/pdf/tir/tir_07_1_colarelli.pdf

3. RightWingNews.com. "Answering 20 Frequently Asked Questions About Conservatism." Retrieved from: http://www.rightwingnews.com/special/conservafaq.php
4. Biehl, Janet and Peter Staudenmaier, *Ecofascism: Lessons from the German Experience* (AK Press, 2001), p. 6
5. Bruggemeier, Franz-Josef, Mark Cioc and Thomas Zeller (editors), *How Green Were the Nazis?: Nature, Environment and the Nation in the Third Reich* (Ohio University Press, 2005), p. 131
6. Biehl, p. 22
7. Kershaw, Ian. *Hitler: 1936-1945: Nemesis* (W.W. Norton & Co., 2001) Pp. 785-786
8. Geman, Ben. "Gore: Republican leaders in a 'global warming denier posture.'" The Hill. December 9, 2009. Retrieved from: http://thehill.com/blogs/e2-wire/677-e2-wire/71461-gore-republican-leaders-in-a-global-warming-denier-posture
9. Palin, Sarah. "Copenhagen's political science." *The Washington Post*. December 9, 2009. Retrieved from: http://www.washingtonpost.com/wp-dyn/content/article/2009/12/08/AR2009120803402.html
10. Krebs, Michael. "Boxer: Climategate hackers should face criminal prosecution." The Digital Journal Web Site. December 2, 2009. Retrieved from: http://www.digitaljournal.com/article/283102
11. The Daily Telegraph. "Climategate: was Russian secret service behind email hacking plot?" December 6, 2009. Retrieved from: http://www.telegraph.co.uk/earth/copenhagen-climate-change-confe/6746370/Climategate-was-Russian-secret-service-behind-email-hacking-plot.html
12. Schweizer, Peter. "Gore isn't quite as green as he's led the world to believe." *USA Today*. December 7, 2006. Retrieved from: http://www.usatoday.com/news/opinion/editorials/2006-08-09-gore-green_x.htm
13. Gibso, Dave. "Al Gore thinks the Earth is actually hotter than the sun." Virginia Beach Conservative Examiner website. November 22, 2009. Retrieved from: http://www.usatoday.com/news/opinion/editorials/2006-08-09-gore-green_x.htm
14. Ask a Scientist: "Temperature of the Earth's core." Newton BBS Home Page. Retrieved from: http://www.newton.dep.anl.gov/
15. Friedman, Thomas L., *Hot, Flat, and Crowded: Why We Need a Green Revolution* (Farrar, Straus and Giroux 2008) p. 308
16. Green Energy Reporter website. "Who Will Be Regulated Under Cap-and-Trade? (Hint: Not Small- and Medium-Sized Businesses)." October 8, 2009. Retrieved from: http://greenenergyreporter.com/2009/10/who-will-be-regulated-under-cap-and-trade-hint-not-small-and-medium-sized-business/
17. Laffer, Arthur and Wayne Winegarden. "The Adverse Economic Impacts of Cap-and-Trade Regulations." Arduin, Laffer & Moore Econometrics.

Notes

September 2007. Retrieved from: http://www.junkscience.com/Cap_and_Trade_Economic_Analysis_September_2007.pdf
18. EPA.gov Web Site. "Endangerment and Cause or Contribute Findings for Greenhouse Gases under the Clean Air Act." Retrieved from: http://www.epa.gov/climatechange/endangerment.html
19. ITplanet.com. "EPA Issues Endangerment Finding. December 8, 2009. Retrievedf from: http://www.enterpriseitplanet.com/blog/article.php/3851786
20. Strassel, Kimberley A. "The EPA's Carbon Bomb Fizzles" *The Wall Street Journal*. December 11, 2009. Retrieved from: http://online.wsj.com/article/SB10001424052748703514404574588120572016720.html

Chapter Eight - Small Matters, Big Steps: The Fascist Way

1. King, Neil Jr. and Jonathan Weisman. "A President as Micromanager: How Much Detail Is Enough?" *The Wall Street Journal*. August 12, 2009. Retrieved from: http://online.wsj.com/article/SB125003045380123953.html
2. "Obama asks Congress to delay digital TV switch." *The Los Angeles Times*. January 8, 2009. Retrieved from: http://latimesblogs.latimes.com/technology/2009/01/obama-digital-t.html
3. DTVTransition.org Web Site. Retrieved from: http://www.dtvtransition.org/
4. Bray, Hiawatha. "FCC rule requires all new TVs to be digital." *The Boston Globe*. February 26, 2007. Retrieved from: http://www.boston.com/business/technology/articles/2007/02/26/fcc_rule_requires_all_new_tvs_to_be_digital/
5. Press Release: "5.7% of U.S. HOUSEHOLDS – OR 6.5 MILLION HOMES – STILL UNPREPARED FOR THE SWITCH TO DIGITAL TELEVISION." The Nielsen Company. January 22, 2009. Retrieved from: http://blog.nielsen.com/nielsenwire/wp-content/uploads/2009/01/press-release-on-dtv-jan-2009_012209.pdf
6. Puzzanghera, Jim. "Delay in switch to digital TV is delayed" *The Los Angeles Times*. January 29, 2009. Retrieved from http://articles.latimes.com/2009/jan/29/business/fi-dtv29
7. King and Weisman
8. Galbraith, Kate. "Obama Toughens Rules for Some Lighting." *The New York Times*. June 29, 2009. Retrieved from: http://www.nytimes.com/2009/06/30/business/energy-environment/30light.html
9. Energy Star Web Site. Retrieved from: http://www.energystar.gov/index.cfm?c=cfls.pr_cfls_mercury
10. Galbraith
11. Galbraith
12. "The Light Bulb Showdown: LEDs vs. CFLs vs. Incandescent Bulbs - What's the Best Deal Now …And in the Future?" The Simple Dollar Web Site. February 10, 2009. Retrieved from: http://www.thesimpledollar.

Notes

com/2009/02/10/the-light-bulb-showdown-leds-vs-cfls-vs-incandescent-bulbs-whats-the-best-deal-now-and-in-the-future/
13. "After Beers, Professor, Officer Plan to Meet Again." CNN.com. July 31, 2009. Retrieved from: http://www.cnn.com/2009/POLITICS/07/30/harvard.arrest.beers/index.html
14. Halloran, Liz. "Obama Beer Summit Choices Make for a Happy Hour." National Public Radio website. July 30, 2009. Retrieved from: http://www.npr.org/templates/story/story.php?storyId=111373030
15. Tomsho, Robert. "White House 'Beer Summit' Becomes Something of a Brouhaha." *The Wall Street Journal*. July 30, 2009. Retrieved from: http://online.wsj.com/article/SB124891169018991961.html
16. Halloran
17. Smith, Ben. "Obama: Cambridge police acted 'stupidly.'" Politico.com Web Site. Retrieved from: http://www.politico.com/blogs/bensmith/0709/Obama_Cambridge_police_acted_stupidly.html
18. CNN.com. "Air Force One is one 'spiffy ride,' Obama says." February 16, 2009. Retrieved from: http://www.cnn.com/2009/POLITICS/02/13/air.force.one/index.html
19. Meacham, Jon. "A Highly Logical Approach." *Newsweek*. May 16, 2009. Retrieved from: http://www.newsweek.com/id/197891
20. Jaffe, Matthew, Karen Travers and Sunlen Miller. "White House Jobs Summit: Real Progress or PR Stunt?" ABCnews.com. December 3, 2009. Retrieved from: http://abcnews.go.com/Politics/white-house-jobs-summit-real-progress-pr-stunt/story?id=9232219
21. Rowland, Kara. "Critics not invited to White House 'jobs summit.'" *The Washington Times*. December 2, 2009. Retrieved from: http://www.washingtontimes.com/news/2009/dec/02/obama-policy-critics-not-invited-to-jobs-summit/
22. Parnes, Amie. "State Dinner: Big tent politics." Politico Click. November 23, 2009. Retrieved from: http://www.politico.com/click/stories/0911/big_tent_politics.html
23. Superville, Darlene. "Evening gowns, sairs at Obama's first state dinner." Associated Press via Yahoo! News. November 25, 2009. Retrieved from: http://news.yahoo.com/s/ap/20091125/ap_on_go_pr_wh/us_state_dinner
24. Parnes
25. Travers, Karen. "Obamas' First State Dinner -- 'Bigger than the Biggest Wedding.'" ABCNews.com. November 24, 2009. Retrieved from: http://abcnews.go.com/Politics/obamas-state-dinner-dos-donts/story?id=9160318
26. Sullivan, Eileen and Julie Pace. "Gatecrashers' e-mail shows no confirmed invitation." Associated Press via Yahoo! News. December 2, 2009. Retrieved from: http://news.yahoo.com/s/ap/20091202/ap_on_en_ot/us_uninvited_guests
27. Associated Press via Yahoo! News. "Obama says 'system didn't work' at state dinner." December 3, 2009. Retrieved from: Obama says 'system didn't work' at state dinner

Notes

28. USA Today, "Obama expresses '100% trust' in Secret Service - The Oval: Tracking the Obama presidency." December 3, 2009. Retrieved from: http://content.usatoday.com/communities/theoval/post/2009/12/obama-could-not-have-more-confidence-in-secret-service-/1
29. Reuters. "Inquisition begins over state dinner gatecrashing." December 3, 2009. Retrieved from: http://blogs.reuters.com/frontrow/2009/12/03/inquisition-begins-over-state-dinner-gatecrashing/
30. Scherer, Michael. "No Testifying for Obama's Social Secretary." Time Magazine. December 3, 2009. Retrieved from: http://www.time.com/time/politics/article/0,8599,1945192,00.html
31. U.S. Supreme Court, UNITED STATES v. NIXON, 418 U.S. 683 (1974). Retrieved from: http://caselaw.lp.findlaw.com/scripts/getcase.pl?court=US&vol=418&invol=683
32. Schere
33. Reuters, "Inquistion," December 3, 2009
34. Tapper, Jake and Sunlen Miller. "White House Staffers Now Posted at Checkpoints for Social Events." ABCNews.com. December 2, 2009. Retrieved from: http://blogs.abcnews.com/politicalpunch/2009/12/white-house-staffers-now-posted-at-checkpoints-for-social-events.html
35. Messina, Jim. Memorandum to White House Staff. WhiteHouse.gov Web Site. December 2, 2009. Retrieved from: http://www.whitehouse.gov/sites/default/files/091202-messing-state-dinner-review-new-guidelines.pdf
36. Reuters UK. "Gate-crasher 'screw up' won't happen again: Obama." December 13, 2009. Retrieved from: http://uk.reuters.com/article/idUKTRE5BD00N20091214
37. Reuters UK. "Gate-crash," December 13

Chapter Nine - The Business of Fascism

1. *Daily Mail*. "Turmoil at top GM as second boss quits." December 3, 2009. Retrieved from: http://www.dailymail.co.uk/money/article-1232735/Turmoil-General-Motors-second-boss-quits.html
2. Stolberg, Sheryl Gay and Bill Vlasic, "U.S. Lays Down Terms for Auto Bailout." *The New York Times*. March 30, 2009. Retrieved from: http://www.nytimes.com/2009/03/30/business/30auto.html
3. Rodrigues, Eva. "Detroit's CEO in Chief." *The Washington Post*. May 3, 2009. Retrieved from: http://www.washingtonpost.com/wp-dyn/content/article/2009/05/01/AR2009050103395.html
4. Adler, Dennis, *Daimler & Benz: The Complete History: The Birth and Evolution of the Mercedes-Benz* (New York, Harper, 2006) Pp. 23-26
5. Abelshauser, Werner, *The Dynamics of German Industry: Germany's Path Towards the New Economy and the American Challenge* (Berghahn Books, 2005) p. 90
6. Abelshauser, p. 90

Notes

7. Wright, David K., *The Story of Volkswagen Beetles (Class Cars: An Imagination Library Series)* (Gareth Stevens Publishing, 2002) p. 4
8. Abelshauser, p. 90
9. CBSNews.com, "Rattner Resigns as Obama's Car Czar." July 13, 2009. Retrieved from: http://www.cbsnews.com/stories/2009/07/13/politics/main5156491.shtml
10. Rattner, Steve. "The auto bailout: How we did it." *Fortune* via CNN/Money.com. October 21, 2009. Retrieved from: http://money.cnn.com/2009/10/21/autos/auto_bailout_rattner.fortune/
11. Rattner
12. Flint, Jerry. "Is Fiat Helping Chrysler - Or Fiat?" *Forbes*. November 3, 2009. Retrieved from: http://www.forbes.com/2009/11/02/chrysler-fiat-automobiles-jerry-flint-business-autos-backseat.html
13. Tomesco, Frederic. "Bush Urges U.S. to Sell Financial, Carmaker Holdings." *Bloomberg*. October 22, 2009. Retrieved from: http://www.bloomberg.com/apps/news?pid=20601103&sid=arZtukNqWYvA
14. Braithwaite, Tom. "Obama favours Tarp fund for jobs." *The Financial Times*. December 7, 2009. Retrieved from: http://www.ft.com/cms/s/0/e9e54962-e2d0-11de-b028-00144feab49a.html
15. Braithwaite
16. Leonhardt, David. "Stimulus Thinking, and Nuance." *The New York Times*. March 21, 2009. Retrieved from: http://www.nytimes.com/2009/04/01/business/economy/01leonhardt.html
17. Boyes, Roger and Adam LeBor, *Seduced by Hitler: The Choices of a Nation and the Ethics of Survival* (Sourcebooks, Inc., 2004). P. 124
18. Aly, Gotz (translated by Chase, Jefferson), *Hitler's Beneficiaries* (New York, Metropolitan Books, 2005) p. 40
19. Patel, Kiran Klaus, *Soldiers of Labor: Labor Service in Nazi Germany and New Deal America, 1933-1945* (Cambridge University Press, 2005) Front Matter, p. iv
20. Patel, p. 64
21. Reuters. "Possible elements of U.S. jobs package." December 7, 2009, updated December 8, 2009. Retrieved from: http://www.reuters.com/article/idUSN0812504420091208
22. Spielvogel, Jackson J., *Hitler and Nazi Germany: A History (5th Edition)* (Prentice Hall, 2004) p. 96
23. Spielvogel, p. 96

Chapter Ten - Fascism at the Community Level

1. Fisher, Robert, The People Shall Rule: ACORN, Community Organizing, and the Struggle for Economic Justice (Vanderbilt University Press, 2009) Pp. 7-8
2. The Sierra Club Web Site, Washington, D.C. Chapter: Politics and Elections. Retrieved from: http://dc.sierraclub.org/politics/

Notes

3. ACORN Web Site: Who is ACORN. Retrieved from: http://www.acorn.org/index.php?id=12342
4. ACORN Web Site: "ACORN, Trom The Ground Up." Retrieved from: http://www.acorn.org/index.php?id=2707
5. Goldberg. *Liberal Fascism*
6. Strom, Stephanie. "Funds Misappropriated at 2 Nonprofit Groups." *The New York Times*, July 9, 2008. Retrieved from: http://www.nytimes.com/2008/07/09/us/09embezzle.html
7. Associated Press via *The New York Times*. "Acorn Offices in New Orleans Are Raided." November 6, 2009. Retrieved from: http://www.nytimes.com/2009/11/07/us/07acorn.html
8. Ibid. Associated Press
9. Stephanopoulos, George. George's Bottom Line: "Obama on ACORN: 'Not Something I've Followed Closely' Won't Commit to Cut Federal Funds." ABCNews.com, September 20, 2009. Retrieved from: http://blogs.abcnews.com/george/2009/09/obama-on-acorn-not-something-ive-followed-closely.html
10. Ibid. Stephanopoulos
11. Garofoli, Joe. "California's ACORN branch splits from group." *San Francisco Chronicle* via SFGate.com, January 14, 2010. Retrieved from: http://articles.sfgate.com/2010-01-14/news/17828120_1_acorn-workers-association-of-community-organizations-voter-registration
12. Jones, Brent, "ACORN's Maryland chapter is shuttered." *The Baltimore Sun*, March 16, 2010. Retrieved from: http://articles.baltimoresun.com/2010-03-16/news/bal-md.acorn16mar16_1_acorn-affiliates-videos-national-scandal
13. Sullivan, Erin, "ACORN Housing Becomes Affordable Housing Centers of America." *City Paper*. March 23, 2010. Retrieved from: http://blogs.citypaper.com/index.php/2010/03/acorn-housing-becomes-affordable-housing-centers-of-america/
14. Bendersky, Joseph W., *A History of Nazi Germany: 1919-45* (Rowman & Littlefield Publishers, Inc., 2000) p. 109
15. Gregory, Mike, "The real Nancy Pelosi - multi-millionaire, resort, dining and winery baroness who profits from non-union and illegal labor." Citizen Journalism Today. January 28, 2009. Retrieved from: http://sadbastards.wordpress.com/2009/01/28/the-real-nancy-pelosi-multi-millionaire-non-union-resort-baroness/
16. Holland, Jesse J. "Mine Workers union endorses Obama for president." AP News via FoxNews.com, May 21, 2009. Retrieved from: http://www.foxnews.com/wires/2008May21/0,4670,ObamaUnions,00.html
17. Conroy, Scott. "Palin Unleashes New Attack Against Obama on Coal." CBSNews.com, November 2, 2009. Retrieved from: http://www.cbsnews.com/blogs/2008/11/02/politics/fromtheroad/entry4564043.shtml

Notes

18. Whitesides, John and Donna Smith. "U.S. Democrats reach deal on 'Cadillac' health tax." Reuters, January 14, 2010. Retrieved from: http://www.reuters.com/article/idUSN1419227420100114
19. Haynes, V. Dion. "U.S. unemployment rate for blacks projected to hit 25-year high." The Washington Post, January 15, 2010. Retrieved from: http://www.washingtonpost.com/wp-dyn/content/article/2010/01/14/AR2010011404085.html
20. Moberg, David. "Obama's Community Roots." The Nation, April 3, 2007. Retrieved from: http://www.thenation.com/doc/20070416/moberg
21. York, Byron. "Obama can't be community organizer for the world." The Washington Examiner, November 3, 2009. Retrieved from: http://www.washingtonexaminer.com/politics/Obama-can_t-be-community-organizer-for-the-world-8474690-68743857.html
22. Greenfield, Jeff. "Obama's Decline in Popularity: What Caused It?" CBSNews.com, January 19, 2010. Retrieved from: http://www.cbsnews.com/blogs/2010/01/18/politics/politicalhotsheet/entry6112366.shtml?tag=cbsnewsLeadStoriesAreaMain;cbsnewsLeadStoriesHeadlines

Chapter Eleven - The Enemy Within

1. Paxton. *The Anatomy of Fascism*, p. 36
2. Wolf, Naomi. " Fascist America, In 10 Easy Steps." April 27, 2007. Retrieved from: http://www.ejfi.org/Civilization/Civilization-14.htm
3. Perez, Evan. "Obama's Detention Plans Face Scrutiny." *The Wall Street Journal*. May 22, 2009. Retrieved from: http://online.wsj.com/article/SB124302633236948169.html
4. Sheppard, Noel. "Martha Stewart Says Sarah Palin 'Dangerous Person.'" Newsbusters.org. November 21, 2009. Retrieved from: http://newsbusters.org/blogs/noel-sheppard/2009/11/21/martha-stewart-says-sarah-palin-dangerous-person
5. WorldNetDaily. "Homeland Security on guard for 'ring-wing extremists.'" April 12, 2009. Retrieved from: http://www.wnd.com/index.php?fa=PAGE.view&pageId=94803
6. Federal of American Scientists Web Site: Department of Homeland Security "Rightwing Extremism: Current Economic and Political Climate Fueling Resurgence in Radicalization and Recruitment." Retrieved from: http://www.fas.org/irp/eprint/rightwing.pdf
7. Cooper, Anderson. "Militia's making a comeback." CNN.com. June 5, 2009. Retrieved from: http://ac360.blogs.cnn.com/2009/06/05/militia-making-a-comeback/
8. "SPLC Report: Return of the Militias." Southern Poverty Law Center Web Site. August 8, 2009. Retrieved from: http://www.splcenter.org/news/item.jsp?aid=392
9. SPLC

Notes

10. IMDB.com: V for Vendetta (2005). Retrieved from: http://www.imdb.com/title/tt0434409/
11. Sheppard, Noel. "Video Shows Media Hypocrisy Concerning Right-wing Hate Speech." Newsbusters.org. March 31, 2010. Retrieved from: http://newsbusters.org/blogs/noel-sheppard/2010/03/31/video-highlights-media-hypocrisy-concerning-rightwing-hate-speech
12. Lewis, Matt. "Chris Matthews' Documentary 'Rise of the New Right': A Curveball From the Left." Politics Daily, June 16, 2010. Retrieved from: http://www.politicsdaily.com/2010/06/16/chris-matthews-documentary-rise-of-the-new-right-a-curveball/
13. "REMARKS BY THE PRESIDENT ON A NEW BEGINNING." The White House Office of the Press Secretary. WhiteHouse.gov. June 4, 2009. Retrieved from: http://www.whitehouse.gov/the_press_office/Remarks-by-the-President-at-Cairo-University-6-04-09/
14. Valhos, Kelley. "House Passes Volunteerism Bill Critics Call Pricey, Forced Service." FoxNews.com. March 18, 2009. Retrieved from: http://www.foxnews.com/politics/2009/03/18/house-passes-volunteerism-critics-pricey-forced-service/
15. Serve.org Web Site. Retrieved from: http://www.serve.gov/
16. Harnden, Toby. "Barack Obama faces 30 death threats a day, stretching US Secret Service." *The Daily Telegraph*. August 3, 2009. Retrieved from: http://www.telegraph.co.uk/news/worldnews/northamerica/usa/barackobama/5967942/Barack-Obama-faces-30-death-threats-a-day-stretching-US-Secret-Service.html
17. Bender, Bryan. "Secret Service strained as leaders face more threats." *The Boston Globe*. October 18, 2009. Retrieved from: http://www.boston.com/news/nation/washington/articles/2009/10/18/secret_service_under_strain_as_leaders_face_more_threats/
18. Ham, Katharine Mary. " Secret Service Director: Threats Against Obama Not Up Over Other Presidents." Blog post for *The Weekly Standard*. December 3, 2009. Retrieved from: http://www.weeklystandard.com/weblogs/TWSFP/2009/12/secret_service_director_threat.asp
19. United States Secret Service Web Site. Retrieved from: http://www.secretservice.gov/faq.shtml#faq1
20. Coleman, Jack. "Post-Party Crashers, Ed Schulz Wants Secret Service to 'Pledge Allegiance' to Obama." Newsbusters.org. December 5, 2009. Retrieved from: http://newsbusters.org/blogs/jack-coleman/2009/12/05/post-party-crashers-ed-schultz-wants-secret-service-pledge-allegiance-
21. Jennings, Brian, *Censorship: The Threat to Silence Talk Radio* (Threshold Editions, 2009) p. 17
22. Almond, Steve. "Who's afraid of the big, bad Fairness Doctrine?" *The Boston Globe*. November 9, 2009.
23. *The Boston Globe*. "Obama for president." October 13, 2008. Retrieved from: http://www.boston.com/bostonglobe/editorial_opinion/editorials/articles/2008/10/13/obama_for_president/

Notes

24. Air America Web Site. Retrieved from: http://airamerica.com/about/
25. Jennings, p. 110
26. Krattenmaker, Thomas G., and Lucas A. Powe, *Regulating Broadcast Programming* (MIT Press, 1994) p. 275
27. Saul, Michael. "Glenn Beck is scarier than Rush Limbaugh, Sean Hannity, says Anti-Defamation League." *The New York Daily News*. November 17, 2009. Retrieved from: http://www.nydailynews.com/news/politics/2009/11/17/2009-11-17_glenn_beck_is_scarier_than_rush_limbaugh_sean_hannity_says_antidefamation_league.html
28. Gerstein, Josh. "NPR vs. Fox." Politico.com. December 7, 2009. Retrieved from: http://www.politico.com/blogs/bensmith/1209/NPR_vs_Fox.html
29. Poor, Jeff. "Obama Blasts Fox News: 'I've Got One Television Station that is Entirely Devoted to Attacking My Administration.'" Business & Media Institute. June 16, 2009. Retrieved from: http://www.businessandmedia.org/articles/2009/20090616181219.aspx
30. Stein, Sam. "Anita Dunn: Fox News An Outlet For GOP Propaganda." The Huffington Post Web Site. October 11, 2009. Retrieved from: http://www.huffingtonpost.com/2009/10/11/anita-dunn-fox-news-an-ou_n_316691.html
31. Nicholas, Peter. "White House communications chief Anita Dunn resigns." *The Los Angeles Times*. November 11, 2009. Retrieved from: http://www.latimes.com/news/nationworld/nation/la-na-dunn11-2009nov11,0,2907854.story
32. *Newsweek*. "The D.C. Powers." January 5, 2009, published online December 20, 2008. Retrieved from: http://www.newsweek.com/id/176312
33. Nordlinger, Jay. "Rise of an Epithet." The National Review. December 7, 2009. Retrieved from: http://nrd.nationalreview.com/article/?q=Mjk1YmRjNzIxNmUwMTI0ZWYxZWU4OWU2MzFiOWJmNDE=
34. Sheppard, Noel. "Garofalo: Tea Party Goers Are Racists Who Hate Black President." Newsbusters.org. April 16, 2009. Retrieved from: http://newsbusters.org/blogs/noel-sheppard/2009/04/16/garofalo-tea-partiers-are-all-racists-who-hate-black-president
35. Spillius, Alex. "Black Democrats: criticism of Barack Obama is rooted in racism." *The Daily Telegraph*. September 15, 2009. Retrieved from: http://www.telegraph.co.uk/news/worldnews/northamerica/usa/barackobama/6194980/Black-Democrats-criticism-of-Barack-Obama-is-rooted-in-racism.html
36. Franke-Ruta, Garance and Sarah Loveheim. "Frank Blasts Nazi Comparisons From LaRouche Backers." *The Washington Post*. August 8, 2009. Retrieved from: http://voices.washingtonpost.com/capitol-briefing/2009/08/town_hall_talk_frank_grills_op.html

Chapter Twelve - The External Enemy

1. Fodor, Denis J., *The Neutrals: World War II* (Time-Life Books, 1982), p.78
2. Ibid, p. 79

Notes

3. Ibid, Pp. 83-84
4. Fremont-Barnes, Gregory, *Essential Histories: The Anglo-Afghan Wars: 1839-1919* (Osprey Publishing, 2009) p. 8
5. Morgan, David S. "Gibbs on Afghanistan: Not Nation-Building." CBSNews.com, December 1, 2009. Retrieved from: http://www.cbsnews.com/blogs/2009/12/01/politics/politicalhotsheet/entry5848072.shtml
6. Crile, George, *Charlie Wilson's War: The Extraordinary Story of How the Wildest Man in Congress and a Rogue CIA Agent Changed the History of Our Times* (Grove Press, 2007) Pp. 521-522
7. Ibid. Crile, p. 522
8. MSNBC.com. "Full text of Obama's Nobel Peace Prize Speech." December 10, 2009. Retrieved from: http://www.msnbc.msn.com/id/34360743/ns/politics-white_house/
9. Yergin, Daniel, *The Prize: The Epic Quest for Oil, Money & Power* (Free Press, 2008) p. 323
10. Sappenfield, Mark. "Obama's Afghanistan timeline adheres to McChyrstal assessment." *The Christian Science Monitor.* December 2, 2009. Retrieved from: http://www.csmonitor.com/USA/Foreign-Policy/2009/1202/p02s04-usfp.html
11. Moore, Michael. "An Open Letter to President Obama from Michael Moore." MichaelMoore.com, November 20, 2009. Retrieved from: http://www.michaelmoore.com/words/mikes-letter/open-letter-president-obama-michael-moore
12. FoxNews.com. "Clinton Demands Unrestricted 'Net Access." January 21, 2010. Retrieved from: http://www.foxnews.com/scitech/2010/01/21/clinton-address-internet-freedom-security/?utm_source=feedburner&utm_medium=feed&utm_campaign=Feed%253A+foxnews%252Fscitech+%2528Text+-+SciTech%2529
13. Farwell, Byron, *Queen Victoria's Little Wars* (W.W. Norton & Company, 1972) p. 13
14. Hanes, W. Travis III, & Frank Sanello, *Opium Wars: The Addiction of One Empire and the Corruption of Another* (Sourcebooks Inc., 2002) p. 295
15. Bodin, Lynn E., *The Boxer Rebellion: Men-At-Arms Series* (Osprey Publishing, 1979) p. 4

Chapter Thirteen - Islamic Fascism

1. Margolis, Eric, "The Big Lie About 'Islamic Fascism." August 26, 2006. LewRockwell.com. Retrieved from: http://www.lewrockwell.com/margolis/margolis46.html
2. Furnish, Timothy. "'Islamic Fascism': Well, It's Half Right." August 14, 2006. History News Network. Retrieved from: http://hnn.us/articles/29162.html
3. Margolis
4. "REMARKS BY THE PRESIDENT ON A NEW BEGINNING."

Notes

5. Esposito, John L., *The Oxford History of Islam* (New York, Oxford University Press, USA, 2000) Pp. 7-8
6. Nicolle, David, *The Great Islamic Conquests AD 632-750 (Essentials Histories)* (New York, Osprey, 2009) p. 7
7. Nicolle, p. 8
8. Krawczyk, Wade. *German Army Uniforms of World War II* (Crowood, 2002) p. 20
9. Whitman-Bradley, Buff, "War on Terrorism Takes New Turn." San Francisco Bay Area Independent Media Center website. June 15, 2006. Retrieved from: http://www.indybay.org/newsitems/2006/06/15/18280842.php
10. *The Guardian*. "Full text: bin Laden's 'letter to America'." November 24, 2002. Retrieved from: http://www.guardian.co.uk/world/2002/nov/24/theobserver
11. *The Guardian*.
12. Pipes, Daniel, *Militant Islam Reaches America* (W.W. Norton & Company, 2002), Pp. 117-118
13. BBC News/Americas. "Obama speech: An analysis." June 4, 2009. Retrieved from: http://news.bbc.co.uk/2/low/americas/8082862.stm
14. Alexiev, Alex. "Obama's Fantasy Islam." National Review Online. June 11, 2009. Retrieved from: http://article.nationalreview.com/?q=YWUwODZjNjhkNDJhNjE5YzllOTZkZjZiZjdlZjZkZjI=
15. Steves, Rick. "Lash a Flute to a Goatskin and Squeeze out some Greece." Rick Steve's Europe Web Site. September 22, 2007. Retrieved from: http://www.ricksteves.com/blog/index.cfm?fuseaction=entry&entryID=160
16. Quataert, Donald, *The Ottoman Empire, 1700-1922* (Cambridge University Press; 2 edition, 2005) p. 76
17. Alexiev
18. Furnish
19. Furnish
20. Matter, Philip, *The Mufti of Jerusalem* (New York, Columbia University Press, Revised Edition, 1988) p. 100
21. Matter, p. 100
22. Karsh, Efraim, *The Arab-Israeli Conflict: The Palestine War 1948 (Essential Histories)* (New York, Osprey Publishing, 2002) Pp. 7-12
23. Lavy, George, *Germany and Israel: Moral Debt and National Interest* (Routledge, 1996) p. 143
24. Lewis, Rand, *The Neo-Nazis and German Unification* (Praeger, 1996) p. 15
25. Lewis, p. 91
26. Hall, Macer. "David Cameron: Brown soft on Muslim fanatics." November 26, 2009. Retrieved from: http://www.express.co.uk/posts/view/142496/David-Cameron-Brown-soft-on-Muslim-fanatics
27. Hall
28. Green, Dominic, *Three Empires on the Nile: The Victorian Jihad, 1869-1899* (New York, Free Press, 2007) Pp. 84-85

Notes

29. Green, p. 114
30. Green, p. 114
31. Associated Press via MSNBC.com. "Model to be Caned for Drinking Beer in Malaysia." August 19, 2009. Retrieved from: http://www.msnbc.msn.com/id/32471704/ns/world_news-asiapacific/
32. Ng, Eileen. "Malaysian state ruler commutes caning sentence for beer-drinking Muslim woman." The Associated Press via The Washington Examiner. April 1, 2010. Retrieved from http://www.washingtonexaminer.com/world/malaysian-state-ruler-commutes-caning-sentence-on-beer-drinking-muslim-woman-89659577.html
33. Ibid
34. Ibid
35. Ibid
36. Paul, Katie. "What Bibi's 'They Hate us for Our Freedom' Moment at AIPAC Means for the Obama Meeting." *Newsweek*. March 23, 2010. Retrieved from http://www.newsweek.com/blogs/the-gaggle/2010/03/23/what-bibi-s-quot-they-hate-us-for-our-freedom-quot-moment-at-aipac-means-for-the-obama-meeting.html
37. FoxNews.com. "Counterterror Adviser Defendes Jihad as 'Legitimate Tenet of Islam." May 27, 2010. Retrieved from http://www.foxnews.com/politics/2010/05/27/counterterror-adviser-defends-jihad-legitimate-tenet-islam/?test=latestnews
38. Ibid
39. CRS Report for Congress. "Al Qaeda: Statements and Evolving Ideology." February 4, 2005. Retrieved from http://www.fas.org/irp/crs/RL32759.pdf

Chapter Fourteen - The Road Ahead

1. Rotella, Sebastian and Christi Parson. "Obama assails intelligence failures in Christmas incident." *The Los Angeles Times*, January 6, 2010. Retrieved from: http://articles.latimes.com/2010/jan/06/nation/la-na-obama-terror6-2010jan06
2. Hosenball, Mark. "Exclusive: Obama Got Pre-Christmas Intelligence Briefing About Terror Threats to 'Homeland.'" *Newsweek*, January 1, 2010. Retrieved from: http://blog.newsweek.com/blogs/declassified/archive/2010/01/01/exclusive-obama-got-pre-christmas-intelligence-briefing-about-terror-threats-to-homeland.aspx
3. Acosta, Jim and Ed Henry, "Obama faces growing to-do list in 2010." CNN.com, January 4, 2010. Retrieved from: http://www.cnn.com/2010/POLITICS/01/04/obama.returns/index.html
4. Krugman, Paul. "What Didn't Happen." The New York Times, January 17, 2009. Retrieved from: http://www.nytimes.com/2010/01/18/opinion/18krugman.html?hp
5. Goldman, Julianna and Ryan J. Donmoyer, "Obama Bank-Fee Plan May Tap Voter Anger Over Bailouts, Bonuses." *BusinessWeek*, January 13, 2010.

Notes

Retrieved from: http://www.businessweek.com/news/2010-01-13/obama-bank-fee-plan-may-tap-voter-anger-over-bailouts-bonuses.html
6. Kuhnhenn, Jim. "Obama tells banks: 'We want our money back.'" Associated Press via Yahoo News, January 14, 2010. Retrieved at: http://news.yahoo.com/s/ap/20100114/ap_on_bi_ge/us_obama_bank_fees
7. Krauthammer, Charles. Transcript from *Special Report with Bret Baier*, January 15, 2010. Retrieved from: http://www.foxnews.com/story/0,2933,583157,00.html
8. Krauthammer
9. Williams, Juan. Transcript from *Special Report with Bret Baier*, January 15, 2010. Retrieved from: http://www.foxnews.com/story/0,2933,583157,00.html
10. Travers, Karen. "President Obama: Federal Government 'Will Go Bankrupt' if Health Care Costs Are Not Reined In." ABC World News: The World Newer Daily Blog. December 16, 2009. Retrieved from: http://blogs.abcnews.com/theworldnewser/2009/12/president-obama-federal-government-will-go-bankrupt-if-health-care-costs-are-not-reigned-in.html
11. The Cap Times. "Closed-door talks on health reform are unhealthy," January 16, 2010. Retrieved from: http://host.madison.com/ct/news/opinion/editorial/article_b3df9402-828f-55e6-a073-01fc3e95e24e.html
12. Krauthammer, Charles, "One year out: President Obama's fall." *The Washington Post*, January 15, 2010. Retrieved from: http://www.washingtonpost.com/wp-dyn/content/article/2010/01/14/AR2010011403558.html
13. Ibid, "One year out."
14. Hurt, Charles. "Pelosi's climate air fare." *The New York Post*, December 17, 2009. Retrieved from: http://www.nypost.com/p/news/national/pelosi_climate_air_farce_Ffs6YfkXfxX3eTFJigpEaP
15. Attkisson, Sharyl. "Copenhagen Summit Turned Junket." CBS News, January 11, 2010. Retrieved from: http://www.cbsnews.com/stories/2010/01/11/cbsnews_investigates/main6084364.shtml
16. Malik Naureen. "Soros Says Copenhagen Climate Summit Was A Failure." NASDAQ.com, January 15, 2010. Retrieved from: http://www.nasdaq.com/aspx/stock-market-news-story.aspx?storyid=201001141826dowjonesdjonline000708&title=soros-says-copenhagen-climate-summit-was-a-failure
17. Elliot, Philip. "Reid apologizes for 'no Negro dialect' comment," Associated Press via Yahoo News, January 9, 2010. Retrieved from: http://news.yahoo.com/s/ap/20100109/ap_on_el_se/us_obama_reid
18. Pergram, Chad. "The Road Ahead." FoxNews.com: The Speaker's Lobby, January 11, 2010. Retrieved from: http://congress.blogs.foxnews.com/2010/01/11/the-road-ahead/
19. Golen, Jimmy. "Limbaugh already down 1 vote in bid to buy Rams." Associated Press via Yahoo News, October 13, 2009. Retrieved from: http://sports.yahoo.com/nfl/news?slug=ap-nfl-limbaugh&prov=ap&type=lgns

Notes

20. Bell, Shannon. "Al Sharpton Rush Limbaugh NFL Controversy: Not Really A Controversy." RightPundits.com, October 13, 2009. Retrieved from: http://www.rightpundits.com/?p=4872
21. Thai, Xuan and Ted Barrett. "Biden's description of Obama draws scrutiny." CNN.com, February 9, 2007. Retrieved from: http://www.cnn.com/2007/POLITICS/01/31/biden.obama/
22. Zeleny, Jeff and Ben Werschkul. "Video: Ten Minutes with Dan Pfeiffer." *The New York Times*, The Politics and Government Blog of the Times, January 18, 2010. Retrieved from: http://thecaucus.blogs.nytimes.com/2010/01/18/video-ten-minutes-with-dan-pfeiffer/
23. Najacht, Norma. "We have a republic if we can keep it." *Custer County Chronicle Online,* September 30, 2009. Retrieved from: http://www.custercountynews.com/cms/news/story-49668.html

Bibliography

"11 Companies that Surprisingly Collaborated With the Nazis." 11 Points Web Site.

Abelshauser, Werner, *The Dynamics of German Industry: Germany's Path Towards the New Economy and the American Challenge* (Berghahn Books, 2005)

ACORN Web Site

Acosta, Jim and Ed Henry, "Obama faces growing to-do list in 2010." CNN.com, January 4, 2010 ActivistCash.com

Adam, Thomas, *Germany and the Americas: Culture, Politics, and History (Transatlantic Relations)* (ABC-CLICO, 2005)

Adler, Dennis, *Daimler & Benz: The Complete History: The Birth and Evolution of the Mercedes-Benz* (New York, Harper, 2006)

Air America Web Site

Alexiev, Alex. "Obama's Fantasy Islam." *National Review Online*. June 11, 2009

Algeo, Matthew, *Last Team Standing: How the Pittsburgh Steelers and Philadelphia Eagles - The "Steagles" - Saved Pro Football During World War II* (Da Capo Press, 2007)

Almond, Steve. "Who's afraid of the big, bad Fairness Doctrine?" *The Boston Globe*. November 9, 2009

Aly, Gotz (translated by Chase, Jefferson), *Hitler's Beneficiaries* (New York, Metropolitan Books, 2005)

Arnold, Peter. 1983, *The Olympic Games: Athens 1896 to Los Angeles 1984* (London: Optimum Books, 1983)

Ask a Scientist: "Temperature of the Earth's core." Newton BBS Home Page

Associated Press via MSNBC.com. "Model to be Caned for Drinking Beer in Malaysia." August 19, 2009

Associated Press via *The Boston Globe*. "Offices Unlikely to offer H1N1 shots." September 17, 2009

Associated Press via *The Boston Globe*, "Prosecutors plan commission case in Cole bombing." November 20, 2009

Associated Press via *The New York Times*. "Acorn Offices in New Orleans Are Raided." November 6, 2009

Associated Press via Yahoo! News. "Obama says 'system didn't work' at state dinner." December 3, 2009

Attkisson, Sharyl. "Copenhagen Summit Turned Junket." CBS News, January 11, 2010 Aued, Blake. "Broun warns of dictatorship." *The Athens Banner-Herald*. September 3, 2009

Axworthy, Mark. *Third Axis Fourth Ally: Romanian Armed Forces in the European War, 1941-1945*. (London, Wellington House, 1995)

BBC News/Americas. "Obama speech: An analysis." June 4, 2009

Beck, Glenn. List of Obama Czar. Glennbeck.com. August 21, 2009

Beekman, Scott, *William Dudley Pelley: A Life in Right-Wing Extremism And the Occult* (Syracuse, New York, USA: Syracuse University Press, 2005)

Bell, Shannon. "Al Sharpton Rush Limbaugh NFL Controversy: Not Really A Controversy." RightPundits.com, October 13, 2009

Bibliography

Bender, Bryan. "Secret Service strained as leaders face more threats." *The Boston Globe*. October 18, 2009

Bendersky, Joseph W., *A History of Nazi Germany: 1919-45* (Rowman & Littlefield Publishers, Inc., 2000) Biehl, Janet and Peter Staudenmaier, *Ecofascism: Lessons from the German Experience* (AK Press, 2001)

Biographiq (Editors). *Herbert Hoover - President of the Great Depression* (Biogrphiq, 2008)

Blume, Elaine. "The truth about trans: hydrogenated oils aren't guilty as charged - trans fats." Nutrition Action Healthletter, March, 1988

Boaz, David, "Hitler, Mussolini, Roosevelt" Reason, October 2007 via The Cato Institute Web Site.

Bodin, Lynn E., *The Boxer Rebellion: Men-At-Arms Series* (Osprey Publishing, 1979)

Boot, Max, *The Savage Wars of Peace: Small Wars and the Rise of American Power* (Basic Books, 2002)

Boston Globe, The. "Obama for president." October 13, 2008

Bosworth, R.J.B, *Mussolini's Italy: Life Under the Fascist Dictatorship, 1915-1945* (New York, Penguin, 2007)

Boyes, Roger and Adam LeBor, *Seduced by Hitler: The Choices of a Nation and the Ethics of Survival* (Sourcebooks, Inc., 2004)

Braithwaite, Tom. "Obama favours Tarp fund for jobs." *The Financial Times*. December 7, 2009

Brands, H.W., *Traitor to His Class: The Privileged Life and Radical Presidency of Franklin Delano Roosevelt* (Anchor, 2009)

Bray, Hiawatha. "FCC rule requires all new TVs to be digital." *The Boston Globe*. February 26, 2007

Brennan, James P. *Peronism and Argentina* (Wilmington, SR Books, 1998)

Bruggemeier, Franz-Josef, Mark Cioc and Thomas Zeller (editors), *How Green Were the Nazis?: Nature, Environment and the Nation in the Third Reich* (Ohio University Press, 2005)

Burleigh, Michael, *The Third Reich: A New History* (New York, USA: Hill and Wang, 2000)

Cap Times, The. "Closed-door talks on health reform are unhealthy," January 16, 2010

Carroll, James R. "Tobacco czar maps new agency's path." Louisville Courier-Journal, November 9

Cary, Lee. "Does the Supreme Court Still Sit." American Thinker Web Site. October 27, 2009

Cashill, Jack, "Who Wrote *Audacity* of Hope?" *American Thinker*. July 12, 2009

CBSNews.com, "Rattner Resigns as Obama's Car Czar." July 13, 2009

Center for Science in the Public Interest Web Site

Clements, Kendrick A., *The Presidency of Woodrow Wilson* (University of Kansas, 1992)

CNN.com. "Air Force One is one 'spiffy ride,' Obama says." February 16, 2009

CNN.com. "After Beers, Professor, Officer Plan to Meet Again." July 31, 2009

Bibliography

Colarelli, Stephen M. "Conservatives Are Liberal, and Liberals Are Conservative - On the Environment." *The Independent Review*. Summer 2002

Coleman, Jack. "Post-Party Crashers, Ed Schulz Wants Secret Service to 'Pledge Allegiance' to Obama." Newsbusters.org. December 5, 2009

Conroy, Scott. "Palin Unleashes New Attack Against Obama on Coal." CBSNews.com, November 2, 2009

Cooper, Anderson. "Militia's making a comeback." CNN.com. June 5, 2009

Corsi, Jerome, *The Obama Nation* (New York, Threshold Editions, 2008)

Cox, Bruce. Green Peace Canada website. September 30, 2008

Crespino, Joseph, *In search of another country: Mississippi and the conservative counterrevolution* (Princeton University Press, 2009)

Crile, George, *Charlie Wilson's War: The Extraordinary Story of How the Wildest Man in Congress and a Rogue CIA Agent Changed the History of Our Times* (Grove Press, 2007)

Curtis, Bryan. "D.W. Griffith in Black and White: Was the Birth of a Nation Director Really a Racist?" Salon.com, January 3, 2003

Daily Mail. "Turmoil at top GM as second boss quits." December 3, 2009

Daily Telegraph, The, "Climategate: was Russian secret service behind email hacking plot?" December 6, 2009

Davis, Derva, *The Secret History of the War on Cancer* (Basic Books, 2009)

Denk, Horst G.; Kenneth Rush, "The German-American Tricentennial: Three Hundred Years of German Immigration to America, 1683 - 1983; Final Report of the Presidential Commission for the German-American Tricentennial to the President and Congress of the United States". Presidential Commission for the German-American Tricentennial (1983).

Dubofsky, Melvyn, *We Shall Be All: A History of the Industrial Workers of the World* (abridged edition) (Working Class in American History). (Abridged Edition, University of Illinois Press, 2000)

Elliot, Philip. "Reid apologizes for 'no Negro dialect' comment," Associated Press via Yahoo News, January 9, 2010

Esposito, John L., *The Oxford History of Islam* (New York, Oxford University Press, USA, 2000) Pp. 7-8

FactCheck.org Web Site. "How many times did Obama vote 'present' as a state senator?" September 25, 2008.

Farwell, Byron, *Queen Victoria's Little Wars* (W.W. Norton & Company, 1972)

Federation of American Scientists Web Site: Department of Homeland Security "Rightwing Extremism: Current Economic and Political Climate Fueling Resurgence in Radicalization and Recruitment." April 7, 2009.

Fest, Joachim C, *Hitler* (Mariner Books, 2002)

Fisher, Robert, *The People Shall Rule: ACORN, Community Organizing, and the Struggle for Economic Justice* (Vanderbilt University Press, 2009)

Flint, Jerry. "Is Fiat Helping Chrysler - Or Fiat?" *Forbes*. November 3, 2009

Fodor, Denis J., *The Neutrals: World War II* (Time-Life Books, 1982)

FoxNews.com. "Clinton Demands Unrestricted 'Net Access." January 21, 2010

Bibliography

FoxNews.com. "Counterterror Adviser Defendes Jihad as 'Legitimate Tenet of Islam." May 27, 2010

FoxNews.com. "Woody Allen says President Obama should be granted dictatorial powers (seriously)." May 17, 2010.

Franke-Ruta, Garance and Sarah Loveheim. "Frank Blasts Nazi Comparisons From LaRouche Backers." *The Washington Post*. August 8, 2009

Fremont-Barnes, Gregory, *Essential Histories: The Anglo-Afghan Wars: 1839-1919* (Osprey Publishing, 2009)

Friedman, Thomas L., *Hot, Flat, and Crowded: Why We Need a Green Revolution* (Farrar, Straus and Giroux 2008)

Friedrich, Otto, Hays Gorey and Ruth Mehrtens Galvin, "F.D.R.'s Disputed Legacy." *Time Magazine*. February 1, 1982.

Furnish, Timothy. "'Islamic Fascism': Well, It's Half Right." August 14, 2006. History News Network

Gage, Beverly, *The Day Wall Street Exploded: A Story of America in its First Age of Terror.* (Oxford University Press, 2009)

Galbraith, Kate. "Obama Toughens Rules for Some Lighting." *The New York Times*. June 29, 2009

Gallagher, Tom, *Portugal A Twentieth-Century Interpretation* (Manchester University Press, 1983)

Garofoli, Joe. "California's ACORN branch splits from group." *San Francisco Chronicle* via SFGate.com, January 14, 2010

Geman, Ben. "Gore: Republican leaders in a 'global warming denier posture.'" The Hill. December 9, 2009

Gerstein, Josh. "NPR vs. Fox." Politico.com. December 7, 2009

Gibson, Dave. "Al Gore thinks the Earth is actually hotter than the sun." Virginia Beach Conservative Examiner website. November 22, 2009

Gilbert, Martin. *Churchill: A Life*, (Holt Paperbacks, 1992)

Goldberg, Jonah. *Liberal Fascism* (New York, Random House, Inc., 2008)

Golen, Jimmy. "Limbaugh already down 1 vote in bid to buy Rams." Associated Press via Yahoo News, October 13, 2009

Goldman, Julianna and Ryan J. Donmoyer, "Obama Bank-Fee Plan May Tap Voter Anger Over Bailouts, Bonuses." *BusinessWeek*, January 13, 2010

Green, Dominic, *Three Empires on the Nile: The Victorian Jihad, 1869-1899* (New York, Free Press, 2007)

Green Energy Reporter website. "Who Will Be Regulated Under Cap-and-Trade? (Hint: Not Small- and Medium-Sized Businesses)." October 8, 2009

Greene, Lisa D, "The USDA Knows Best: The Food Pyramid." December 2002, http://iml.jou.ufl.edu

Greenfield, Jeff. "Obama's Decline in Popularity: What Caused It?" CBSNews.com, January 19, 2010

Greenspan, Alan, *The Age of Turbulence: Adventures in a New World* (New York, Penguin, 2008)

Gregor, Neil, *Nazism* (New York, USA: Oxford University Press, 2000)

Bibliography

Gregory, Mike, "The real Nancy Pelosi - multi-millionaire, resort, dining and winery baroness who profits from non-union and illegal labor." Citizen Journalism Today. January 28, 2009

Griffith, Roger, *The Nature of Fascism* (New York, Routledge, 1993)

Gross, Bertram, *Friendly Fascism: The New Face of Power in America.* (South End Press, 1999)

Guardian, The. "Full text: bin Laden's 'letter to America'." November 24, 2002

Hall, Macer. "David Cameron: Brown soft on Muslim fanatics." November 26, 2009

Halloran, Liz. "Obama Beer Summit Choices Make for a Happy Hour." National Public Radio website. July 30, 2009

Ham, Katharine Mary. " Secret Service Director: Threats Against Obama Not Up Over Other Presidents." Blog post for *The Weekly Standard*. December 3, 2009

Harnden, Toby. "Barack Obama faces 30 death threats a day, stretching US Secret Service." *The Daily Telegraph*. August 3, 2009

Hanes, W. Travis III, & Frank Sanello, *Opium Wars: The Addiction of One Empire and the Corruption of Another* (Sourcebooks Inc., 2002)

Harper, Jim. "A Flagging Obama Transparency Effort." Cato @ Library. April 9, 2009

Hawley, Ellis W., *Herbert Hoover as Secretary of Commerce: Studies in New Era Though and Practice* (Iowa State Press, 1982)

Haynes, V. Dion. "U.S. unemployment rate for blacks projected to hit 25-year high." The Washington Post, January 15, 2010

Hedges, Chris, *American Fascist: The Christian Right and the War on America.* (New York, Free Press 2007)

Heller, Steven, *The Swastika: Symbol Beyond Redemption?* (New York, Allworth Press, 2008)

HereComesTheScience.com. "The Genius of the Obama Campaign Logo." February 6, 2008

Higham, John, *Strangers in Land Patterns of American Nativism, 1860-1925* (Rutgers University Press, 2002)

The History Place. "Hitler's Boyhood." 1996.

Holland, Jesse J. "Mine Workers union endorses Obama for president." AP News via FoxNews.com, May 21, 2009

Hoover, Herbert, *The Memoirs of Herbert Hoover: The Great Depression, 1929-1941* (Kessinger Publishing, LLC., 2009)

Hosenball, Mark. "Exclusive: Obama Got Pre-Christmas Intelligence Briefing About Terror Threats to 'Homeland.'" *Newsweek*, January 1, 2010

Hough, Emerson, *The Authorized History of the American Protective League* (Reilly & Lee Company, 1919)

Huffington Post, The. "CNN Fact Checks SNL Sketch Detailing Obama's Failures." October 6, 2009

Hurt, Charles. "Pelosi's climate air fare." *The New York Post*, December 17, 2009

Bibliography

Hurwitz, Michael, *D.W. Griffith's Film, The Birth of a Nation: The Film that Transformed America* (BookSurge Publishing, 2006)

IMDB.com bio for William Dudley Pelley

IMDB.com: V for Vendetta (2005)

Ingram, Billy. "Cigarette Commercials." TV Party Web Site

ITplanet.com, "EPA Issues Endangerment Finding. December 8, 2009

Jaffe, Matthew, Karen Travers and Sunlen Miller. "White House Jobs Summit: Real Progress or PR Stunt?" ABCnews.com. December 3, 2009

Jennings, Brian, *Censorship: The Threat to Silence Talk Radio* (Threshold Editions, 2009)

Jones, Brent, "ACORN's Maryland chapter is shuttered." *The Baltimore Sun*, March 16, 2010

Kaplan, Jeffrey, *Encyclopedia of White Power: A Sourcebook on the Radical Right* (AltaMira Press, 2000)

Karsh, Efraim *The Arab-Israeli Conflict: The Palestine War 1948 (Essential Histories)* (New York, Osprey Publishing, 2002)

Karash, Efraim, *The Iran-Iraq War 1980-1988 (Essential Histories)* (New York, Osprey Publishing, 2002)

Kershaw, Ian. *Hitler: 1889-1935* (New York, W.W. Norton & Co., 2000)

Kershaw, Ian. *Hitler: 1936-1945*: Nemesis (W.W. Norton & Co., 2001)

King Jr., Neil and Jonathan Weisman. "A President as Micromanager: How Much Detail Is Enough?" *The Wall Street Journal*. August 12, 2009

King Jr., Neil. "Role of White House Czars Sparks Battle." *The Wall Street Journal*. September 11, 2009

Klein, Aaron. "American flag disappears from Obama campaign jet." WorldNetDaily. July 21, 2008

Krattenmaker, Thomas G., and Lucas A. Powe, *Regulating Broadcast Programming* (MIT Press, 1994)

Krauthammer, Charles. Transcript from *Special Report with Bret Baier*, January 15, 2010

Krauthammer, Charles, "One year out: President Obama's fall." *The Washington Post*, January 15, 2010

Krawczyk, Wade. *German Army Uniforms of World War II* (Crowood, 2002)

Krebs, Michael. "Boxer: Climategate hackers should face criminal prosecution." The Digital Journal Web Site. December 2, 2009

Krugman, Paul. "What Didn't Happen." The New York Times, January 17, 2009

Kuhnhenn, Jim. "Obama tells banks: 'We want our money back." Associated Press via Yahoo News, January 14, 2010

Laffer, Arthur and Wayne Winegarden. "The Adverse Economic Impacts of Cap-and-Trade Regulations." Arduin, Laffer & Moore Econometrics. September 2007

Lanier, Carlotta Walls and Lisa Frazier Page, *A Mighty Long Way: My Journey to Justice at Little Rock Central High School* (New York, One World/Ballantine, 2009)

Bibliography

Lavy, George, *Germany and Israel: Moral Debt and National Interest* (Routledge, 1996)

Leonhardt, David. "Stimulus Thinking, and Nuance." *The New York Times*. March 21, 2009

Leuchtenburg, William E., *Herbert Hoover: The American Presidents Series: The 31st President, 1929-1933* (Times Books, 2009)

Levitas, Daniel, *The Terrorist Next Door: The Militia Movement and the Radical Right* (St. Martin's Griffin, 2004)

Lewis, Rand, *The Neo-Nazis and German Unification* (Praeger, 1996)

Lieberman, Jethro K, *A Practical Companion to the Constitution: How the Supreme Court Has Ruled on Issues from Abortion to Zoning, Updated and expanded Edition of The Evolving Constitution* (University of California Press, 1999)

Liebknecht, Wilhelm, "Our Recent Congress" (1896). Marxists.org

Los Angeles Time, The. "Obama asks Congress to delay digital TV switch." January 8, 2009

Lozowick, Yaacov and Haim Watzman (translator), *Hitler's Bureaucrats: The Nazi Security Police and the Banality of Evil* (Continuum, 2005)

Malik Naureen. "Soros Says Copenhagen Climate Summit Was A Failure." NASDAQ.com, January 15, 2010

Malkin, Michelle. "I pledge to be of service to Barack Obama." Michelle Malkin Web Blog. September 2, 2009

Margolis, Eric, "The Big Lie About 'Islamic Fascism." August 26, 2006. LewRockwell.com

Martin, George Whitney, *The Red Shirt and the Cross of Savoy: The Story of Italy's Risorgimento, 1748-1871.* (Dodd Mead, 1969)

Matter, Philip, *The Mufti of Jerusalem* (New York, Columbia University Press, Revised Edition, 1988)

McCelland, Edward. "Why Chicago Didn't Want the Olympics." October 2, 2009

Meacham, Jon. "A Highly Logical Approach." *Newsweek*. May 16, 2009.

Meneses, Filipe de., *Salazar: A Political Biography* (New York, Enigma Books, 2009)

Messina, Jim. Memorandum to White House Staff. WhiteHouse.gov Web Site. December 2, 2009

Mission: Readiness website. "Ready, Willing and Unable to Serve." November 2009

Moberg, David. "Obama's Community Roots." The Nation, April 3, 2007

Moore, Michael. "Pinch Me... A message from Michael Moore." MichaelMoore.com website. November 5, 2008.

Moore, Michael. "An Open Letter to President Obama from Michael Moore." MichaelMoore.com, November 20, 2009.

Moore, Michael Scott. "Insanity on the Spree." *Spiegel International*. March 20, 2008

Bibliography

Morgan, David S. "Gibbs on Afghanistan: Not Nation-Building." CBSNews.com, December 1, 2009

Morris, Aldon D., *Orgins of the Civil Rights Movement* (Free Press, 1986)

Mostret, Mary. ConservativeTruth.org. November 10, 2008

MSNBC.com. "Full text of Obama's Nobel Peace Prize Speech." December 10, 2009

Mussolini, Benito; Schnapp, Jeffery Thompson (ed.); Sears, Olivia E. (ed.); Stampino, Maria G. (ed.). "Address to the National Corporative Council (14 November 1933) and Senate Speech on the Bill Establishing the Corporations (abridged; 13 January 1934)". *A Primer of Italian Fascism*. (Lincoln, University of Nebraska Press, 2000)

Najacht, Norma. "We have a republic if we can keep it." *Custer County Chronicle Online*, September 30, 2009

Neocleous, Mark, *Fascism (Concepts in Social Thought)* (University of Minnesota Press, 1997)

Newsweek. "The D.C. Powers." January 5, 2009, published online December 20, 2008

Newton-Small, Jay. "Senators Take On Obama's Czars." *Time Magazine*. October 22, 2009

New York Times, The, "JUSTICES UPHOLD A TEACHERS' OATH; Back State Law Requiring a Constitutional Pledge." January 23, 1968

Ng, Eileen. "Malaysian state ruler commutes caning sentence for beer-drinking Muslim woman." The Associated Press via The Washington Examiner. April 1, 2010

Nicholas, Peter. "White House communications chief Anita Dunn resigns." *The Los Angeles Times*. November 11, 2009

Nicolle, David, *The Great Islamic Conquests AD 632-750 (Essentials Histories)* (New York, Osprey, 2009)

Nielsen Company, The. Press Release: "5.7% of U.S. HOUSEHOLDS – OR 6.5 MILLION HOMES – STILL UNPREPARED FOR THE SWITCH TO DIGITAL TELEVISION." January 22, 2009

Nordlinger, Jay. "Rise of an Epithet." *The National Review*. December 7, 2009

Palin, Sarah. "Copenhagen's political science." *The Washington Post*. December 9, 2009

Parnes, Amie. "State Dinner: Big tent politics." Politico Click. November 23, 2009

Patel, Kiran Klaus. *Soldiers of Labor: Labor Service in Nazi Germany and New Deal America, 1933-1945* (Cambridge University Press, 2005)

Paul, Katie. "What Bibi's 'They Hate us for Our Freedom' Moment at AIPAC Means for the Obama Meeting." *Newsweek*. March 23, 2010

Paxton, Robert O. 2005. *Anatomy of Fascism*. (New York, Vintage, 2005)

Pergram, Chad. "The Road Ahead." FoxNews.com: The Speaker's Lobby, January 11, 2010

Perez, Evan. "Obama's Detention Plans Face Scrutiny." *The Wall Street Journal*. May 22, 2009

Bibliography

Pestritto, Ronald J. and William J. Atto, *American Progressivism: A Readers.* (Lexington Books, 2008)

Pestritto, Ronald J., *Woodrow Wilson and the Roots of Modern Liberalism* (Rowman & Littlefield Publishers, Inc., 2005)

Pipes, Daniel, *Militant Islam Reaches America* (W.W. Norton & Company, 2002)

Pitts, Edward Lee. "Czarist Rule." Worldmag.com. November 9, 2009

Poor, Jeff. "Obama Blasts Fox News: 'I've Got One Television Station that is Entirely Devoted to Attacking My Administration.'" Business & Media Institute. June 16, 2009

Price, R.G. 2004. "Rise of American Fascism." RationalRevolution.net

Proctor, Robert N, *The Nazi War on Cancer* (Princeton University Press, 2000)

Puzzanghera, Jim. "Delay in switch to digital TV is delayed" *The Los Angeles Times*. January 29, 2009

Quataert, Donald, *The Ottoman Empire, 1700-1922* (Cambridge University Press; 2 edition, 2005)

Rattner, Steve. "The auto bailout: How we did it." *Fortune* via CNN/Money.com. October 21, 2009

Rempel, Gerhard, *Hitler's Children: The Hitler Youth and the SS* (University of North Carolina Press, 1990)

Reuters. "Inquisition begins over state dinner gatecrashing." December 3, 2009

Reuters. "Possible elements of U.S. jobs package." December 7, 2009, updated December 8, 2009

Reuters UK. "Gate-crasher 'screw up' won't happen again: Obama." December 13, 2009

RightWingNews.com. "Answering 20 Frequently Asked Questions About Conservatism."

Rodrigues, Eva. "Detroit's CEO in Chief." *The Washington Post.* May 3, 2009

Roosevelt, Theodore, *The Letters of Theodore Roosevelt, Volume 3, The Square Deal: 1901-1903* (Harvard University Press, 2004)

Rotella, Sebastian and Christi Parson. "Obama assails intelligence failures in Christmas incident." *The Los Angeles Times*, January 6, 2010

Rowland, Kara. "Critics not invited to White House 'jobs summit.'" *The Washington Times*. December 2, 2009

Sappenfield, Mark. "Obama's Afghanistan timeline adheres to McChyrstal assessment." *The Christian Science Monitor*. December 2, 2009

Saul, Michael. "Glenn Beck is scarier than Rush Limbaugh, Sean Hannity, says Anti-Defamation League." *The New York Daily News*. November 17, 2009

Schaap, Jeremy, *Triumph: The Untold Story of Jesse Owens and Hitler's Olympics* (New York: Mariner Books, 2007)

Scherer, Michael. "No Testifying for Obama's Social Secretary." *Time Magazine*. December 3, 2009

Schilling, Chelsea. "Is Obama's face on U.S. flag illegal?" WorldNetDaily. October 14, 2009.

Bibliography

Schlesinger, Arthur M., Jr., *The Coming of the New Deal, 1933-1935 (The Age of Roosevelt, Vol. 2)* (Mariner Books, 2003)

Schmaltz, William H., *Hate: George Lincoln Rockwell and the American Nazi Party* (Potomac Books, 2008)

Schweizer, Peter. "Gore isn't quite as green as he's led the world to believe." *USA Today*. December 7, 2006

Scrapbookpages.com. "Work in the Dachau camp"

Sheppard, Noel. "Garofalo: Tea Party Goers Are Racists Who Hate Black President." Newsbusters.org. April 16, 2009

Sheppard, Noel. "SNL Skewers Obama: So Far I've Accomplished Nothing! Nada!" Newsbusters.org. October 4, 2009

Sheppard, Noel. "Martha Stewart Says Sarah Palin 'Dangerous Person.'" Newsbusters.org. November 21, 2009

Sheppard, Noel. "Video Shows Media Hypocrisy Concerning Right-wing Hate Speech." Newsbusters.org. March 31, 2010

Shirer, William L., *The Rise and Fall of the Third Reich: A History of Nazi Germany*. (New York, Simon & Schuster; 1st Touchstone edition, 1990)

Simonelli, Frederick J, *American Fuehrer: George Lincoln Rockwell and the American Nazi Party* (Chicago, USA, University of Illinois Press 1997)

Simple Dollar, The. "The Light Bulb Showdown: LEDs vs. CFLs vs. Incandescent Bulbs - What's the Best Deal Now …And in the Future?" February 10, 2009.

Smith, Ben. "Obama: Cambridge police acted 'stupidly.'" Politico.com Web Site. July 22, 2009

Smith, Richard, "Making a Pledge of Allegiance is a Serious Matter" Cross Resources Web Site, August 6, 2009

Southern Poverty Law Center Web Site. "SPLC Report: Return of the Militias." August 8, 2009

Spicer, Kevin P, *Antisemitism, Christian Ambivalence, and the Holocaust*. (Indiana University Press, 2007)

Spielvogel, Jackson J., *Hitler and Nazi Germany: A History (5th Edition)* (Prentice Hall, 2004)

Spillius, Alex. "Black Democrats: criticism of Barack Obama is rooted in racism." *The Daily Telegraph*. September 15, 2009

"State Cigarette Excise Tax Rates & Rankings." Tobaccofreekids.org. October 12, 2009

Staudenmaier, Peter. "Fascist Ecology: The 'Green Wing' of the Nazi Party and its Historical Antecedents." Spunk Library and AK Press

Stein, Sam. "Anita Dunn: Fox News An Outlet For GOP Propaganda." The Huffington Post Web Site. October 11, 2009

Stelter, Brian. "Fox's Volley With Obama Intensifying." *The New York Times*. October 11, 2009

Stephanopoulos, George. George's Bottom Line: "Obama on ACORN: 'Not Something I've Followed Closely' Won't Commit to Cut Federal Funds." ABCNews.com, September 20, 2009

Bibliography

Steves, Rick. "Lash a Flute to a Goatskin and Squeeze out some Greece." Rick Steve's Europe Web Site. September 22, 2007

Stokes, Melvyn, *D.W. Griffith's the Birth of a Nation: A History of the Most Controversial Motion Picture of All Time* (New York, The Oxford University Press, 2008)

Stolberg, Sheryl Gay and Bill Vlasic, "U.S. Lays Down Terms for Auto Bailout." *The New York Times*. March 30, 2009

Stone, Geoffrey R., *Perilous Times: Free Speech in Wartime from the Sedition Act of 1798 to the War on Terrorism*. (New York, W.W. Norton & Company, 2004)

Strassel, Kimberley A. "The EPA's Carbon Bomb Fizzles." *The Wall Street Journal*. December 11, 2009

Strom, Stephanie. "Funds Misappropriated at 2 Nonprofit Groups." *The New York Times*, July 9, 2008

Sullivan, Eileen and Julie Pace. "Gatecrashers' e-mail shows no confirmed invitation." Associated Press via Yahoo! News. December 2, 2009

Sullivan, Erin, "ACORN Housing Becomes Affordable Housing Centers of America." *City Paper*. March 23, 2010

Superville, Darlene. "Evening gowns, sairs at Obama's first state dinner." Associated Press via Yahoo! News. November 25, 2009

Sweeney, Michael S., *Secrets of Victory: The Office of Censorship and the American Press and Radio in World War II* (University of North Carolina Press, 2001)

Tapper, Jake and Sunlen Miller. "White House Staffers Now Posted at Checkpoints for Social Events." ABCNews.com. December 2, 2009

Thai, Xuan and Ted Barrett. "Biden's description of Obama draws scrutiny." CNN.com, February 9, 2007.

The Sierra Club Web Site, Washington, D.C. Chapter: Politics and Elections

Tolzmann, Don Heinrich, *German Immigration to America The First Wave* (Westminster, Maryland, Heritage Books, 2009)

Tomesco, Frederic. "Bush Urges U.S. to Sell Financial, Carmaker Holdings." *Bloomberg*. October 22, 2009

Tomsho, Robert. "White House 'Beer Summit' Becomes Something of a Brouhaha." *The Wall Street Journal*. July 30, 2009

Travers, Karen. "Obamas' First State Dinner -- 'Bigger than the Biggest Wedding.'" ABCNews.com. November 24, 2009

Travers, Karen. "President Obama: Federal Government 'Will Go Bankrupt' if Health Care Costs Are Not Reined In." ABC World News: The World Newer Daily Blog. December 16, 2009

Trimborn, Jürgen, *Leni Riefenstahl: a life*. (New York: Faber & Faber, 2007)

Valhos, Kelley. "House Passes Volunteerism Bill Critics Call Pricey, Forced Service." FoxNews.com. March 18, 2009

Videovat.com. " Eric Moussambani - Worst Olympic Swimming Performance Ever?" August 8, 2008

Bibliography

Wade, Wyn Craig, *The Fiery Cross: The Ku Klux Klan in America* (Oxford University Press, 1998)

Wallace, Max, *The American Axis: Henry Ford, Charles Linbergh, and the Rise of the Third Reich* (St. Martin's Griffin, 2004)

Wall Street Journal, The, "The Bloomberg Diet: The nanny state reaches into the kitchen." December 9, 2006

Walters, Guy, *Berlin Games: How the Nazis Stole the Olympic Dream* (New York: Harper Perennial, 207)

Watson, Bruce, "Crackdown! When bombs terrorized America, the Attorney General launched the 'Palmer Raids.'" *Smithsonian Magazine*. February 2002

Weisman, Steven R., *The Great Tax Wars: Lincoln - Teddy Roosevelt - Wilson How the Income Tax Transformed America*. (New York, Simon & Shuster, 2004)

Whitman-Bradley, Buff, "War on Terrorism Takes New Turn." San Francisco Bay Area Independent Media Center website. June 15, 2006

Whitesides, John and Donna Smith. "U.S. Democrats reach deal on 'Cadillac' health tax." Reuters, January 14, 2010

Williams, Juan. Transcript from *Special Report with Bret Baier*, January 15, 2010

Wolf, Naomi. " Fascist America, In 10 Easy Steps." April 27, 2007

Wolf, Richard, "Obama says he's just getting warmed up." *USA Today*. October 29, 2009

WorldNetDaily. "Homeland Security on guard for 'ring-wing extremists.'" April 12, 2009

Wright, David K., *The Story of Volkswagen Beetles (Class Cars: An Imagination Library Series)* (Gareth Stevens Publishing, 2002)

Yergin, Daniel, *The Prize: The Epic Quest for Oil, Money & Power* (Free Press, 2008) p. 323

York, Byron. "Obama can't be community organizer for the world." *The Washington Examiner*, November 3, 2009

Yue, Lorene and Brandon Glenn. "Chicago designers create Obama's logo." *Crane's Chicago Business*. February 22, 2007

Zeleny, Jeff and Ben Werschkul. "Video: Ten Minutes with Dan Pfeiffer." The New York Times, The Politics and Government Blog of the Times, January 18, 2010

Zeskind, Leonard, *Blood and Politics: The History of the White Nationalist Movement from the Margins to the Mainstream* (Farrar, Straus and Giroux, 2009)

Government Web Sites:

DTVTransition.org
Energy Star Web Site
EPA.gov

Bibliography

Thomas Jefferson: Reply to the Legislature of Vermont, 1807. ME 16:293
Lincoln Bicentennial Web Site
Open Congress Web Site
The President's Council on Physical Fitness and Sports Web Site
Serve.org Web Site
Title 4, Chapter 1, Section 4, US Code
U.S. Constitution Online
US Immigration Support Web Site
United States Secret Service Web Site
WhiteHouse.gov

Legal Rulings:

A.L.A. SCHECHTER POULTRY CORPORATION v. UNITED STATES, 295 U.S. 495 (1935)
295 U.S. 495
U.S. Supreme Court, UNITED STATES v. NIXON, 418 U.S. 683 (1974)

Index

2008 Presidential Race 46, 49, 52–55
Academy Award 94, 97
ACORN
   2008 Presidential campaign 123
   ACCE split 127
   membership (400,000 families) 124
   philosophy 124–125
ActivistCash.com 84
Afghanistan 7, 60, 62, 63, 69, 74, 79, 101, 109, 112, 133
Ahlus Sunnah wal Jamaah 172
Air America 144–146, 148
Allah
   Adhan, Muslim call to prayer 47
Al-Qaeda
   attacks U.S. embassies 62
   attacks U.S.S. Cole 62
   attacks World Trade Center 62, 133, 138, 165
   Christmas Day attack 177
American Civil War 13, 16, 17, 20
American Nazi Party (ANP)
   founded 40
   name change New Order 42
   name change NSWPP 42
   reborn as the German American Bund 36
   white power 42
American Protective League 22, 220
AmeriCorps 140
Amerika 71, 108
Anti-Defamation League 146, 210, 224
Anti Yellow Dog League 22
Associated Press 57, 109, 110
Balfour Declaration 170
Barton, Joe L. 103
Beck, Glenn 69, 146, 147, 189
Biden, Vice President Joe 105, 106

bin Laden, Osama 62, 162, 165
Birmingham, Alabama
   nickname Bombingham 43
   nickname Dynamite Hill 43
Birth of a Nation, The 13
Bloomberg, Mayor Michael 86
Blue Eagle 17, 28–29
Bolshevik Revolution 17–18
Boxer, Barbara 95
British Union of Fascists 2, 37
Broun, Paul (R-Georgia) 65, 140
Brüder Schweign
   aka as Silent Brotherhood 43
Bush, President George W. 31, 46, 53–54, 58–60, 61–62, 64, 65, 69–70, 97, 104, 108, 109, 119–120, 132–136, 141, 149, 154, 155, 165
Cap and Trade 98–100
Carter, President Jimmy 155, 171
Castro, Fidel 74
Center for Science in the Public Interest 83, 104
Cheney, Vice President Dick 46, 61, 65, 136, 179
Chicago
   and Olympics 76–80
   Columbian Exposition of 1893 80
   German immigrants 34
Choudary, Anjem 172
Chrysler 114–115, 117–119, 181, 184
Churchill, Winston 71
Civil Rights Act of 1964 44
Clark, General Wesley 83
Clean Air Act 99, 100, 203
Climate-gate 94–95
Clinton, Hillary Rodham 49, 52
Clinton, President Bill 31, 59–60, 62, 69, 109, 111, 142
Codreanu, Corneliu Zelea 7

Index

Colarelli, Stephen M. 91
Communist Party 18
Conservatism 5, 6, 12
Constitution
   12th Amendment 31
   14th Amendment 129
   22nd Amendment 31
   Article I 70, 136
   Article II 68
Cosmotheism 42
Creel Commission 22
Crowley, Sgt. James 105, 107
C-SPAN 182–183
Czars
   issue with Czars by Democrats 70
   number under Clinton 69
   number under George W. Bush 69
   number under Obama 67
   number under Roosevelt 69
   number under Truman 69
   origin of term 67, 68
Democratic National Convention 49
Democratic Party 27, 49
Dent, Charles 111
Department of Energy 96
Detroit 34, 110, 118, 205, 224
Deutsche Arbeitsfront 122
Deutscher Reichsbund für Leibesübungen 80
Dickstein, Samuel 35
Drexler, Anton 50
Dunn, Anita 66, 147, 210, 223, 225
Edwards, John 52
Eisenhower, President Dwight
   Council on Physical Fitness 82
   desegregation as national security 44
Fairey, Shepard 57
Fairness Doctrine 135, 143–144, 209, 216

Fasces 1, 2
Fascism
   10 Easy Steps 133–136
   in Britain 2
   Islamic. *See* Chapter 13 Islamic Fascism
   response to capitalism 3–5, 6, 7, 12
   state Socialism 4–5
Faubus, Governor Arkansas 44
Favreau, Jon 52
FBI 19, 39, 44, 65
FCC 102, 145
Food and Drug Administration's Center for Tobacco Products 90
Fox News 135, 146–147
Franco, Francesco 8, 101
Franklin, Franklin 190
Frank, Rep. Barney (D-Mass.) 149
Free Society of Teutonia (FTS) 34–35
Frías, Hugo Rafael Chávez 58
Friends of New Germany
   absorbs the FTS 35
   Boycott 35
   Newark branch 35
Garibaldi, Giuseppe 38
Garofalo, Janeane 60, 148
Gates, Jr., Henry 105–107
General Motors 114
Generations Invigorating Volunteerism and Education Act 140
German American Bund
   Brown scare 37
   rally, Madison Square Garden 36
German immigration 33
Gestapo 64–65
Gibbs, Robert 111
Gissibl, Fritz and Peter 34
Gitmo. *See* Guantanamo Bay Naval Base

Index

Giuliani, Mayor Rudy 52
Goebbels, Joseph 66–67, 90, 147, 161
GOP. *See* Republican Party
Gore, Vice President Al 94–97
Great Britain
   wars in Afghanistan 153–154
   wars in China 159
Great Depression
   and the New Deal 25–26
   rise of fascism 25
Great War. *See* World War One
Greenpeace 91
Guantanamo Bay Naval Base 62, 74, 135
Gulag 134
Hannity, Sean 143
Health and Human Services, Department of 68, 82, 87
Hess, Rudolf
   as Deputy Führer 34
   disbanding Friends of New germany 35
   supporter of "green wing" 93
Himmler, Heinrich 64, 85
Hindenburg, Paul von 50, 65
Hitler, Adolf
   and Olympic Games 76–78
   and SS 64, 85, 140
   and Volkswagen 116
   as a vegetarian 85, 93
   as Chancellor of Germany 34, 50, 65–66
   Beer Hall Putsch 50
   calls for scorched earth 93
   closeness to mother 47
   compared to Obama 47
   did not smoke 89
   first world leader to fly 71
   in World War I 48
   relationship to father 47
   view towards American Nazis 35
   writes Mein Kampf 50–51
Hitler Youth 23, 81
Homeland Security, Department of 65, 68, 137
Hoover, J. Edgar
   and the Silver Legion 39
   attacks on Klan by FBI 44
Hoover, President Herbert
   and Efficiency Movement 24
   and Goodwill Tour 24
   criticism by Roosevelt 25
   discussing the New Deal 26
   during Boxer Rebellion 23, 24
   Great Depression 23
   loses 1932 election 25
   Medicine-Ball Cabinet 69
House Committee on Un-American Activities
   early activities 35
   testifmony from J. Edgar Hoover 39
   testimony from William Pelley 39
   the German-American Bund 37
House Homeland Security Committee 110–111
Hussein, Saddam 62–63
Industrial Workers of the World (IWW) 18
Integralism
   Brazilian 7
   the symbol of integralism 8
International Olympic Committee 76
International Worker's Day 18
Iraq 54, 60, 62, 63, 65, 74
Iron Guard 7
Islam
   and terrorists 62, 133, 135, 138, 162, 165
   and the Mahdi 172
   blaming colonialism 167
   conflict with Israel 169–170

Index

Obama: "what Islam is, not what it isn't" 140
President Obama's speech at Cairo University 140, 167
Islamaic Law. *See* Shari'a Law
Islamofascism 161–162
Jackson, Jesse 189
Jackson, President Andrew 68
Jamestown 33
Jefferson, President Thomas 30
Johnson, Hugh Samuel 27
Johnson, President Lyndon 44, 63, 153
Kellman, Jerry 130
Kennedy, Edward M. 140
Kennedy, President John F. 5, 82, 142
Koehl, Matt
 as leader 42
 succeeds Rockwell 42
Kuhn, Fritz Julius
 criticism of F. D. Roosevelt 36
 embezzlement 37
 head of the American Nazi Party 36
Ku Klux Klan
 and The Birth of a Nation 13
 assassinations 44
 as terrorist group 44
 bombings 44–45
 daytime talk shows 44
 forced busing 44
 modern rally points 45
 political alliances 43
 prosecution of Klan 44
 rise in 1920s 19
 Southern Poverty Law Center, 137
LaRouche, Lyndon 150
Legiunea Archanghelu Mihai. *See* Iron Guard
Lewis, Sinclair 13
Liberalism 5–6, 9, 12, 90

Limbaugh, Rush 143, 144
Liuzzo, Viola 44
Lott, Trent 187–188
Mahdi Muhammad Ahmad 172–173
McCain, John 54, 59
McKinley, President William 20–21, 31, 142–143
McVeigh, Timothy 42, 138
Mission: Readiness 82–83
Moore, Michael 61, 132
Mosley, Sir Oswald 2, 37–38
Motorisierung 116
MoveOn.org 123–124, 157
Muhammad 48, 163, 169, 172
Muslim Arabs 164, 168
Mussolini, Benito
 elected to Chamber of Deputies 50
 march on Rome 19, 49–50
 on planned victory parade 156
 on the third way 3, 5
 ousting Luigi Facta 49
 rise to power 3
NAACA 13
Nader, Ralph 84
National Industrial Recovery Act. *See* New Deal
National Public Radio 146
National Socialism
 and Fascism 1–14
National Socialist Institute for Corporatism. *See* Nazi Party
Nazi Party
 and fitness 80–82
 and German Labor Front 122
 and Islam 169
 and the National Socialist Institute for Corporatism 9
 and the SA 23, 28
 and tobacco 89–90
 and Volkswagen 116–117

Index

Anti-Semitic 6–7
  a people's party 10
  as environmentalists 85
  control of business 117
  control of labor 121–122
  Nationalsozialistischer Reichsbund für Leibesübungen 80
  oaths 16
  Reich's Nature Protection Law of 1935 93
  rise of 50
Neo-Nazi
  as Koehl, Matt 42–43
  as Pierce, William 42–43
  daytime talk shows 33, 42
  in Germany 171
  in the United States 40
New Deal
  and National Recovery Administration 17, 27
  and the Blue Eagle 17, 28
  and The Corporate State 28
  called Jew Deal 36
  National Industrial Recovery Act 25, 27
  origin of 26
  support from Mussolini 26
New Party 37
New York 18, 35–37, 41, 46, 52, 57, 79, 86, 88, 118, 170
Nielsen Company 102–103
Nobel Peace Prize
  won by former Vice President Al Gore 94, 97
  won by President Obama 21, 23
  won by President Roosevelt 21
  won by President Wilson 23
Oath of Allegiance
  taken by Southerners 16
  under Nazi Germany 16
Obama, Barack
  at Harvard Law School 48
  bail outs 37
  Beer Summit 105
  book, Audacity of Hope 51–53
  book, Dreams From My Father 51
  childhood in Hawaii 47, 48
  closeness to mother 47
  compared himself to Mr. Spock 107
  compared to a Marxist 3
  compared to Lincoln, Kennedy, Roosevelt and Reagan 5
  elected 44th President 46
  elected Senator 49
  elected to Harvard Law Review 52
  goes to Denmark for Olympics 76
  on Islam 140, 163, 167
  on job summit 109
  on light bulbs 103–105
  on posters 28
  on the Third Way 3, 79
  on winning the Nobel Peace Prize 21, 23
  ordered Chrysler to merge with Fiat 114, 117–119
  Presidential Campaign 3
  promise of hope and change 17, 50, 75
  relationship to father 47
  speaks at Democratic National Convention 49
  spoofed on Saturday Night Live 72
Office of Censorship 26
Oklahoma City Bombing 42
Olbermann, Keith 148
Olympics 76–80
Opium Wars 159
O'Reilly, Bill 143
Ottoman Empire 168, 170
Owens, Jesse 77
Pakistan 69, 155
Palin, Sarah 95, 135
Partito Nazionale Fascista 3
Patler, John 42

Index

Pelley, William Dudley
  arrest of 40
  as a foreign correspondent 38
  as screenwriter 38
  as writer 40
  called Star-Spangled Fascist 38
  founder of Silver Legion and the Christian Party 39
  metaphysics 39
  president campaign 39
  publications Revelation and Roll Call 39
  Soulcraft Press 40
Pelosi, Nancy 183, 186
Perkins, Francis 28
Peronism 7
Perón, Juan 7
Pfeiffer, Dan 189
Phillips, Macon 73
Pierce, William Luther
  believed in Holocaust 43
  National Alliance 42
  pseudonym Andrew MacDonald 42
  Turner Diaries, The 42
Pledge of Allegiance
  comparison to Oath of Citizenship 15
  origin of 14
  revision of 15
Podesta, John 101
Porsche, Ferdinand 117
President's Council on Physical Fitness and Sports 82
Progressive tax 21
Public Health Cigarette Smoking Act 89
Qing Dynasty 159
Rathke, Dale and Wade 125
Rattner, Steven 118
Red Scare 18, 35

Reid, Senator Harry 31
Republican Party 12, 21, 53, 147
Richardson, Bill 52
Rockwell, George Lincoln
  anti-Jewish teachings 41
  as Holocaust denier 40
  contact with Nation of Islam 42
  founds World Union 40
  parallels with Hitler 41
  shooting of 42
  use of Swastika 41
Rogers, Desiree 110–112
Roman Republic 2
Roosevelt, President Franklin D.
  cadre of advisers 69
  called Franklin Rosenfeld 36
  Civilian Conservation Corps 121
  compared to Mussolini by Hoover 25
  fourth progressive President 25
  labeled warmonger 39
  New Deal 25
  seven food groups 88
  snubs Jesse Owens 78
Roosevelt, President Theodore
  and Square Deal 21
  Bull Moose Party 21
  move Republican Party into progressive camp 21
  Obama, compared to 21
  on winning Nobel Peace Prize 21
  Spanish-American War 21
  Vice President 21
  youngest president at 42 20
Salahi, Tareq and Michaele 110
Salazar, António de Oliveira 8
Salgado, Plinio 7–8
Schulz, Ed 132, 143
Secret Service 110–112, 141–142
Sedition Act of 1918 22
Seinfeld, television show 36

Index

Shari'a Law 166–168, 171, 173–175
Sharpton, Al 189
Shirts, colors of
  black 38
  brown 23, 34, 38
  red 38
  silver 37–40
Silver Legion of America
  influence of Mussolini, Hitler 37
  scarlet L 37
  uniform worn 38
Sima, Horia 7
Southern Poverty Law Center 137
Spanknobel, Heinz 35
Stalin, Josef
  and definition of fascism 1
  Gulag system 134
State Socialism 4, 5
Storm Troopers
  Sturmabteilung, SA 34
Sullivan, Mark 110, 142
Supreme Court 17, 18, 29, 32, 111, 132
Taft, President William Howard 21, 31
TARP 119–120
Tea Baggers 133, 134
Tea Party 134, 148
Thirty Years War 89
Tojo, Hideki 151
Trans fat 83, 85–86, 104
Truman, President Harry S. 29, 69, 178
UAW 181
United Nations 40, 170
U.S. Chamber of Commerce 108
Utopia 17, 20, 33
Vargas, Getulio 8
Versailles Treaty 9, 23, 34

Victor Emmanuel III, King of Italy 50
Vietnam War 42, 63, 153, 154
Volkswagen 116, 117
Voting Rights Act 44
Wagoner, Rick 114, 117, 135
Wall Street
  1919 bombing of 18
  fat cats 5
  given money 119
  Wall street crash 1929 19, 23
Weimar Republic 4, 121–122
Whitacre, Ed 114
White House
  and Jobs Summit 108
  and State Dinner 107, 109–110
  Obama's road to 49
  WhiteHouse.gov 73
Why We Fight, propaganda film 36
Wilhelm II, Kaiser of Germany 22, 63
Willkie, Wendell 28
Wilson, Woodrow
  and American progressive tax 21
  and food guide 88
  and Fourteen Points 23
  on The Birth of a Nation 13
  on winning Nobel Peace Prize 23
  on Word War I 22
  wins 1912 election 21
  wins 1916 election 31
Winfrey, Oprah 52, 79, 135
Wolf, Naomi 132, 140
World Trade Center
  9/11 165
  9/11 as an inside job 46
  1993 bombing 18, 62
World War One
  caused rise of Fascism 2, 4, 6, 9, 63
  German migration 33
  Hitler joins the army 48
  Ku Klux Klan 19

Index

    Muslim Arabs uprising 168
    Ottoman Empire 168
    Palestine Mandate 170
    President Wilson enters the war 22
    Red Scare 18

World War Two
    American Fascists 33
    attack on Pearl Harbor 37
    FDR's media manipulation 26
    French of British mandates 168
    Great Depression 26
    Hitler as leader 71
    influence of German-American Bund 37
    Mein Kampf 51
    Nazis view of the Arabs 169
    Portuguese involvement 8
    post war concepts 3
    post war Neo-Nazi groups 40
    the Silver Legion 39
    Zionist conference of 1942 170

Wright, Jeremiah 51, 126